Scarlett Slept Here

Scarlett Slept Here

A BOOK LOVER'S
GUIDE TO THE SOUTH

Joy Dickinson

CITADEL PRESS
Kensington Publishing Corp.
www.kensingtonbooks.com

CITADEL PRESS books are published by

Kensington Publishing Corp.
850 Third Avenue
New York, NY 10022

All Kensington titles, imprints, and distributed lines are available at special quantity discounts for bulk purchases for sales promotions, premiums, fund raising, educational, or institutional use. Special book excerpts or customized printings can also be created to fit specific needs. For details, write or phone the office of the Kensington special sales manager: Kensington Publishing Corp., 850 Third Avenue, New York, NY 10022, attn: Special Sales Department, phone 1-800-221-2647.

Citadel Press logo Reg. U.S. Patent and Trademark Office
Citadel Press is a trademark of Kensington Publishing Corp.

First printing March 2001

10 9 8 7 6 5 4 3 2 1

Printed in the United States of America

Library of Congress Cataloging-in-Publication Data

Dickinson, Joy.
    Scarlett slept here : a book lover's guide to the South / Joy Dickinson.
        p. cm.
    "A Citadel Press book."
    Includes bibliographical references and index.
    ISBN 0-8065-2092-2
    1. Literary landmarks—Southern States Guidebooks. 2. American literature—
    Southern States—History and criticism. 3. Southern States—In literature.   I. Title.
PS144.S67D53   2001
810.9'975—dc21   99-39097
                                                                                CIP

You knew someone for years, then suddenly one day
. . . you were seized with love for them.
You said to yourself: How could I have not known it before?
There is the man I love.

—Nancy Lemann, *The Fiery Pantheon*

For Jim, my love
How could I have not known it before?

Contents

Acknowledgments

*L*ike babies, bake sales, and Bingo, books never spring full-blown as the creative expression of just one person. The author's name goes on the cover, but dozens of friends, family members, and professional colleagues deserve a hefty portion of the credit. I'm blessed to have a particularly devoted cheering section, and it's my pleasure and privilege to acknowledge them here. You are all loved and appreciated more than you'll ever know.

First, heartfelt love and gratitude to my parents, Marjorie and Eugene Wilson, who once again provided the concern, encouragement, and support that got me through some very "long dark nights of the book." The much-loved friends of the JEN (Joy Emergency Network) soothed and calmed my midnight I'll-never-write-again terrors; they were the cushion that softened every blow along the way to birthing this baby—Dena Hill Bennett, Michael Bennett, Kathy Hartley, Melinda Rice, Amy Logan, Lori Neal Racine, Brenda Barrett, Angela Wilson and Jennifer Wilson, with a special thanks for on-site comfort to Bert Pigg and Adriana Bate in New Orleans.

Jim Tipping, love of my life, you've been the angel gently perching on my shoulder, whispering in my ear and keeping me going. I love you with all my heart. Spencer, Price, and Drew, thanks for putting the PlayStation on low volume during the final throes of editing and keeping the lightsaber attacks to an endurable minimum.

Along the research road, I received especially helpful guidance from: Dave Tomsky of the Grove Park Inn Resort, Marla Tambellini of the Asheville Convention and Visitors Bureau, and Ted Mitchell of the Thomas Wolfe Memorial, all in Asheville, North Carolina; authors Jan

Karon, Charles Frazier, and Allan Gurganus on the importance of place in Southern writing; and, in New Orleans, Ellen Johnson of the Tennessee Williams New Orleans Literary Festival, Beverly Gianna and Christine DeCuir of the Greater New Orleans Convention and Visitors Bureau, Robert Florence of Historic New Orleans Walking Tours, and Ritchie Champagne of Anne Rice's Vampire Lestat Fan Club.

I'd also like to thank the readers, many of whom have become friends, of my first book, *Haunted City*. Their enthusiasm and encouragement went a long way toward giving me the courage to plunge into the risky waters of writing another one.

Finally, heartfelt gratitude to my agent, Linda M. Kruger, of the Fogelman Literary Agency, and editors Monica Harris, Linda Regan, Bruce Bender, and Margaret Wolf.

Introduction

Moonlight, Mules, and Madness— The Quirky Allure of Southern Literature

There is no frigate like a book
To take us lands away
Nor any coursers like a page
Of prancing poetry

—Emily Dickinson

Tell about the South, what it's like there. What do they do there?
Why do they live there? Why do they live there at all?

—William Faulkner, *Absalom, Absalom!*

*M*iss Emily wasn't known primarily as a world traveler, spending virtually her entire life cosseted away in the village of Amherst, Massachusetts. But she knew her stuff when it came to the ability of literature to figuratively transport readers, and to inspire them to set out for those "lands away" they had so yearningly read about. The connection between literature and travel boasts a lengthy, often lofty pedigree: No less a literary achievement than the Bible owes a great deal of its excitement to travel—Moses leading the exodus out of Egypt, God himself taking a heaven-to-earth journey to hand down the Ten Commandments, Mary and Joseph's trek to Bethlehem (where a good guidebook, frankly, would have come in handy). Every year, tens of thousands of spiritual pilgrims retrace the footsteps of biblical characters. For nearly 2,000 years, travelers have responded to the palpable tug of wanting to see and experience biblical settings for themselves, transforming the once-quiet Holy Land into one of the world's greatest tourist attractions.

Fast-forward two millennia, and the book-loving traveler can find solace and like-minded readers in Wordsworth's Lake Country, Jane Austen's English countryside, Peter Mayle's French Provence, and Stephen King's Maine, not to mention the current mecca of book-related travel: Savannah, Georgia. Since the 1994 publication of John Berendt's *Midnight in the Garden of Good and Evil*, swarms of people have fervently sought out the sites in "the Book," as those in Savannah succinctly refer to *Midnight*. Travelers fiercely clutching their dog-eared copies whisper excitedly outside Mercer House, where the book's infamous murder took

Anne Rice's Garden District mansion, also the home of her fictitious Mayfair Witches.

place; they perch atop Conrad Aiken's tomb-disguised-as-a-bench in
moss-draped Bonaventure Cemetery to have their photos taken; they line
up in droves to hear the Lady Chablis sing the blues at Club One.
According to the local tourism office, *Midnight* has become the number
one reason vacationers choose Savannah.

Similarly, gothic novelist Anne Rice has lured thousands of her fans
to New Orleans. Those who have read her erotically charged, dangerous
adventures of the Vampire Lestat and the Mayfair Witches can't wait to
sip coffee at Cafe du Monde, or to take a stroll through shadowy
Lafayette Cemetery. Like Berendt in Savannah, Rice has had a stunning
effect on New Orleans's economy. She's one of the most popular reasons
people visit the Crescent City—just behind jazz and Creole food. Want
to hit the Big Easy at Halloween? Better book several months in advance;
the hotels are typically filled to overflowing with Rice fans, in town for
her fan club's annual "Gathering of the Coven."

Berendt and Rice fans are just the most dramatic examples of a literary-
travel phenomenon. According to *literarytraveler.com*, a Web site devoted
to book-loving wanderers, "Literary travelers have helped make cultural
and historical tourism one of the most popular sectors of the travel industry. In a recent survey by the Travel Industry Association of America,
53.6 million adults said they visited a museum or historical site in the
past year and 33 million adults attended a cultural event such as a theater,
arts, or music festival." You know something's made it into the pop-
culture pantheon when Alex Trebek gives it his blessing, and sure
enough, the category "literary tourism" has recently appeared on that
most cultural of quiz shows, *Jeopardy!*

Literature lovers seem inexorably drawn to the places they've read
about, whether it's the New Orleans of Anne Rice, the South Carolina
coast of Pat Conroy, or the northern Mississippi immortalized by William
Faulkner.

And the South, with its rich literary heritage, seduces more than its
share of readers-turned-adventurers. Virtually every guidebook to the area
below the Mason-Dixon line lists, at the very least, books set in the area
and has fleeting references to its most famous authors: William Faulkner,
Flannery O'Connor, Eudora Welty, and Tennessee Williams.

Historically, however, not everyone has agreed on the South's contribution to the collective culture, notably the critic H. L. Mencken. In
a column for the *New York Evening Post* in 1917, Mencken dubbed the

South "the Sahara of the Bozarts," condemning the region as "almost as sterile, artistically, intellectually, culturally as the Sahara Desert." By his day's standards, this was regrettably accurate. Were he looking at the South's literary output during the remaining eighty-three years of the twentieth century, however, Mencken's words would undoubtedly have been considerably kinder.

While generalizations by their very nature can be misleading, most Southern literature bears what Flannery O'Connor called an almost palpable sense of place. Moreover, Southern works of the late nineteenth and early twentieth centuries, and many even in the latter half of the last century, frequently draw their conflict from the Civil War and its still-echoing reverberations.

Mark Twain describes this phenomenon in his 1884 essay "Southern Sports":

> In the North one hears the war mentioned in social conversation, once a month; sometimes as often as once a week; but as a distinct subject for talk, it has long ago been relieved of duty. . . . The case is very different in the South. There, every man you meet was in the war; and every lady you meet saw the war. The war is the great chief topic of conversation. The interest in it is vivid and constant; the interest in other topics is fleeting. . . . In the South, the war is what A.D. is elsewhere: they date from it.

Naturally, the literary output of the South would be considerably different if they had, say, *won.*

Losing gave the South an endless wellspring of indignation and reason to put 'em up, as articulated (if you can call it that) by Walsh Jones, a Faulkner character: "Well, Kernel, they mought have kilt us, but they ain't whupped us yet, air they?"

And that, according to Padgett Powell in his preface to *New Stories From the South 1998,* just about sums it up:

> The literature of the South is full of people running around admitting or denying their whippedness. The blend of this confession and denial can be complex—and you can have the less interesting stark extremes of all denial, all confession—but finally that is the key: the people have been whipped, and whipped good.
>
>   This is why, in real life, as my daughter puts it, the dogfight— at which one party will not be beaten, on pain of death, and one

will, is a distinctly Southern thing, excepting anomalous Boston, where they also, curiously, last turned over school buses.

One could, I suppose, attribute the hotheaded tendencies of both Southerners and Bostonians to the predominance of Irish ancestry running through both areas, but that's another book.

Some Southern writers contend that without the still-lingering racial inequities that the War of Northern Aggression (as it is called south of the Mason-Dixon) crystallized, Southern literature would have little to distinguish it. Ironically, slavery actually *created* an advantage for writers by producing an underclass and thus conflict, says Mississippi native and Civil War chronicler Shelby Foote. Foote says in *Growing Up Southern: How the South Shapes Its Writers:*

> Imagine a Russian novel without any peasants in it. I don't know where southern literature would have been without blacks to write about. It would be very different. A writer can place a value on terrible, terrible things. With the South and slavery, you had a society that was stacked up in different parts. That makes you conscious of your relationships with other people and what happens when their rules are crossed or broken. You have no grounds for moral indignation anymore.

Folks from all over the country, the South included, have found moral unworthiness in many of the South's writers. The tradition of censorship, alive and well in classrooms across America, has resulted in the banning of books by Southerners Erskine Caldwell, William Faulkner, Alice Walker, and Tennessee Williams, among others. One gets the notion reading these authors, however, that controversy wasn't something that much troubled them.

Then there are those, such as North Carolina's Doris Betts, who see a New South literary canon emerging, fueled by marked shifts in class. She says in *Growing Up Southern:*

> These days you don't have aristocratic plantation writers, like Faulkner. You have people who have come out of beauty shops and trailer parks—plebian middle class and lower class writers who never went to war and are not that much interested in traditions of glory and valor. . . . The land of cotton is the integrated, urbanized, crowded land of the computer. In the Kmart checkout line, Dilsey's

descendants and those from the Compton and Sartoris clans are all wearing jeans.

Whether their passions are fed by old wounds or causes of a more contemporary nature, Southerners continue to take stands in the most fiery and obstinate ways. Logic doesn't play much part when a Southerner of any generation perceives a threat to his or his family's honor—and the legitimacy of that honor is also inconsequential. This, too, shows up in the writing.

As editor Susie Mee says in *Downhome: An Anthology of Southern Women Writers*:

> Heaven and hellfire may have faded and dimmed for some postmodern Yankees, but not for Southerners. Words such as guilt, retribution, vexation, the smite of God, iniquities—all found in the Book of Job—have been part of the Southern vocabulary since Civil War days, and even before. Along with the language comes a strong belief in a miraculous cause-and-effect. In a Biblical universe, everything is possible, and everything, even a gesture, can have repercussions.

Along with the "recent unpleasantness between the states" (many a Southern lady's gentle euphemism for the bloodiest war in American history), several sources have pointed out another defining indicator of true Southern literature: the dead mule.

In what the *New York Times* dubbed a "minor classic of mock scholarship," University of North Carolina scholar Jerry Leath Mills published a paper in 1997 called "Equine Gothic: The Dead Mule as Generic Signifier of Southern Literature." Mills's hilarious treatise appeared in no less an august publication than *The Southern Literary Journal*.

Mills dug up, so to speak, more than two hundred references to *Equus caballus x asinus (defunctus)*—as he calls the mule—in the works of Faulkner, Richard Wright, Caldwell, Truman Capote, Thomas Wolfe, and Zora Neale Hurston, as well as in Doris Betts's definitive piece, *The Dead Mule*. Cormac McCarthy, though best known for his novels about the western part of Texas and the Mexican border, killed fifty-nine mules in *Blood Meridian*, making him, by Mills's reckoning, the undisputed king of Southern prose.

Still-breathing mules also make frequent appearances in the literature of the South. Padgett Powell, in his introduction to *New Stories From the South 1998*, begins a discussion of "What Southern Literature Is" with this passage:

> A mule runs through Durham. There is something on his back. Memaw gives chase, with a broom, with which she attempts to whap out the fire on the mule. The mule keeps running. The fire appears to be fueled by paper of some sort, in a saddlebag tied on the mule.
>
> There is of course a measure of presumption in crediting Memaw with trying to put out the fire; it is difficult for the innocent witness to know that she is not just beating the mule, or hoping to, and that the mule happens to be on fire, and that that does not affect Memaw one way or another. But we have it on private authority, our own, that Memaw is attempting to save the paper, not gratuitously beat the mule, or even punitively beat the mule. Memaw is not a mule beater.

For those unfamiliar with the imagery of the mule, it has been interpreted to symbolize Southern character—equal parts innocence, bravado, and intractable stubbornness—and the Southern laborers from slaves to migrant farmworkers, who were downtrodden and ill-respected, and who literally built the South on a sweat-slicked foundation of grief, hopelessness, and blood. For other readers and critics, they're just mules.

Sadly—and to my unending horror as a Southern girl—my own adventures aboard a vessel of papyrus began not with Faulkner or Foote, or even a recently deceased mule, but with Laura Ingalls Wilder's *Little House* series, a collection that I so adored that I spent one entire summer, at the age of eight, reading the entire set from start to finish four times.

I longed to see Laura's Big Woods, Plum Creek, and Silver Lake, to spend a winter someplace where snow wasn't merely a miracle (as it was in northern Texas, where I grew up), it was a threat. The places in the *Little House* books didn't seem to belong to America; they were part of that glorious, mysterious planet called Out There. Out beyond the norm of everyday life, out past the safety line.

When I was about twelve and living in suburban Dallas, I developed an intense yearning to see Alabama, thanks to the haunting, evocative prose of Harper Lee. *To Kill a Mockingbird* gave me a taste of small-town values and vices that I'd never understood growing up in the suburbs of a large city. I remember my mother saying she couldn't wait to get away from Holdenville, Oklahoma, where she grew up and graduated in a high school class of about fifty, because *everyone* knew *everything* that happened in town. I thought that would be great, to be so connected to a group of people that they knew you so intimately they could see inside your very soul—until Harper Lee helped me see the ugly side of that situation. At about that same time in my life, I desperately, irrationally, longed to live in a Brooklyn walk-up with a fire escape, where I could read on summer afternoons (complete with a glass of ice water and a bowl of peppermint candy). This desire came courtesy of *A Tree Grows in Brooklyn*.

The wanderlust continued as I grew older. At seventeen, I developed an almost painful need to go to New Orleans, an inner fire started by Anne Rice and *Interview With the Vampire*. After being kicked out of English class for reading *Interview* when I was supposed to be reading *An American Tragedy* (which I'd finished), I became convinced that Dallas, Texas, was full of hicks with no sense of adventure or romance. Clearly, I was destined for the wilder, more accepting atmosphere of the Big Easy. I didn't set foot on Louisiana soil till I was twenty-five, and by then New Orleans had become, like Laura Ingalls's Minnesota, a place far bigger than life in my eyes. I couldn't wait to explore the streets where Lestat and Louis played and preyed, to picnic in Lafayette Cemetery, in the shadow of the Mayfair tomb.

I realized as I grew older, never without a book on my nightstand (usually a tottering stack, truth be told), that I had come to love travel as much as I loved reading—and that virtually every place on my "must visit" list stemmed from a beloved book. Cruising down the Mississippi on a paddle wheeler: *Life on the Mississippi*, Mark Twain. A weekend in Asheville, North Carolina: *Look Homeward, Angel*, Thomas Wolfe. Drinking in the exuberant vibrancy of New Orleans from under the D. H. Holmes clock on Canal Street: *A Confederacy of Dunces*, John Kennedy Toole. Dipping my toes in the South Carolina marshes: *The Prince of Tides*, Pat Conroy. And on and on and on.

I could never enjoy three-day cruises to nowhere or packaged eight-week "tomorrow is Venice!" European jaunts, no matter how glamorous they sounded. I wanted to *experience*, I wanted to *discover*, I wanted to *explore*, just as my favorite characters had, and in the places they had. For me, a Caribbean cruise couldn't even begin to compete with a weekend in out-of-the-way languid little Oxford, Mississippi, otherwise known as Yoknapatawpha County to Faulkner readers.

One of the best ways to prepare for a trip is to read the literature of that region—not just the travel essays and other nonfiction, but also the fiction that stems from a particular place. And not just the "approved fiction," either. Even if they don't want to admit it, there are people who are fans of *both* literary sons of Oxford: William Faulkner, the one whose statue graces the town square, and John Grisham, the one whose name graces the bestseller lists. And Grisham, for all the critical bullets he's taken, can still summon more perceptive, unclouded descriptions of the South—with all its charms, peculiarities, and prejudices—than the most critically lauded Northerner. If you haven't lived it, you probably can't write it, and that applies to nothing so much as life in Dixie.

There are exceptions to every rule, of course, and John Berendt is a prime example. Berendt is a Northerner from, of all places, *New York*. (Pause here for appropriate cringes of horror.) But Berendt utterly immersed himself in Savannah's culture and quirks for years before picking up a pen. That dedication shows; you'll find out more about Savannah from his 388-page book than from all the guidebooks the local chamber of commerce could produce from now until the dawn of the *next* millennium.

Fiction, even fiction disguised as nonfiction (as in the case of *Midnight*), enjoys a luxury strict, factual accounts lack: the ability to be completely, brutally honest without making anyone mad enough to sue, disinherit, or murder you. After all, it's fiction, right? Of course, Faulkner and Wolfe might disagree with that assessment, especially Wolfe, who was virtually disowned by the entire town of Asheville, North Carolina, after the publication of *Look Homeward, Angel*. The house in Asheville that served as the model for *Angel's* Dixieland was nearly destroyed by arson in mid-1998. One has to wonder if the prejudices against Wolfe's acidic view of his hometown still linger.

Scarlett Slept Here will attempt to take readers on a sort of whirlwind fantasy literary itinerary, visiting dozens of places with literary significance, whether it's where a beloved author was born, lived for a time, or set a favorite book. On just one of many research trips for *Scarlett*, I put 3,700

Bonaventure Cemetery in Savannah, setting for several scenes in *Midnight in the Garden of Good and Evil.*

miles on my trusty little Chevy in seventeen frenzied days of "if it's Tuesday, it must be Memphis" travel. I returned home with ten cities and endless hamlets and backwoods competing for space in my head, thirty rolls of film, fourteen humidity-crinkled notebooks, and a carload of pamphlets, books, and other "research materials" (I'm not sure what purpose the tiny church made of matchsticks, picked up at a Tennessee roadside stand, will serve in this book. I trust that will become apparent in due time).

My advice: Don't try this. But do read *Scarlett* with an open heart and an imaginary passport, collecting mind-stamps as you travel with me.

I hope the book will bring back memories of your own favorite Southern authors, some perhaps long forgotten, as well as inspire you to check out authors you may have not yet discovered. As delightful as the classics of Southern literature are, they're matched by dozens of modern novelists: Ellen Gilchrist, Allan Gurganus, Sharyn McCrumb, Charles Frazier, Kaye Gibbons, Reynolds Price, Sheila Bosworth. The list is as long as your imagination and your reading time. And then you can narrow your travel plan down to a weekend in Oxford or a romantic week at the Grove Park Inn in Asheville—which boasts connections to Frazier and F. Scott Fitzgerald, as well as Wolfe, its most famous hometown boy.

Scarlett will take you to Anne Rice's homes in New Orleans, as well as the domiciles of her fictional vampires and witches. You'll visit both the townhouse where Tennessee Williams lived while writing *A Streetcar Named Desire* and the run-down building on Elysian Fields Avenue that Stanley and Stella Kowalski called home. It will ferry you to Pat Conroy's hometown of Beaufort, South Carolina, and to the bed-and-breakfast where Barbra Streisand filmed portions of the movie version of Conroy's *The Prince of Tides*. You'll explore Savannah's supposedly haunted Bonaventure Cemetery, where one of readers' favorite scenes from *Midnight in the Garden of Good and Evil* is set, and the home of the city's pre-Berendt literary scion, Flannery O'Connor. In Atlanta, you'll see the place where Margaret Mitchell lived while writing *Gone With the Wind* and the hotel where Hollywood's Scarlett, Vivien Leigh, and other cast members stayed during the gala premiere of the 1939 movie.

Whether you can actually travel to the literary sites detailed in these pages or must limit your adventures to those of the armchair variety, I hope *Scarlett Slept Here* will enhance your literary sightseeing with vivid details, "you can almost touch it" images, and side trips down alleyways you might not otherwise have ventured into. If you spot omissions or (Faulkner forbid) errors, or have suggestions for future editions of *Scarlett*, throw 'em at me (joylynnd@earthlink.net).

Joy Dickinson
Corrales, New Mexico
November 2000

Only in Savannah: a testament to the qualities that Southern writing most celebrates: eccentricity, loyalty, and a stubborn refusal to ever give up hope.

1

Alabama

My mother and father were born in the most beautiful place on earth, in the foothills of the Appalachians along the Alabama-Georgia line. It was a place where gray mists hid the tops of low, deep-green mountains, where redbone and bluetick hounds flashed through the pines as they chased possums into the sacks of old men in frayed overalls, where old women in bonnets dipped Bruton snuff and hummed "Faded Love and Winter Roses" as they shelled purple hulls, canned peaches, and made biscuits too good for this world.

It was a place where playing the church piano loud was near as important as playing it right, where fearless young men steered long, black Buicks loaded with yellow whiskey down roads the color of dried blood, where the first frost meant hog killin' time and the mouthwatering smell of cracklin's would drift for acres from giant, bubbling pots.

It was a place where the screams of panthers, like a woman's anguished cry, still haunted the most remote ridges and hollows in the dead of night, where children believed they could choke off the cries of night birds by circling one wrist with a thumb and forefinger and squeezing tight, and where the cotton blew off the wagons and hung like scraps of cloud in the branches of trees.

—Rick Bragg, All Over but the Shoutin'

*A*labama's beautiful rolling hills, thousands of miles of lake-shore, and fertile river valleys make it one of the most visually nurturing places imaginable, as evocatively captured by one of its most prolific authors, Rick Bragg. Bragg's career has been spent mostly as a journalist, with stints at papers in his home state of Alabama as well as a long stay at the *St. Petersburg Times* in Florida. But his best work has been as chief chronicler of the South for the *New York Times*, where he recently became the Miami bureau chief.

The state's amazingly diverse literary offspring also include Monroeville's Harper Lee and Truman Capote, Birmingham's Walker Percy and Fannie Flagg, and Montgomery's Zelda Fitzgerald, who met F. Scott while he was stationed at Camp Sheridan. Winston Groom, author of *Forrest Gump*, also hails from Alabama.

A marvelous overview of Alabama's rich literary harvest can be found in *Many Voices, Many Rooms* (a 1997 wordplay based on Capote's first book, *Other Voices, Other Rooms*), edited by Philip D. Beidler. Beidler also edited the excellent *The Art of Fiction in the Heart of Dixie: An Anthology of Alabama Writers*, published in 1987.

SOUTHERN SIGHTS

Alabama Bureau of Tourism and Travel, 401 Adams Ave., P.O. Box 4927, Montgomery, AL 36103–4927; (334) 242–4169 or (800) ALA–BAMA.
Bed-and-Breakfast Association of Alabama, P.O. Box 707, Montgomery, AL 36101.

Monroeville

Millions of schoolchildren have gotten their first real glimpse of the South through the eyes of Scout Finch, the young heroine of Harper Lee's *To Kill a Mockingbird*. Through her preadolescent protagonist, Lee paints an unforgettably vivid portrait of the South and all its contradictions—justice and revenge, prejudice and tolerance, black and white. Lee's southwest

Alabama hometown of Monroeville—"a small town two hours of hard driving from any place one had ever heard of," in the words of author George Plimpton—was immortalized as Maycomb in *Mockingbird*.

Despite its out-of-the-way locale—a little more than one hundred miles southwest of Montgomery—nearly half a century after *Mockingbird*'s publication, Monroeville still attracts hundreds of tourists every year, all looking for Boo Radley's tree and the courtroom where Atticus Finch took on the racial bigotry that ran like an acid river through the Deep South in the 1930s.

For many, the book has taken the bite out of their hatred. Political strategist James Carville, himself a product of Louisiana Cajun country, has said the book changed his attitudes and his life: "I just knew, the minute I read it, that she [Harper Lee] had been right and I had been wrong." A former governor of Georgia, urging his constituents to bury the past and the Confederate flag with it, reminded them of Scout's courage in the face of the rednecks who'd come to string up the wrongfully accused Tom Robinson.

Monroeville's centerpiece is the Old Courthouse, whose upstairs courtroom served as Lee's inspiration for the pivotal trial scenes in *Mockingbird*. None of the 1962 movie, which came out two years after the book's publication, was actually filmed in Monroeville. But a plaque over the courtroom door reads, "This room was used as a model for the courtroom scene in *To Kill a Mockingbird*." The Old Courthouse isn't used these days for trials; a more modern courthouse was built next door in 1991.

The Old Courthouse, built in 1903, was designed by renowned Southern architect Andrew Bryan. Its gorgeous original tin ceilings remain, stamped with a dogwood design, and the floors were hewn from local pine and blackgum. The historic treasure now houses the Monroe County Heritage Museum and Gift Shop, which features local-interest exhibits, including a section devoted to the War of 1812 and a corner alcove featuring mementos from the town's two literary offspring, Harper Lee and her next-door neighbor, Truman Capote.

The exhibit includes photos signed by Gregory Peck, who played lawyer Atticus Finch in the movie version of *Mockingbird*, signed copies of Capote's books, copies of letters in which he mentions Monroeville, and the *Life* magazine cover of Capote and the two actors (Robert Blake and Scott Wilson) who played the killers in the film version of his most famous book, *In Cold Blood*.

The courtroom of the Old Monroe County Courthouse. (photo courtesy of the Monroe County Heritage Museums)

The courthouse grounds also feature three houses from the movie set, carted up and moved from California, where the movie was filmed. Visitors can peek inside the Finch house, Miss Blanche Dubose's, and Boo Radley's. Every year the museum presents a locally produced stage version of *To Kill a Mockingbird*.

Oddly, the courthouse exhibit features nothing donated by the notoriously reclusive Harper Lee, save a handwritten note saying the courthouse in the movie version of *Mockingbird* is nearly an exact replica of the Monroeville courthouse. Lee lives in New York most of the year but returns to Monroeville every winter to stay with her sister, Alice, who is a title lawyer in town.

Lee, now in her seventies, seems to have devoted the four decades since her sole book's publication to eschewing any attention that might result from it. Nelle (or "Nail," in Southern Alabamian), as she's known locally—Harper is her middle name—might have lunch at the Sweet Tooth or browse through the fripperies at Finishing Touches, a gift shop that sells autographed copies of *Mockingbird*. She'll buy a few groceries at Piggly Wiggly or attend services at the First United Methodist Church.

A scene from the annual Monroeville production of *To Kill a Mockingbird.* (photo courtesy of the Monroe County Heritage Museums)

The townspeople leave her to herself, content with the occasional hello. The justifiably proud Monroeville city fathers have for years wanted a Harper Lee Day, or at least a billboard honoring their Pulitzer Prize–winner, but Lee steadfastly refuses.

She describes her hometown in realistic, if not always flattering terms, in *Mockingbird:* "Maycomb was an old town, but it was a tired old town when I first knew it. In rainy weather the streets turned to red slop;

grass grew on the sidewalks, the courthouse sagged in the square. Some-how, it was hotter then: a black dog suffered on a summer's day; bony mules hitched to Hoover carts flicked flies in the sweltering shade of the live oaks on the square. Men's stiff collars wilted by nine in the morning. Ladies bathed before noon, after their three o'clock naps, and by night-fall were like soft teacakes with frostings of sweat and talcum."

Lee's father, Amasa Coleman Lee, was a lawyer (the role model for Atticus) and publisher of the *Monroe Journal*. The elder Lee died in 1962, but people in town still recall him fondly. In a 1999 interview with Y'all.com, a Web site devoted to the South, pharmacist and town histo-rian Dickie Williams says, "I used to serve him a Co'cola every day. He'd come in here and get him a nickel Coke. No ice."

The town jail, Harper Lee writes in *Mockingbird:*

> . . . was the most venerable and hideous of the county's build-ings. Atticus said it looked like something Cousin Joshua St. Clair might have designed. It was certainly someone's dream. Starkly out of place in a town of square-faced stores and steep-roofed houses, the Maycomb jail was a miniature Gothic joke one cell wide and two cells high, complete with tiny battlements and flying buttresses. Its fantasy was heightened by its red brick facade and the thick steel bars at its ecclesiastical windows. It stood on no lonely hill, but was wedged between Tyndal's Hard-ware Store and the *Maycomb Tribune* office. The jail was May-comb's only conversation piece: its detractors said it looked like a Victorian privy; its supporters said it gave the town a good solid respectable look, and no stranger would ever suspect that it was full of niggers.

Harper Lee's Monroeville neighbor, Truman Capote, was born in New Orleans in 1924. As a young child, he was brought to Monroeville to live with an aunt and stayed until 1931—long enough to become Lee's best friend and the role model for Dill, the quirky, startlingly incisive little boy who lived next door to the Finches.

"I'm Charles Baker Harris. I can read," Dill introduces himself, naming the one talent sure to make him irresistibly attractive to Scout. Lee's description of Dill leaves little doubt as to Capote's influence:

He wore blue linen shorts that buttoned to his shirt, his hair was snow white and stuck to his head like dandruff; he was a year my senior but I towered over him. As he told us an old tale his blue eyes would lighten and darken; his laugh was sudden and happy; he habitually pulled at a cowlick in the center of his forehead. . . . We came to know him as a pocket Merlin, whose head teemed with eccentric plans, strange longings, and quaint fancies.

And that's about as accurate a description of Truman Capote as one could hope for.

Before Harper Lee used him as a character in a book, Capote had beaten her to the literary punch, modeling the tomboy Idabel after her in *Other Voices, Other Rooms*, his critically hailed first novel, published in 1948, which has as its protagonist a thirteen-year-old boy growing up in the rural South.

In second grade, Capote learned that he was being sent back north to live with his mother. He wanted a party, an elaborate Halloween party that all the neighborhood kids would remember forever (this could be viewed as a preadolescent precursor to his legendary Black and White Ball, thrown in honor of the *Washington Post*'s Kay Graham in 1966). Little Truman's Halloween party was memorable all right, but not exactly for the reasons Truman might have intended.

In a 1997 article in *Vanity Fair* magazine, writer James Wolcott quotes Jennings Faulk Carter, a cousin of Truman's, as recalling that "the party was nearly stampeded by a visit from the Ku Klux Klan, who had heard tell there might be Negroes present and set upon one scared [white] boy dressed as a robot, whose cardboard legs prevented him from fleeing." Harper's daddy and other powerful townfolk dealt with the bullies, and "the sheeted rednecks slunk off to their cars."

After he left Monroeville, Capote never returned to live in the South, except for brief periods in New Orleans and Key West. He once toyed with the idea of buying a place in Monroeville, as recounted by Jennings Faulk Carter in Plimpton's *Capote*:

Daddy had told him about a piece of land . . . with a small house on it, for sale. Truman immediately wanted to buy it. The jeweler in Monroeville owned it. They almost closed the deal. But Daddy got to thinking . . . and came to the conclusion that if Truman bought that little piece of property, all these strange people from the North that wrote and did movies would come down.

And so, he just took it upon himself to tell Truman that Mr. Jones, the jeweler, had decided not to sell. It wasn't six months after that Truman came up to Mother's in his red Jaguar. He had this funny boy in there with him, a nice-looking young man. I didn't know that anything was going on, but Mother saw right through it and she just had this screaming fit. She got that broom and ran the boy off . . . Well, after Mother had the fit, we all knew.

Thus ended Capote's brief sojourn back to the town that had once nurtured him.

Capote's and Lee's homes once stood two blocks south of the square on South Alabama Avenue. All that remains on the Capote lot is a stone wall around the yard, a remnant from Capote's time. A historical marker notes the Capote connection: "On this site stood the home of the Faulk family of Monroeville, relatives of writer Truman Capote. Capote himself lived in this home from 1927 to 1933, and for several years he spent his summer vacations here. Two of the Faulk sisters operated a highly successful millinery shop on the town square, and the third sister, affectionately known as Sook, was the inspiration for characters in *The Grass Harp*, *The Thanksgiving Visitor*, and *The Christmas Memory*. The original structure on this site burned to the ground in 1940 and the second home was demolished in 1988. Monroeville remained important to Capote throughout his life and he returned to the area many times before his death in 1984 to visit relatives."

The plaque also features a short quote from *The Grass Harp*, but does not mention Capote's friendship with Lee or his being the inspiration for Dill—there is no reference to Lee at all, in fact. Lee's lawyer—her sister Alice, still practicing law in her late eighties—made it clear when the marker was erected that Lee would have no part of it; she simply didn't want the attention. On the back corner of the Faulk lot stands a snow-cone stand that gets plenty of customers from nearby Monroeville Elementary, which both Capote and Lee attended.

The Grass Harp gives great insight into the oddly egotistical but sharing nature of Capote's soul mate, Sook, whom he called Dolly in the book: "She saw everything first, and it was her one real vanity to prefer that she, rather than you, point out certain discoveries: a birdtrack bracelet, an eave of icicles—she was always calling come see the cat-shaped cloud, the ship in the stars, the face of frost."

There's no historical marker next door on the Lee lot, now home to Mel's Dairy Dream. Behind the ice-cream store is a thick grove of trees and brush. Push your way through and you can see the playground at the elementary school, where Nelle and Truman spent hours dreaming up stories and tussling in the red Alabama dirt. An assistant principal at the school has a three-foot-long piece of oak in his office, supposedly from the tree where Boo Radley hid his friendship offerings for the Finch children. The tree was chopped down in 1976, and the house on Alabama Avenue that was rumored to be the inspiration for Boo's has been replaced by a gas station.

A handsome stone in the town cemetery memorializes Lillie Mae Faulk, Truman's mother, and her two consorts: Julien Persons, Truman's biological father, and Joseph Capote, his adoptive father. Truman is listed at the bottom, although his date of death is a day off. In actuality, neither Truman's remains nor his mother's rest there. Lillie Mae was cremated, and the ashes were misplaced after Joe Capote neglected to pay the mausoleum rent. Truman's ashes were scattered along with those of his longtime companion, Jack Dunphy, on a pond near Sag Harbor, New York.

Capote and Lee remained close as they grew older. In 1959, when Capote was researching the murders of the Clutter family in Kansas for his classic true-crime novel, *In Cold Blood*, he took Nelle with him as a research assistant. Their friendship made sense given Capote's oft-quoted advice to young writers: "My point to young writers is to socialize. Don't just go up to a pine cabin all alone and brood. You reach that stage soon enough anyway." Capote and Lee together went through the house where the Clutter murders had taken place, and she stayed for several weeks helping him gather facts on the grisly crime, in which four members of a farm family were terrorized and murdered.

The friendship between Capote and Lee fueled still-standing speculation about the true authorship of *To Kill a Mockingbird*; there are those who swear Capote wrote most or all of it. Lee, for her part, has never written another book. Like Margaret Mitchell, whose only book published during her lifetime was the Pulitzer-winning *Gone With the Wind*, Harper Lee wrote her groundbreaking Southern saga, won her Pulitzer, and put down her pen.

Author Mark Childress, born in Monroeville in 1957, uses small-town Alabama as the setting for his most successful novel, *Crazy in Alabama,* a wildly comic coming-of-age story about a young boy living with his undertaker uncle at the beginning of the Civil Rights Movement. Childress started his career in journalism but turned to fiction in the early 1980s. Like that of Lee and Capote, his work often chronicles the racially charged atmosphere in the South, which hadn't changed all that much from the 1930s to the 1960s. One suspects that Atticus Finch would have hung his head from the shame of it.

LITERARY LURES AND SOUTHERN SIGHTS

Finishing Touches, 18 E. Claiborne Street; (334) 575–2066.

Mel's Dairy Dream (on the lot where Harper Lee's home stood), 216 S. Alabama Avenue; (334) 743–2483.

Monroe County Heritage Museum, Courthouse Square, (334) 575–7433; www.tokillamockingbird.com; open 8 A.M. to 4 P.M. weekdays, 10 A.M. to 2 P.M. Saturdays. Free admission.

Monroeville Area Chamber of Commerce, 27 N. Mount Pleasant Avenue; (334) 743–2879; www.frontiernet.net/~monroecol.

Monroeville Elementary School, 420 S. Mount Pleasant Avenue; (334) 743–3474.

Sweet Tooth Bakery, 5 W. Claiborne Street; (334) 575–7040.

Montgomery

Montgomery, in the central part of the state, seems at first like any other mid-size American city of 200,000—clean, fairly conservative, bustling in a not-quite-type A way. But flick away just a bit of the dusty surface, and Montgomery gleams, subtly showcasing its enormous store of Southern history, from the Civil War to the Civil Rights Movement, as well as a seemingly bottomless wellspring of arts and culture.

This is the city where Rosa Parks sparked a movement by refusing to give up her seat on the bus. Ten years after Parks's 1955 stance, the Selma-to-Montgomery Civil Rights March culminated at the capitol steps, led by Dr. Martin Luther King Jr. This is also the city whose fashionable Cloverdale suburb gave us Zelda Sayre and nurtured the romance between a teenage Zelda, as yet untainted by the schizophrenia that would torture her later in life, and a young serviceman named F. Scott Fitzgerald, who was stationed at nearby Camp Sheridan in 1918.

Montgomery served as the first capital of the Confederacy, and it was at its capitol building atop Goat Hill that Mississippian Jefferson Davis was inaugurated as the first (okay, *only*) president of the Confederate States of America. To this day, Alabama's governors are still sworn in using the same Bible that Davis used. The Capitol, built in 1851, still serves as a working house of government but is also a museum chock-full of fascinating Southern history. Civil War buffs can also visit the first White House of the Confederacy downtown, the 1835 home Davis used when he and his family lived here.

Not far across town stands a more modern-day monument to the struggle that began in Davis's day: sculptor Maya Lin's Civil Rights Memorial. Lin, who also designed the Vietnam Veterans Memorial in Washington, D.C., here used a curved, circular black granite table engraved with the names of forty martyrs of the Civil Rights Movement. The names shoot out from the center like bursts from an exploding star. Water flows from the center across the surface, reflecting the words of Martin Luther King Jr., carved into the wall behind: "We will not be satisfied until justice rolls down like waters and righteousness like a mighty stream."

In the fashionable suburb of Cloverdale, at 915 Felder Avenue, literary wanderers can catch an almost eerie glimpse into the mind of one of Montgomery's most famous—and infamous—daughters, Zelda Sayre Fitzgerald. The Cloverdale area is on the National Register of Historic Places and makes a lovely driving or walking tour. Other historic Montgomery neighborhoods include the Garden District and Cottage Hill.

Zelda, Cloverdale's most famous flapper, was born in 1900, the daughter of an Alabama Supreme Court justice. When she was eighteen, Zelda met her future husband, Jazz Age icon F. Scott Fitzgerald. At that time, he wasn't anyone's icon, he was merely an Army grunt stationed at nearby Camp Sheridan. They met at a country club dance. In 1919, she wrote him a letter that's preserved with others under the glass top of a bureau in the Cloverdale house.

"Darling heart," it begins, "Our fairytale is almost ended, and we're going to marry and live happily ever after." She was right about the first and second parts, but not about the "happily ever after." The Fitzgeralds lived in the Cloverdale house, now nearly a century old, with their daughter, Scottie, from October 1931 to April 1932. Zelda had suffered her first mental breakdown—the then-generic term for depression and schizophrenia—in 1930, and it was thought that a return to her hometown might soothe Zelda's tortured soul.

The house is full of Fitzgerald memorabilia: photos, hundreds of paper dolls that Zelda drew for Scottie, and Zelda's paintings and letters, both from the hopeful early years and the darker later days. Her paintings, mostly in shades of purple and blue, line the walls. Some are subtly sensuous, others, like her dancing nudes, deliberately provocative. The floral subjects exhibit an almost wispy tenderness, as if they, like Zelda, are skating just along the edge of reality and might vanish with a strong breeze. Some of Zelda's artwork also hangs in the Montgomery Museum of Fine Art, Alabama's oldest fine-arts museum, which also boasts an impressive collection of Southern regional art.

During their stay in Montgomery, Scott worked on *Tender Is the Night*, which was published in 1934. He had already seen his first great success in the 1920s, with *The Great Gatsby* and *This Side of Paradise*. Zelda also began her first and only novel, *Save Me the Waltz*, while living in Cloverdale. Zelda's novel was published in 1932, but despite her own gifts as a writer, she never matched her husband's acclaim—a horrible humiliation for the girl who once was known as the prettiest and smartest in all Montgomery. Some say that Scott's derision of Zelda's work led to her breakdowns.

He hated her novel, claiming she had based it on their marriage. That seems a tad hypocritical, given that the book Scott began in Montgomery, *Tender Is the Night*, featured a character named Nicole Driver, whose life seemed to mirror Zelda's. She wasn't amused. "What made me so mad," Zelda wrote, "was that he made the girl so awful and kept on reiterating how she had ruined his life."

The Fitzgerald house, once seemingly doomed to destruction, was saved in the mid-1980s by local businessman Julian McPhillips, a devotee of both history and literature. "My wife and I knew it was the only house in town where either Scott or Zelda had lived that was still standing," he told a reporter from the *Birmingham Post-Herald* in 1991. "A developer could have knocked it down and built 20 town homes on that property and made a million."

McPhillips and his wife, Leslie, weren't about to let that happen. They bought the house—long since divided into apartments—in 1986 and kept it as an apartment building. In 1989, the McPhillipses turned one of the first-floor apartments into the Fitzgerald Museum. Most of the home's artifacts were bought from Zelda's friends and family. They include items as diverse and poignant as Zelda's cigarette holder and her mother's pink baby booties. Visitors to the home can watch a twenty-five-minute video about the Fitzgeralds' life in Montgomery.

LITERARY LURES AND SOUTHERN SIGHTS

Alabama Shakespeare Festival, Wynton M. Blount Cultural Park, off Woodmere Boulevard; (334) 271–5353 or (800) 841–4ASF; www.asf.net.

Alabama State Capitol, Capitol Hill, east end of Dexter Avenue (downtown); (334) 242–3184. Open 9 A.M. to 4 P.M. Mondays through Saturdays. Free admission.

Civil Rights Memorial, 400 Washington Street (on the grounds of the Southern Poverty Law Center); (334) 264–0286. Open 24 hours daily. Free admission.

Dexter Avenue King Memorial Baptist Church (where Martin Luther King Jr. became pastor in 1954), 315 S. Jackson Street; (334) 269–5327. Guided tours at 10 A.M. and 2 P.M. Mondays through Thursdays and Saturdays, and at 10 A.M. only on Fridays. Donation.

First White House of the Confederacy, 644 Washington Street; (334) 242–1861. Open 8:30 A.M. to 4 P.M. weekdays. Donation.

The Fitzgerald Museum, 919 Felder Avenue, Cloverdale; (334) 264–4222. Open 10 A.M. to 2 P.M. Wednesdays through Fridays, 1 P.M. to 5 P.M. weekends. Donation.

Old Alabama Town, 301 Columbus Street; (334) 240–4500. Open 9:30 A.M. to 3:30 P.M. Mondays through Saturdays, 1:30 P.M. to 3:30 P.M. Sundays. Admission fee.

Montgomery Area Chamber of Commerce, Convention & Visitor Division, 401 Madison Avenue, P.O. Box 79, Montgomery, AL 36101; (334) 834–5200; www.montgomerychamber.org.

Montgomery Museum of Fine Art, 1 Museum Drive; (334) 244–5700. Open 10 A.M. to 5 P.M. Tuesdays, Wednesdays, Fridays, and Saturdays; 10 A.M. to 9 P.M. Thursdays, and noon to 5 P.M. Sundays. Free admission.

Montgomery Area Visitor Center, 300 Water Street; (334) 261–1100 or (800) 240–9452.

ACCOMMODATIONS AND RESTAURANTS

Chantilly, 1931 Vaughn Road; (334) 271–0509. Elegant continental dining.

Country Barbecue, 5336 Atlanta Highway; (334) 270–0126; and 2610 Zelda Road; (334) 262–6211. This is where the locals get their barbecue fix.

Governor's House, 2705 E. South Boulevard; (334) 228–2800. Nice accommodations close to the downtown sights.

Guest House Hotel and Suites, 120 Madison Avenue; (334) 264–2231. The best hotel in downtown Montgomery.

Lattice Inn, 1414 S. Hull Street; (334) 832–9931. Comfortable and cozy, this inn has two guest rooms furnished with antiques. A one-bedroom cottage for four is also available, as are two modern rooms than can be turned into a suite.

Red Bluff Cottage, 551 Clay Street; (334) 264–0056. Exquisite bed-and-breakfast convenient to downtown, with four antiques-decorated guest rooms. From the upstairs porch, guests can see the Alabama River and the Capitol.

Sassafras Tea Room, 532 Clay Street; (334) 265–7277. Historic Queen Anne–style home on the Alabama River. You'll be humming "Swanee" before you get your bread pudding or pecan pie.

Vintage Year, 405 Cloverdale Road; (334) 264–8463. Cool artsy decor and an Italian menu.

Birmingham

Northern Alabama is infused with a culture and character all its own, even though it's not that far geographically from its more southerly brethren. It's a little rougher, a lot hotter, much less inclined toward culture and the arts (except for Birmingham), and more concerned with simply getting by.

Rick Bragg describes the oppressive Southern heat in *All Over but the Shoutin'*:

You begged the sky for a single cloud. The sun did not shine down, it bored into you, through your hat and hair and skull, until you could feel it inside your very brain, till little specks of that sun seemed to break away and dance around, just outside your eyes. . . .

Your sweat did not drip, it ran, turning the dust to mud on your face, soaking your T-shirt and your jeans, clinging like dead skin. . . . Every now and then you or some man beside you would uncover a ground rattler, and you would chop it to little pieces with your shovel or beat it to mush with rakes, not just because it could bite you, kill you, but because it got in your way, because you had to take an extra step, to raise your arms an extra time, under that sun.

The racial tensions of the southern part of the state were felt strongly here, especially in Birmingham, but in the more rural areas blacks and whites commingled more amicably, and many white Alabamians had the grace to be ashamed of the bigoted leaders who claimed to speak for all of them. Bragg wrote:

I know I grew up in a time when a young man in a baggy suit and slicked-down hair stood spraddle-legged in the crossroads of history and talked hot and mean about the colored, giving my poor and desperate people a reason to feel superior to somebody, to anybody. I know that even as the words of George Wallace rang through my Alabama, the black family who lived down the dirt road from our house sent fresh-picked corn and other food to the poor white lady and her three sons, because they knew their daddy had run off, because hungry does not have a color.

Bragg's family was white, but hardly of a privileged class: "These were people who remembered the weight of the cotton sack, people with grease under their fingers that no amount of Octagon soap would ever scrub away, people who built redwood decks on their mobile homes and have no idea that smart-aleck Yankees think that is somehow funny. People of the pines. My people," he writes. And prejudice was something they were accustomed to. As his family walked from home to town and back, he recalls, "People rode by us and stared, because no one—no one—walks in the Deep South. You ride, and if you don't have something to ride in, you must be trash."

Birmingham, a north-central Alabama city of nearly a million, is the state's largest city and also its most cosmopolitan. The University of Alabama is the city's pride and joy, as well as its largest employer. Despite its sophistication, though, the city was home to some of the most divisive confrontations of the Civil Rights era, earning it the unflattering nickname of America's Most Segregated City.

More than fifty racially motivated bombings took place here in the early 1960s during the tenure of the notorious Eugene "Bull" Connor, ostensibly the commissioner of public safety. The bombings included one in 1963 that killed four little girls at the 16th Street Baptist Church. After that tragedy and the national disdain it earned the city, things slowly began to turn more positive. A black mayor was elected in 1979.

For all its problems, Birmingham retains an almost indefinable allure.

In *The Fiery Pantheon,* Southern girl Nancy Lemann writes about a character's affinity for all things Alabamian:

> After living in Tuscaloosa, Alabama, Monroe wanted to live in Birmingham. Mobile, Tuscaloosa, Birmingham—*Alabama* was the source of all knowledge. He wanted to show Grace Birmingham . . . People in Birmingham had a quality that many Southerners have: They had this world-weary, worldly-wise air as if they had just been standing at the edge of a yawning abyss, looking down into a yawning vortex of ruin, and had seen it all—as if they were possessed of the most tragic knowledge the world could know. It was as if the Civil War were transpiring in their very hearts, for they had some inner knowledge of destruction.

In that same book, Lemann further describes the "Birmingham anomaly":

> The people had the personality of New Orleans, with their mad drawls and world-weary knowledge, their bemusing hopelessness; but Birmingham is a postbellum town—unlike New Orleans or Charleston or Savannah. It is a gutsy-looking industrial town overlooked by suburban hills. . . . Birmingham was the type of

town where you kept running into people you knew even though you didn't know anyone there and had never been there before in your life.

In *Fried Green Tomatoes at the Whistle Stop Cafe* (1987) by Birmingham native Fannie Flagg, the character Artis expresses an undeniable, if illogical, adoration of the city:

> Birmingham, the town that during the Depression had been named by FDR "the hardest hit city in the U.S." . . . where people had been so poor that Artis had known a man that would let you shoot at him for money and a girl that had soaked her feet in brine and vinegar for three days, trying to win a dance marathon . . . the place that had the lowest income per capita of any American city and yet was known as the best circus town in the South.
>
> Birmingham, which at one time had the highest illiteracy rate, more venereal disease than any other city in America, and at the same time proudly held the record for having the highest number of Sunday School students of any city in the U.S. . . . where Imperial Laundry trucks had once driven around town with WE WASH FOR WHITE PEOPLE ONLY written on the side, and where darker citizens still sat behind wooden boards on streetcars that said COLORED and rode freight elevators in department stores.
>
> Birmingham, Murder Capital of the South, where 131 people had been killed in 1931 alone. All this, and yet Artis loved his Birmingham with an insatiable passion, from the south side to the north side, in the freezing-cold rainy winter, when the red clay would slide down the sides of hills and run into the streets, and in the lush green summers, when the green kudzu vine covered the sides of the mountains and grew up in trees and telephone poles and the air was moist and heavy with the smell of gardenias and barbecue. . . . He missed Birmingham like most men miss their wives.

Folks in Flagg's fictitious Whistle Stop, though, don't share Artis's ardor. In the *Weems Weekly*, Whistle Stop's weekly bulletin, an editorial of July 12, 1930, reads: "I, for one, am delighted at the addition to our busy street. Just think, now you can mail a letter, have a meal, and get your hair done all on the same block. All we need now is a picture show to open up, then none of us would ever need to go over to Birmingham again."

Whistle Stop also has its share of the literary-minded, as shown in the occasional *Weems Weekly* theatrical review: "The Whistle Stop Drama put on their annual play Friday night, and I want to say, good work, girls. The name of the play was *Hamlet,* by the English playwright Mr. William Shakespeare, who is no stranger to Whistle Stop because he also wrote last year's play."

Despite its disdain of big bad Birmingham, Whistle Stop had its own notoriety. When a boy loses his arm to an oncoming freight train, the newspaper editor scolds the citizenry: "That makes a foot, an arm and an index finger we have lost right here in Whistle Stop this year. And also, the colored man that was killed, which just says one thing about us, and that is that we need to be more careful in the future. We are tired of our loved ones losing limbs and other things."

Flagg, an actress as well as a writer and now a resident of California, says her careers in both fields began in the fifth grade, when she wrote, produced, directed, and starred in a three-act comedy, *The Whoopee Girls,* "which got the audience hysterical and got Fannie expelled because it contained the word *martini.*" She later entered the Miss Alabama contest and won a scholarship to the Pittsburgh Playhouse, where she "distinguished herself as the only girl in the history of the school to fail ballet."

Her writing credits include dozens of television specials; *Fried Green Tomatoes,* which was made into a much-beloved movie starring Kathy Bates and Jessica Tandy; and *Welcome to the World, Baby Girl!,* published in 1998.

Fans of *Fried Green Tomatoes* will no doubt want to visit the Irondale Cafe, about seven miles east of Birmingham. The homey restaurant— yes, fried green tomatoes are available—was the inspiration for the book's Whistle Stop Cafe. The current owners have redecorated one room to resemble a 1930s cafe, and another evokes the fifties and sixties.

Walker Percy, best known for the time he spent in New Orleans, was also born in Birmingham, in 1916, the son of a financially successful Birmingham lawyer. Walker's father, Leroy Pratt Percy, was the son of a prominent Mississippi Delta family whose members included civic lead-

The Irondale Cafe, inspiration for the restaurant in *Fried Green Tomatoes at the Whistle Stop Cafe*. (photo courtesy of the Irondale Cafe)

ers, politicians, and writers, both men and women. In 1929, at the age of forty, Leroy Percy committed suicide, as had his father and several other male ancestors before him. The entire family suffered from chronic depression and ill health, which had a profound effect on Walker Percy and his writings.

Young Walker spent his childhood in a Birmingham that biographer Lewis Lawson called "New-South Birmingham, living in a contemporary home just off the number six fairway of the New Country Club." Walker's mother, Martha Susan (called Mattie Sue) Phinizy, who was from Athens, Georgia, was killed in an auto accident in 1932. After the deaths of their parents, Walker and his two brothers were adopted by his father's first cousin, William Alexander Percy. So at age sixteen, Walker Percy moved from New South Birmingham to Old South Greenville, Mississippi, where he lived in the old Percy House on Percy Street.

A more recent Birmingham native is Vicki Covington, born in the 1950s. Covington's novels include *Gathering Home*, *Bird of Paradise*, and *Night Ride Home*. In her latest, *The Last Hotel for Women*, Covington's sharp but surprisingly gentle gaze turns on 1960s Birmingham and the violence that ensued. She uses the reprehensible real-life character of Bull Connor to make the point that, as Y'all.com puts it, for him and "the entire South, moral awareness comes as a painful but necessary awakening, with the hope of redemption always one step ahead."

Covington, a self-described "Christian liberal," told Y'all.com why she included Bull Connor in the novel: "We will never be completely healed in Birmingham until we understand and forgive Connor. We haven't yet. But he is part of the story of who we are. If we forgive him, we can forgive ourselves. Every story has a villain; the story can't exist without it. In many ways, he is the sacrificial lamb."

She also described the Southern writer's deep affinity for place. "It's my subjective belief that Southerners are a mystical people," she said. "They are more likely to embrace the spirit, to call it by its name. A writer's imagination is totally shaped by the place in which she lives, and place is the most important element of creation, especially for Southerners."

Covington grew up in Birmingham's Woodlawn neighborhood. In 1994, *Birmingham* magazine asked her to name her favorite place in the city. Her choice? The viaduct passing over Sloss Furnace—she liked its sense of connection, its aura of possibility. "On the viaduct, we're crossing over. We're going somewhere, somewhere good," she writes.

LITERARY LURES AND SOUTHERN SIGHTS

Birmingham Civil Rights Institute, 520 Sixteenth Street N.; (205) 328–9696; www.bcri.bham.al.us/. This moving monument includes historic film footage of police dogs being turned on peaceful demonstrators, the charred shell of the bus that was burned during the Freedom Rides, and the door from Dr. Martin Luther King Jr.'s Birmingham jail cell. Open 10 A.M. to 5 P.M. Tuesdays through Saturdays, 1 P.M. to 5 P.M. Sundays. Admission fee.

Greater Birmingham Convention and Visitors Bureau, 2200 Ninth Avenue N., Birmingham, AL 35203; (205) 458–8000 or (800) 458–8085; www.bevb.org.

Sloss Furnaces National Historic Landmark, 20 Thirty-Second Street N.; (205) 324–1911. Open 10 A.M. to 4 P.M. Tuesdays through Saturdays, noon to 4 P.M. Sundays. Free admission.

Accommodations and Restaurants

Bombay Cafe, 2839 Seventh Avenue S.; (205) 322–1930. Great food, reasonable prices. Try the Big Easy crabcake sandwich—but get there early, 'cause they go fast.

Dreamland Bar-B-Que, 1427 Fourteenth Avenue S.; (205) 933-2133. Serves *only* pork ribs, so don't ask. Think I exaggerate? Well, check out the servers' T-shirts emblazoned with the restaurant's motto: "No Slaw, No Beans, No Potato Salad. Don't ask."

Irondale Cafe, 1906 First Avenue N., Irondale; (205) 956–5258.

John's Restaurant, 112 Twenty-first Street N. (downtown); (205) 322–6014. Serves seafood and incredible coleslaw.

Meadowlark Farms, County Road 66-534 Industrial Road, Alabaster (about twenty minutes from downtown); (205) 663–3141. A former farmhouse-turned-European country inn with yummy specialties, such as chateaubriand and duck with brandy fruit sauce.

Pete's Famous Hot Dogs, 1925 Second Avenue N.; (205) 252–2905. A Birmingham tradition since 1915. Pete's gone, but relatives are still serving up dogs at amazingly nominal prices.

Pickwick Hotel, 1023 Twentieth Street S., in Five Points South; (205) 933–9555 or (800) 255–7304. Built in 1931 as an office buidling and converted in 1986 to a bed-and-breakfast hotel. Charming Art-Deco style includes pink walls, green carpets, and period furnishings. High tea served from 3 P.M. to 5 P.M. Mondays through Thursdays.

Redmont Hotel, 2101 Fifth Avenue N.; (205) 324–2101. Built in the Jazz Age, in the roaring Twenties, the Redmont is the oldest operating hotel in Birmingham. Recently underwent a multi-million dollar renovation.

Rib-It-Up, 830 First Avenue N., near the Arlington Mansion; (205) 328–7427. Traditional, mouthwatering barbecue with traditional Southern sides. Kiss your diet goodbye.

Tutwiler Hotel, 2021 Park Plaza N.; (205) 322–2100. The grande dame of Birmingham hotels, this elegant jewel was built in 1913 as luxury apartments and converted to a hotel in 1986. It retains its old-world style, with marble floors, chandeliers, brass banisters, and antiques in the lobby. Guest rooms are filled with period reproductions.

The Shoals

In the northwestern corner of Alabama is an area so flush with huge lakes, formed by dams on the Tennessee River, that it has been dubbed the Great Lakes of the South. The area boasts more than 1,200 miles of lake shoreline. The so-called Quad Cities—Muscle Shoals, Tuscumbia, Sheffield, and Florence—are tucked near the banks of the Tennessee.

The cottage at Ivy Green where Helen Keller lived with her teacher, Annie Sullivan. (photo courtesy of Ivy Green)

Tuscumbia, situated on the south side of the Tennessee River about six miles from Florence, has as its primary claim to fame being the birthplace of Helen Keller. Keller was born in June 1880, a perfectly normal, healthy child. But nineteen months later she was stricken with a mysterious illness that left her blind and deaf, trapping her in an internal cell to which only one person had the key. Twenty-four-year old Annie Sullivan arrived at Ivy Green—the Keller home—on March 3, 1887, the day Helen would later call her soul's birthday.

Just a month later, Helen—who had acted like nothing so much as a small terrified wild animal when Annie arrived—emerged from isolation,

The pump at Ivy Green. (photo courtesy of Ivy Green)

borne on the power of one word: W-A-T-E-R, spelled into her hand in sign language by Annie as she pumped water on Helen's hand. Suddenly, Helen *got it*. She understood. Annie would forever be remembered by Helen and her family, and immortalized on stage and screen as *The Miracle Worker*.

Helen described the moment in her autobiography, *The Story of My Life*:

> As the cool stream gushed over one hand, she spelled into the other the word "water," first slowly, then rapidly. I stood still, my whole attention fixed upon the motions of her fingers. Suddenly, I felt a misty consciousness as of something forgottten—a thrill of returning thought; and somehow the mystery of language was revealed to me.

After her "reawakening," Helen's eagerness and intellectual prowess led her to become, in the words of Mark Twain, "the most marvelous person of her sex who existed on the earth since Joan of Arc." She graduated *magna cum laude* from Radcliffe College and published her autobiography while still in college. Keller became a women's rights crusader, particularly in the area of birth control. "The incalculable mischief of an uncontrolled birth rate sucks up the vitality of the human race," she wrote.

In 1915, writing about women's suffrage, she said, "Let us see how the votes of women will help solve the problems of living wisely and well." Keller traveled tirelessly as a lecturer, and in 1964, four years before she died, she was awarded the Presidential Medal of Honor.

William Gibson's 1959 play based on Keller's early days with Annie Sullivan, *The Miracle Worker,* is staged every summer on the grounds of Ivy Green, now a permanent shrine in her honor. The cottage where Helen and Annie lived—a former playhouse—contains personal belongings, including Keller's braille typewriter and library. Outside, the pump at which she first learned the meaning of water still stands. The simple white-frame house and cottage were built in 1820 by Keller's grandfather.

LITERARY LURES AND SOUTHERN SIGHTS

Anderson's Bookland, 114 N. Court Street, Florence; (256) 766–1163.

Colbert County Tourism and Convention Bureau, U.S. Highway 72 West, P.O. Box 440, Tuscumbia 35674; (256) 383–0783 or (800) 344–0783; www.alabamatravel.org/north/cctcb.html.

Florence/Lauderdale Tourism, One Hightower Place, Florence 35630; (256) 750–4141; www.flo-tour.org.

Ivy Green, birthplace of Helen Keller, 300 W. North Commons, Tuscumbia; (256) 383–4066. Open 8:30 A.M. to 4 P.M. Mondays through Saturdays, 1 P.M. to 4 P.M. Sundays. Advance reservations required. Admission $2.50. Every June a Helen Keller festival takes place in Tuscumbia, featuring a parade, tours of historic sites, puppet shows, and performances of *The Miracle Worker.*

Pope's Tavern, 203 Hermitage Drive, Florence; (256) 760–6439. Open 10 A.M. to 4 P.M. Mondays through Saturdays. Admission fee. One of Florence's oldest structures, the tavern is one block from Court Street, on a street that used to be called Military Road and was the most direct route from New Orleans to Nashville. During the Civil War, the tavern was used as a makeshift hospital for wounded soldiers from both sides. In 1874 it became a private home, and in 1965 it was purchased by the city of Florence. Now it's furnished as a tavern again.

Frank Lloyd Wright's Rosenbaum House, 601 Riverview Dr., Florence. Tours of this house, designed and built in 1939 by architect Frank Lloyd Wright, are not available at present but are expected to resume soon. Check the www.flo-tour.org Web site for updates. The Rosenbaum house is the only Wright house in Alabama and the best example of a do-it-yourself "Usonian" house in the country—*Usonian* was Wright's word for things related to the United States; apparently North American wasn't specific enough for him. The home sits on two acres overlooking the Tennessee River. Until tours are available, it's still worth a drive by.

ACCOMMODATIONS AND RESTAURANTS

Dale's Restaurant, 1001 Mitchell Boulevard, Florence; (256) 766–4961. Don't miss Dale's famous marinade.

Holiday Inn-Sheffield, 4900 Hatch Boulevard, Sheffield; (256) 381–4710. Serves both Florence and Sheffield; amenities include an exercise room and hot tub.

Homestead Inn, Florence, 504 S. Court Street; (256) 766–2331 or (800) 248–5336. Renovated red-brick building near the center of Florence, built in the 1960s as a Holiday Inn. Olympic-size swimming pool, restaurant.

Joe Wheeler State Park Lodge, U.S. 72 (near Rogersville, between Decatur and Florence); (256) 729–8288 or (800) 544–5639. Three-story, fieldstone-and-redwood lodge with views of Wheeler Lake from every room.

Key West Inn, 1800 U.S. 72, Tuscumbia; (256) 383–0700. Comfy, clean, with budget prices.

Louisiana, the Restaurant, 1311 E. Sixth Street, Muscle Shoals; (256) 386–0801. Heavily influenced by the Cajun and Creole styles of New Orleans's French Quarter.

Renaissance Grille, One Hightower Place, Florence; (256) 718–0092. Perched atop the Renaissance Tower overlooking the Tennessee River basin, this is a perfect place to watch an Alabama sunset.

Wood Avenue Inn, 658 N. Wood Avenue, Florence 35630; (256) 766–8441. An 1880 Victorian bed-and-breakfast.

2

Mississippi

I discovered that my little postage stamp of native soil was worth writing about and that I would never live long enough to exhaust it. It opened up a gold mine of people, as I created a cosmos of my own.

—William Faulkner

ississippi has taken so many intellectual hits over the years, it seems almost the natural thing to continue the bombardment. But the state has probably produced more outstanding writers per capita than any other in the South, with the possible exception of North Carolina. Authors born in Mississippi include—along with the big guns, Eudora Welty, William Faulkner, and Tennessee Williams—contemporary writers such as Ellen Gilchrist, who was born in Vicksburg; Elizabeth Spencer, born in Carrollton and now living in North Carolina; and Richard Ford, who now lives in New Orleans. Larry Brown, a former firefighter whose critically adored novels include *Father and Son* and *Big Bad Love*, lives in Oxford.

In *Growing Up Southern*, a collection of interviews with Southern authors, the editor relates a story about Greenville, Mississippi, native Shelby Foote, whose Civil War narrative is widely considered definitive. While Foote was in New York in the 1950s, someone asked him, "You're from Mississippi, aren't you?" At Foote's affirmative reply, the stranger asked, "What in the world do you do down there?"

Foote said, "Not much."

"So, how can you stand it?"

Foote carefully explained, "Well, we've got certain things down there that amount to something. For example, who do you think is the best writer in the United States?"

"William Faulkner."

"He's from Mississippi. Who do you think is the best woman writer in the United States?"

"Eudora Welty."

"Well, she's from Mississippi. Who do you think is the greatest playwright in America?"

"Tennessee Williams."

"He's from Mississippi. I guess we do a few things down there."

The *Growing Up Southern* editor suggested an addendum to the list: "Who do you think is the greatest chronicler of the Civil War?"

"Shelby Foote. He's from Mississippi."

SOUTHERN SIGHTS

Mississippi Division of Tourism Development, P.O. Box 849, Jackson, MS 39205; (601) 359–3297 or (800) WARMEST; www.visitmississippi.org.

Jackson

The central Mississippi city of Jackson, originally known as LeFleur's Bluff, was renamed to honor General Andrew Jackson, hero of the War of 1812. During the Civil War, Jackson was torched three separate times by the dreaded general William Tecumseh Sherman, with only a few public buildings spared the blaze: the old Capitol, the governor's mansion, and city hall. For a time, residents called the town Chimneyville because that's just about all that Sherman had left standing. Today, Jackson is by far the state's largest city, with a population of nearly 400,000.

In literary terms, Jackson belongs to one woman. Eudora Welty, born there in April 1909, has lived there most of her life and remains the town treasure. The affection felt by Jacksonians and readers alike for Welty is unmatched in this century's literary world. Ann Hyman, the *Times-Union* book editor, summed up Welty's allure in a story about the author's ninetieth birthday in 1999: "She's that kind of writer, a writer whose work you can literally reminisce about. There are only a few writers who can make us ask, in wonder and delight, how did she (or he) do that? Welty is one."

Mary Hood, a novelist and short story writer who lives in Woodstock, Georgia, told Hyman for that same article that Welty's vision "is complete, not made. It's the gift. There's no one like her." Welty has written thirty-two books and won the Pulitzer Prize, the Presidential Medal of Freedom, and several O. Henry Prize awards, as well as the National Institute of Arts and Letters' Gold Medal for Fiction.

Despite her unequaled acclaim, however, Miss Eudora, as she is called, remains uncommonly modest about her accomplishments, exhibiting particular sensitivity to her literary brethren from the same state. She once said that sharing a literary landscape with William Faulkner was "like living near a mountain."

Welty scholars beg to differ. Noel Polk, an English professor at the University of Southern Mississippi, told the *Boston Globe* in 1999: "She was thought of as female, and somehow inferior to Faulkner. But what goes unsaid is that what usually lies near a mountain is another mountain. Miss Welty has established herself as a new mountain."

In the autobiographical *One Writer's Beginnings*, Miss Eudora poked fun at the controversy stirred up by the mountain himself, on publication of Faulkner's scandalous—i.e., sexy and violent—*Sanctuary*. In describing the real-life Jackson character of Gypsy Smith, a firebrand evangelist, Welty notes that his influence was such that he even made a believer out of the editor of the evening newspaper. "It made him lastingly righteous so that he knew just what to say in the *Jackson Daily News* when one of our fellow Mississippians had the unmitigated gall to publish, and expect other Mississippians to read, a book like *Sanctuary*."

It should be noted that Faulkner, for his part, contributed to the scandal surrounding *Sanctuary* by admitting more than once that he wrote the book—the tale of a society girl's kidnapping into the seamy underworld of Memphis—not out of any great literary urge but simply because he was broke and needed the money a potboiler could quickly generate. "I took a little time out," he said, "and speculated what a person in Mississippi would believe to be current trends, chose what I thought was the right answer and invented the most horrific tale I could imagine and wrote it in about three weeks."

Welty, on the other hand, enjoyed a long career unsullied by controversy, although her fierce intelligence was matched by the courage she showed during the troubled 1960s. Novelist Ellen Douglas, who lives near Welty in Jackson, recalls that Welty once was asked if she was afraid that the Ku Klux Klan, in retribution for her outspoken liberal attitude, might attack her home.

"You know," Miss Eudora replied, "people who burn crosses don't usually read *The New Yorker.*"

In 1963, shortly after the leader of the National Association for the Advancement of Colored People, Medgar Evers, was murdered in Jackson, Welty wrote one of her strongest pieces, a first-person essay in a man's voice for *The New Yorker.* "Where Is the Voice Coming From?" tells of consuming racial hatred, spit out in harsh vitriol many found strikingly similar to that of Byron De La Beckwith—the man who killed Evers. Welty's ear for internal and spoken dialogue brought the killer's depths of pure meanness to chilling life: "I done what I done for my own pure-D satisfaction . . . we ain't never now never going to be equals and you know why? One of us is dead."

Welty was born in April 1909 at 741 North Congress Street, in Jackson. She describes a lasting impression from early childhood in *One Writer's Beginnings:*

> At our house on North Congress Street . . . we grew up to the striking of clocks. . . . I don't know whether or not my father's Ohio family, in having been Swiss back in the 1700s before the first three Welty brothers came to America, had anything to do with this; but we all of us have been time-minded all our lives. This was good at least for a future fiction writer, to be able to learn so penetratingly, and almost first of all, about chronology.

In 1925, the Weltys moved a few blocks across town, near the state Capitol, and Welty has lived ever since in that Tudor-style house her parents built at 1119 Pinehurst Street. In *One Writer's Beginnings*, the author gives a glimpse of herself as an impish youngster who along with her brother, rode her bike or roller-skated through the capitol to the Carnegie Library on the other side.

Everyone knows where Miss Eudora lives, but people in Jackson leave her be. In an article for *Southern Living* magazine, Welty friend and fellow author Willie Morris notes the two items on Miss Eudora's front door: a Clinton-Gore bumper sticker and a handwritten sign requesting "No autographs please." The unspoken rule is that no one shows up unannounced or uninvited, and Jacksonians take it as a given that visitors will respect this.

Wright paints a wonderful picture of his friend, noting that Welty "has a lovely, evocative Southern voice, quiet and lilting, punctuated by laughter and the ebullient retort, and all sorts of questions solicitously addressed to her companions. If the oral history of the South lives in her written words, it flourishes also in her spoken ones."

Richard Ford, himself a Pulitzer Prize–winner who grew up in Jackson and now lives in New Orleans, has said he believes that between Faulkner and Welty, Welty is the stronger writer. "She is much less an elitist than Faulkner," Ford told the *Boston Globe*. "She's much better educated than Faulkner. She benefited from coming along after Faulkner. He established a camp farthest out, and it had a good effect on her because it encouraged her to be more accessible. . . . Nobody is better at taking the density of lived experience that seems imperceptible and making it thrilling."

Indisputably, Welty boasts an uncanny knack for description, as shown in this passage from *The Optimist's Daughter*, the novel that won her the Pulitzer Prize: "Perhaps she was forty. There was little even of forty in her looks except the line of her neck and the backs of her little square, idle hands," she writes, describing a selfish, provincial widow. "She was bony and blue-veined; as a child she had very possibly gone undernourished. Her hair was still a childish tow. It had the tow texture, as if, well rubbed between the fingers, those curls might have gone to powder. She had round, country-blue eyes and a little feist jaw."

In *Eudora Welty: Writers' Reflections Upon First Reading Welty*, Tony Earley recalls how reading Welty made him realize the power of the Southern voice. "Incredibly, the voice had the same accent I did. It was the first time I had realized that literature could speak in a language I recognized as my own."

That voice, he contends, may have led to a consequence Welty never intended: "I have a theory—perhaps unformed and, without question, unsubstantiated—that most bad Southern writing is descended directly from Eudora Welty's 'Why I Live at the P.O.,'" Earley wrote in an essay in *The Oxford American* in 1999. He continues:

Welty's story smacks of a certain now-familiar sensibility, rife with caricature, overstated eccentricity, and broadly drawn humor, that has come to represent Southern writing, and through that representation, the South itself. . . . The characters in "Why I Live at the P.O." possess the prototypical, colorful Southern names that, in the musical sound of their regional specificity, have come to promise colorful Southern doings: Papa-Daddy, Uncle Rondo, Stella-Rondo, Shirley T., Sister. They eat green-tomato pickle and, on the Fourth of July, sport about in flesh-colored kimonos while impaired by prescription drugs. They live in Mississippi. They grow long beards and illegitimate children and mismatched sets of breasts.

In a 1972 interview, Welty explained what she calls the "narrative sense of human destiny" that she believes Southerners possess:

There's someone to remember a man's whole life, every bit of the long way. I think that's a marvelous thing, and I'm glad I got to know something of it. . . . In the South, where people don't move about as much, and where they once hardly ever moved at all, the pattern of life was always right there.

Readers in Jackson can be reminded of Welty's enormous influence, in any number of ways, at the Eudora Welty Library, the state's largest public library. The facility, which opened in 1986, includes a forty-two-foot-long circulation desk, hand-crafted in rosewood and maple by local artisan Fletcher Cox. The Mississippi Writers' Room is a cornucopia of delectable literary treats, with exhibits on Welty, Faulkner, Williams, Shelby Foote, Richard Wright, Larry Brown, Ellen Douglas, and many others. For the literary traveler, this is a must-stop on the itinerary.

LITERARY LURES AND SOUTHERN SIGHTS

Boyd House, "the Oaks," 823 N. Jefferson Street; (601) 856–0347. Greek Revival cottage, circa 1846, rumored to have served as Sherman's headquarters during the 1863 siege. Period furnishings include a sofa from Abraham Lincoln's law office in Springfield, Illinois. Open 10 A.M. to 3 P.M. Tuesdays through Saturdays. Admission fee.

Eudora Welty Library, 300 N. State Street; (601) 968–5811. Open 9 A.M. to 9 P.M. Mondays through Thursdays, 9 A.M. to 6 P.M. Fridays and Saturdays, and 1 P.M. to 5 P.M. Sundays. Admission free.

Governor's Mansion, 300 E. Capitol Street; (601) 359–6421. Tours every half hour from 9:30 A.M. to 11 A.M. Tuesdays through Fridays. Admission is free. Built in 1842 at a cost of about $61,000 (somewhat over the budget of $10,000). Classic Greek Revival structure, saved from destruction in 1904 by an outraged citizenry who asked, "Will Mississippi destroy what Sherman would not burn?" It was restored several times instead, including an early 1970s $2.7 million program that reinstated the original floor plan. Everyone from John Fitzgerald Kennedy to novelist William Styron has slept here, many in the sumptuous "Cream Bedroom," which features a massive Renaissance Revival half-canopied bed.

Jackson City Hall, 219 S. President Street; (601) 960–1084. Admission free, with 30- to 45-minute tours offered daily except during state events. Completed in 1847, this beautiful building was used during the Civil War as a hospital for the wounded from both sides. It was one of only three public buildings to survive the three separate Yankee torchings of the city during the war.

Jim Buck Ross Mississippi Agriculture and Forestry-National Aviation Museum, 1150 Lakeland Drive; (601) 713–3365 or (800) 844–8687. This wonderful museum features a re-created 1920s Mississippi town with a general store, gas station, school, church, newspaper office, doctor's office, and gardens. An 1860s farmstead includes cabins, a sawmill, and farm animals. Summertime hours are 9 A.M. to 5 P.M. Mondays through Saturdays, and 1 P.M. to 5 P.M. Sundays; from Labor Day to Memorial Day it's closed on Sundays. Admission fee. The Jackson Convention and Visitors Bureau also has an office here; (601) 969–1800.

Lemuria Book Store, 4465 Interstate 55 North, No. 202; (601) 366–7619. One of the best bookstores in the South, right up there with Square Books in Oxford.

Medgar Evers Home, 2332 Margaret Walker Alexander Drive; (601) 977–7839. Open for tours by appointment. The small, plain frame house where Civil Rights leader Medgar Evers was assassinated.

Metro Jackson Convention and Visitors Bureau, P.O. Box 1450, Jackson, MS 39215–1450; (601) 960–1891 or (800) 354–7695; www.visitjackson.com.

Mississippi Department of Archives and History, 100 S. State Street; (601) 359–6850; www.mdah.state.ms.us. Free.

Mississippi Heritage Festival, held each June at Jackson City Zoological Park; (601) 352–2580.

Mississippi Museum of Art, 201 E. Pascagoula Street; (601) 960–1515. The largest art museum in Mississippi, with more than five thousand pieces, including the world's largest collection by Mississippi artists. Contemporary collections include works by Georgia O'Keeffe and Andy Warhol. Admission $3.

Old Central High School, 259 N. West Street, now owned by Mississippi and used for state offices. This is the high school from which Eudora Welty graduated at the age of sixteen. The main building was designed in collegiate Gothic style, with crenellated towers and an arched entrance.

State Historical Museum (Old Capitol), State at Capitol Streets; (601) 359–6920. Beautifully restored 1833 building, one of only three antebellum buildings left unscathed by Sherman's troops. The mezzanine features a Eudora Welty photo exhibit. Open from 8 A.M. to 5 P.M. weekdays, 9:30 A.M. to 4:30 P.M.. Saturdays, 12:30 P.M. to 4:30 P.M. Sundays. Admission is free.

Southern Literary Festival, every April; (601) 974–1302.

State Capitol Building, High at President Street; (601) 359–3114. The new Capitol, circa 1903, built in the Beaux Arts Classical style.

ACCOMMODATIONS AND RESTAURANTS

Bully's Restaurant, 3118 Livingston Road; (601) 362–0484.

Chimneyville Smokehouse, 970 High Street; (601) 354–4665.

Edison-Walthall Hotel, 225 E. Capitol Street; (601) 948–6161 or (800) 932–6161. Jackson's most elegant hotel, all dark wood and whispered conversations, also features an elegant restaurant.

Fairview Bed and Breakfast, 734 Fairview Street; (601) 948–3429 or (888) 948–1908. Colonial Revival bed-and-breakfast, circa 1908, listed on the National Register of Historic Places and named Top Inn of 1994 by *Country Inns* magazine.

Hal and Mal's Restaurant and Brewery, 200 S. Commerce Street; (601) 948–0888. Owned by music promoter Malcolm White, who has papered the walls with autographed pictures of recording stars and other celebrity diners. Great catfish, quiche, and burgers, and a fabulous place to hear music. A little tricky to find, but it's very close to the old capitol. Ask anybody in Jackson; they can tell you how to get there.

Keifer's, 705 Poplar Boulevard; (601) 355–6825. Marvelous Greek restaurant with an inexpensive, varied menu.

Mayflower Cafe, 123 W. Capitol Street; (601) 355–4122. A local institution run by two aging Greek brothers who serve up Southern favorites, most dripping with cream gravy.

Millsaps-Buie House, 628 N. State Street; (601) 352–0221 or (800) 784–0221. Three-story, Victorian bed-and-breakfast with a view of the State Capitol. Circa 1888.

The Old Capitol Bed and Breakfast Inn, 226 N. State Street; (601) 359–9000 or (888) 359–9001. Luxury suites with hot tubs, a swimming pool, and off-street parking. A room dubbed Faulkner's Flat features a headboard constructed of enormous bindings of the Mississippi author's classic works.

Sun-n-Sand Motel, 401 N. Lamar Street; (601) 354–2501. A funky, fun little place for those in an adventurous mood, this is a relic of the old 1950s road hotels. Just a block from the stately Capitol Building, the Sun-n-Sand is a wild pastiche of orange and turquoise, accented with tasteful Polynesian touches and a trapezoidal pool and sundeck.

Oxford

The lushly beautiful little college town of Oxford, population about 10,000, sits nestled in the green hills south of Holly Springs National Forest. It's in the northern part of Mississippi, about sixty miles southeast of Memphis, Tennessee. William Faulkner, the man many have dubbed the greatest American author, called Oxford home, especially the antebellum house he named Rowan Oak, where he lived from 1930 to 1962.

He was born William Cuthbert Falkner (he added the "u" later in life) on September 25, 1897, in New Albany, Mississippi, near Tupelo. But he lived most of his life, until just prior to his death in July 1962, at Rowan Oak. Faulkner died at a hospital in Byhalia, Mississippi, of a heart attack after a three-week bout of back pain. His death was doubtless hastened by a lifelong fondness for drinking liquor in vast quantities.

Rowan Oak, the stately yet simple home of William Faulkner for much of his life.

As a youth, Faulkner briefly attended the University of Mississippi in Oxford, where he made a D in English and was refused membership in a literary society. For a while he ran the university post office, reading the magazines before distributing them to mail patrons. For this he was fired, an indignity that haunted him for years. In 1987, at a ceremony Faulkner would no doubt have enjoyed enormously, the U.S. Postal Service issued a commemorative Faulkner stamp at the Oxford Post Office. His inauspicious career with the postal service apparently had been forgotten.

Despite his lack of success at Ole Miss, Faulkner's literary stature eventually was such as to strike awe in the hearts of many another Southern writer. Georgia's Flannery O'Connor, no slouch herself, once said, "The presence alone of Faulkner in our midst makes a great difference in what the writer can and cannot permit himself to do. Nobody wants his mule and wagon stalled on the same tracks the Dixie Limited is roaring down."

Some took the risk, though, becoming friends with the grand man of letters, notably Shelby Foote and Walker Percy, both from the west-central Mississippi river town of Greenville. Once, sowing their oats, the two young men drove to Oxford, walked right up to Rowan Oak's front door, unannounced, to express their admiration for their hero. Faulkner took them for a stroll through the cedars and told them he'd just finished a book about the Mississippi Delta. Sure enough, *The Wild Palms* came out six months later, but Foote and Percy didn't realize it was the same book until years later. When they'd talked to Faulkner, the book's working title was *If I Forget Thee, Jerusalem*.

Faulkner was later a great fan of Foote's, especially of his Civil War novel, *Shiloh*. One friend reportedly told Faulkner, "Bill, you ought to write Shelby Foote and tell him that. It would give him great pleasure to hear that from you." Faulkner's reply: "You don't stop a running horse to give him sugar." Apparently, Foote got word of Faulkner's fascination with Shiloh, though. On the ninetieth anniversary of the Battle of Shiloh, Foote stopped in Oxford on his way to the Tennessee battlefield. He drove to Rowan Oak and asked Faulkner if he'd like to join him on the pilgrimage. Faulkner accepted.

For Faulkner, born just thirty-three years after the end of the Civil War, the horrors still resonated, both for him and his characters. Toward the end of his career, he wrote:

> For every Southern boy fourteen years old, not once but whenever he wants it, there is the instant when it's still . . . 1863, the brigades are in position behind the rail fence, the guns are laid and ready in the woods, and the furled flags are already loosened to break out and Pickett himself with his long, oiled ringlets and his hat in one hand probably and his sword in the other looking up the hill waiting for Longstreet to give the word and it's all in the balance, it hasn't happened yet.

Faulkner won the Nobel Prize for Literature in 1949, and in 1955 won both the Pulitzer Prize and the National Book Award for *A Fable*. Many of his books were set in and around Oxford, thinly veiled as Jefferson, seat of the fictitious Yoknapatawpha County. As in this chapter's opening notation, he once said that his "little native postage stamp of soil" would provide fertile ground for a lifetime of writing, so why on earth should he venture elsewhere? And in Faulkner's world, Oxford took on mythic proportions, becoming a sort of Everytown in its thrifty consolidation of humanity, both good and evil.

Civil War battlefields such as Shiloh, in Tennessee, have drawn writers such as William Faulkner and Shelby Foote for more than a century.

Faulkner's most controversial novel, *Sanctuary*, contains some of his most evocative descriptions of his homeland:

> It was a bright, soft day, a wanton morning filled with that unbelievable soft radiance of May, rife with a promise of noon and of heat, with high fat clouds like gobs of whipped cream floating lightly as reflections in a mirror, their shadows scudding sedately across the road. It had been a lavendar spring. The fruit trees, the white ones, had been in small leaf when the blooms matured, they had never attained that brilliant whiteness of last spring, and the dogwood had come into full bloom after the way also, in green retrograde before crescendo.
>
> But lilac and wisteria and redbud, even the shabby heaven trees, had never been finer, fulgent, with a burning scent blowing for a hundred yards along the vagrant air of April and May. The bougainvillia against the veranda would be large as basketballs and lightly poised as balloons.

For those who might agree with critics that Faulkner's lengthy descriptions went a bit overboard, Oxford hosts the annual Faux Faulkner contest, challenging entrants to submit their adjective-laden best. The 1996 winner, for instance, by New Orleans lawyer Lance Martin, ran a breath-sapping 470 words—all one sentence that began:

> Streaks of rainbow light and voices of ill-placed mirth emanated through the deep woods, piercing its teeming sanctum and illuminating tangled roots and ancient mounds (erected, occupied and foolishly thought owned by Indian settlers of old as if anyone could own or even tame these woods but long since vacated without so much of a trace of their existence save the names attending its topography, ghost names of long-vanished warriors, loosely fashioned on its devastated, weary soul) now trampled by a cacophonous crowd, townsfolk and hill dwellers, degenerates and socialites, gathered, comingled . . .

You get the idea.

The love lives of Faulkner's characters were often hopeless at best, downright deranged at worst. "Even if you're a fictional character, it's difficult to cope with such emotional excess," wrote Amy Weldon for Y'all.com, a Web site devoted to all things Southern, in a 1999 Valentine's Day article titled "Falling in Love the Faulkner Way." Weldon also helpfully provided a list of ways to tell if you're in love (if you're a Faulkner character). Some examples:

> No. 12. You track down the father of your illegitimate child at his hunting camp, even though you already know he won't talk to you (*Delta Autumn*).
>
> No. 10. If somebody sends you obscene letters, you act shocked but kind of enjoy them (*Intruders in the Dust*).
>
> No. 9. To avoid your feelings, you embark on a thirty-year hunting trip (*Go Down, Moses*).
>
> No. 4. You love your girlfriend despite her differences—including differences in species (*The Hamlet*, in which Isaac Snopes falls in love with a cow and lives in sin, in the barn, until she's taken from him and shot).
>
> No. 2. You sleep with your boyfriend every night, even though he's been dead for twenty years (*A Rose for Emily*).

And the No. 1 reason, according to Weldon, you recognize you're in love if you're a Faulkner character: You don't smell like trees—but you did when you left the house three hours ago. In *The Sound and the Fury*, Caddy Compson's younger brother accuses her of "not smelling like trees" anymore after a virginity-losing romp with an admirer.

Like many of his characters, Faulkner seemed distinctly lacking in romanticism, at least when it came to writing. "If a writer has to rob his mother, he will not hesitate," he once remarked. "The 'Ode on a Grecian Urn' is worth any number of old ladies."

His trilogy about the Snopes clan—*Sanctuary, Light in August*, and *A Green Bough*—and *Absalom, Absalom!*, all considered among his best work, were some of the books he wrote while living at Rowan Oak. His downstairs office still bears the outline, written on the walls in red grease pencil and ordinary graphite pencil, of his Pulitzer Prize–winning *A Fable*.

The office remains exactly as it was when Faulkner died in 1962, with his portable black Underwood typewriter perched atop the desk he made himself. Upstairs in Faulkner's bedroom, many of his clothes remain folded away in the drawers, some with "Faulkner" still hand-lettered inside by a

William Faulkner's downstairs office at Rowan Oak. The outline of a book, in fading grease pencil, is still visible on the walls.

Faulkner's bedroom, upstairs at Rowan Oak, is essentially the same as he left it.

Paris laundry. His mud-caked, worn boots, once left out for visitors to see, have now been stored away and replaced by a pair of dusty shoes.

When Faulkner bought his estate, Oxford was a sleepy little town of about 1,500 souls, and Faulkner's new homestead was known simply as the Bailey place. He renamed it Rowan Oak after the legend of the mythic Rowan tree, which the Celtic people believe to harbor magic powers of safety and protection. He made many of the improvements to the home himself, such as the plain, white pine shelves in the library. Faulkner's books are still shelved there, in the same order he had them. Underneath the shelves, he had built locking compartments to store shotgun shells away from the children of the house. Faulkner's funeral took place in the downstairs parlor.

In 1997, Oxford installed a bronze, seated statue of Faulkner on the southern side of the courthouse square. Until then, the only public reminders of the town's most famous son were Faulkner Alley, a murky little passageway off the square, a portrait on display at the local McDonald's (much to Faulkner's relatives' chagrin), and a plaque affixed to the courthouse.

The bronze statue, by local sculptor William Beckwith, cost $50,000 and stirred a cauldron of rancor among townsfolk, businesspeople, and the Faulkner estate. A stately four-story magnolia tree had to be razed to make room for the statue and the bench it's sitting on, and Faulkner's family was aghast. Faulkner's love of nature—at least of the plant and tree variety—was legendary.

He loved to hunt, though, and considered some animals mere nuisances that he couldn't be bothered with—but he certainly didn't mind if others got rid of the critters. In 1959, he ran a notice in the *Oxford Eagle* that read:

> The posted woods on my property inside the city limits of Oxford contain several tame squirrels. Any hunter who feels himself too lacking in woodcraft and marksmanship to approach a dangerous wild squirrel might feel safe with these. These woods are a part of the pasture used by my horses and milk cow; also, the late arrival will find them already full of other hunters. He is kindly requested not to shoot either of these.

Jimmy Faulkner, a nephew of "Brother Will," predicted grimly when the statue was being built that next thing you knew, Faulkner keyrings and other kitschy memorabilia would be sold on the courthouse lawn. He told the *Dallas Morning News* in 1997 that Oxford was interested only in his uncle's money when he was alive, and not much has changed on that account.

"Very few Oxford people read his books, really," Jimmy Faulkner said. "Some read them to try to pick themselves out in them. And when they found themselves, they got mad about it. If Brother Will could come back to life, he would find that he has a hell of a lot more friends here than he had when he was alive."

"They want to use him to make money. They're the ones behind this statue. It's being built by the Snopeses," [the family that personified low-class, vicious Southern evil in Faulkner's work]. "It's a Snopes statue."

The statue was put in place, however, and remains despite the adamant objections of Faulkner's family and others. But some say the bitterness it sparked will stain Oxford for generations. William Ferris, director of the Center for the Study of Southern Culture at the University of Mississippi, told Doug Swanson of the *Dallas Morning News* just before the statue's unveiling: "The cutting of that tree will haunt the town for years to come. Like Faulkner said, 'The past is never dead. It's not even past.'"

Oxford resident Martha Glenn Cofield told the *Morning News* that Faulkner was a quiet man who kept to himself and ignored the controversy sometimes stoked by his fictionalization of the town's citizenry.

> He would create some obnoxious character and give him the name of someone real. Sometimes people didn't like it. There were people who thought his books were just terrible. Especially *Sanctuary*. It was just so *shocking*. It upset everybody.
>
> My great-aunt Jenniebelle Stevens—she married a Smith— was the librarian in New Albany, about thirty miles from here over in Union County, where Mr. Faulkner was born. She wouldn't have his books on the shelves of *her* library. Until he won the Nobel Prize. Then she had to concede.

As author Elizabeth Spencer, also a native Mississippian, told Willie Morris in an interview, Faulkner was

> . . . one of us, right over here at Oxford, shocking us and exposing us to people elsewhere with story after story, drawn from the South's own private skeleton closet . . . the hushed-up family secret, the nice girl who wound up in a Memphis whorehouse, the suicides, the idiot brother kept at home, the poverty and ignorance of the poor whites . . . the revenge shootings, the occasional lynchings, the real life of the blacks. What was this man trying to do?

Near Oxford is the little town of Taylor, which you get to by taking Old Taylor Road. Taylor has three—count 'em, three—buildings: two grocery stores and a potter's shop. Taylor Grocery has a restaurant in back where catfish and trimmings are served Thursday through Sunday nights. The town is achieving cult status among Faulkner fans; this is the area he called Frenchman's Bend in his books. The Taylor studio of sculptor William Beckwith, who crafted the controversial Faulkner statue on the courthouse square, features his rendering of Temple Drake, who waited for the train in Taylor in Faulkner's novel *Sanctuary*. Yes, as Miss Welty would tell you, there's *that* book again.

Some who knew Faulkner claim he's never really left town. According to Willie Morris in a *National Geographic* article in 1989, "His niece, Dean Faulkner Wells, says that late one night in the house on South Lamar she awakened suddenly to the smell of his pipe. She knew his ghost was there."

Another Oxford writer whose name might ring a bell with readers: John Grisham, who grew up about thirty miles north, in Southaven, and attended law school at Ole Miss in the late 1970s. Grisham has written nearly a dozen legal thrillers, all bestsellers that have sold more than fifty million copies in dozens of countries worldwide. His detractors will tell you he's "no Faulkner," but then Grisham doesn't claim to be. His first book, *A Time to Kill*, was set in northern Mississippi and took on the time-honored Southern burr of racial injustice. Grisham now spends most of his time in Charlottesville, Virginia, but maintains strong ties to Oxford, where he lived for years, raised his family, and for several years coached a Little League baseball team.

Several years ago Grisham rescued the barely breathing *Oxford American* literary magazine and, as publisher, turned it into a thriving oasis for new Southern writing, criticism of books about the South, and essays and interviews on subjects as diverse as the Southern devotion to football, Southern music and art, and Padgett Powell's recent "What Southern Literature Is."

LITERARY LURES AND SOUTHERN SIGHTS

Center for the Study of Southern Culture, University of Mississippi Campus; (662) 915–5993; www.olemiss.edu/dept5/south. Research center for Southern literature, music and folklore in a restored antebellum observatory. Open 8 A.M. to 5 P.M. weekdays. Admission free.

Maud Faulkner's House, University Avenue at South Lamar Street, south of the courthouse square. This was the home of William Faulkner's mother, Maud Butler Falkner. Today it's distinguishable from its neighbors by the concrete block at the bottom of the front steps. The word "Falkner" is carved on the block, with the "n" turned backward.

Faulkner and Yoknapatawpha Conference, held annually in July at the University of Mississippi; (662) 915–7282. This quarter-century tradition takes one Faulknerian issue and dissects it thoroughly through lectures, discussions, readings, and other scholarly pursuits. Past topics have included "Faulkner at 100: Retrospect and Prospect," "Faulkner in America," and "Faulkner and Gender."

Faulkner Trail, a ten-minute walk through Bailey's Woods, adjacent to Rowan Oak, toward the Ole Miss baseball stadium. Ask at Rowan Oak or Ole Miss for directions.

First National Bank of Oxford, 101 Courthouse Square, northeast corner, Faulkner's father established this bank in 1910 in the smaller building to the east. Faulkner used it as the Sartoris Bank in *Intruders in the Dust* and *The Unvanquished*. The building has housed a funeral home, a men's clothing store, and today it's Duvall's, a women's clothing store. The bank is now in the larger building next door.

Freeland and Freeland Law Office, 1013 Jackson Avenue; (662) 234–3414. The law offices founded in 1958 by T. H. Freeland III and Phil Stone, who became good friends with Faulkner. The author's first manuscripts, in fact, were typed by Stone's secretaries in the Victorian-style building just a couple of blocks from the square.

Lafayette County Courthouse, on the square. The original courthouse, built in 1840, was burned in 1864 by Union troops. The current building dates from 1873. As depicted in *The Sound and the Fury*, a Confederate soldier stands guard outside, peering down South Lamar Avenue.

Oxford Conference for the Book, every April, University of Mississippi; (662) 915–7439. Annual conference initiated in 1994, gathers writers and editors to ponder the processes of creation and publication. Speakers at the 1998 conference included such literary luminaries as Stephen E. Ambrose, Rick Bragg, Oxford residents Larry Brown and Barry Hannah, Tony Horwitz, and Elizabeth Spencer.

Oxford-Lafayette County Chamber of Commerce, 299 Jackson Avenue East; (662) 234–4651.

Oxford Tourism Council; 115 South Lamar Boulevard; (662) 234–4680 or (800) 880–6967.

Rowan Oak, Old Taylor Road; (662) 234–3284. Antebellum home of Nobel Prize–winner William Faulkner, now owned by the University of Mississippi. The outline of Faulkner's novel *A Fable* is still where he left

The offices of lawyer Phil Stone, a good friend of William Faulkner's, where many of his first manuscripts were typed by the firm's secretaries.

it—written on the walls of his downstairs study—and Faulkner's dusty shoes sit upstairs by his bed, as if just waiting for his feet to plop back into them. Beautiful grounds. Picnickers (and their dogs, especially squirrel-chasers) are welcome. The house is open from 10 A.M. to noon and 2 P.M. to 4 P.M. Tuesdays through Saturdays, 2 P.M. to 4 P.M. Sundays. The grounds are open during daylight hours seven days a week.

Square Books, 160 Courthouse Square; (662) 236–2262. Open 9 A.M. to 9 P.M. Mondays through Thursdays, 9 A.M. to 10 P.M. Fridays and Saturdays, 10 A.M. to 6 P.M. Sundays. A truly marvelous Southern bookstore, tucked in a building constructed in the 1860s, Square Books has treasures awaiting in every nook and cranny, with a droolworthy section of Southern literature. Readers can sip coffee or tea in the upstairs cafe, or take a book and a muffin out on the balcony, which features a lovely view of the courthouse and square. Owner Richard Howarth and his staff know their stuff—they could probably even tell you the proper pronunciation of Yoknapatawpha, although I neglected to ask—and they often host

The Lafayette County courthouse in Oxford, Mississippi, featured in Faulkner's books, including *The Sound and the Fury*.

local and regional writers for readings and signings. Even the restrooms here are stocked with reading material. Just down the block, Off Square Books has used and overstocked titles at great prices.

St. Peter's Cemetery (Faulkner's grave). The cemetery is about a half-mile northeast of Rowan Oak, on Jefferson Avenue at Sixteenth Street. Walk down Sixteenth to the base of the hill; the family grave is a few steps in under a towering oak tree. This is the same cemetery Benjy visits weekly in *The Sound and the Fury*. Literary pilgrims frequently leave small offerings at Faulkner's grave—flowers, candy kisses, bottles of bourbon.

Tallahatchie Riverfest and William Faulkner Birthday Celebration; (888) 534-8232. Held every year in nearby New Albany, Faulkner's birthplace, on the weekend closest to his September 25 birthday.

University of Mississippi, Lamar Boulevard at University Avenue; (662) 915-7211. Walking tours available. Founded in 1848, Ole Miss was one of the few landmarks to survive the burning of Oxford in 1864. Throw a quarter in the air, and it'll probably land on a famous or soon-to-be famous author on the English faculty, one of the nation's best.

ACCOMMODATIONS AND RESTAURANTS

Barksdale-Isom House, 1003 Jefferson Avenue; (662) 236–5600. Circa 1838 bed-and-breakfast on the National Register of Historic Places. For non-guests, tours available by appointment only. Renovated in the 1990s, the house was constructed completely of native timber and handcrafted by Indian and slave labor, a classic example of planter-type architecture.

Bottletree Bakery, 923 Van Buren Avenue, north of the square; (662) 236–5000. The cinnamon rolls alone are worth the short walk from the square. On Sundays during the school year, you can see Southern society in all its glory—Ole Miss girls fresh from church in dresses, hose, and heels, no matter how high the temperature and heat index.

City Grocery, 152 Courthouse Square; (662) 232–8080. Once a grocery store, now a trendy bistro serving dishes like shrimp and grits alongside bananas Foster bread pudding.

Downtown Grill, 110 Courthouse Square; (662) 234–2659. Specialties include seafood gumbos and Mississippi catfish.

Oliver-Britt House Inn and Tea Room, 512 Van Buren Avenue; (662) 234–8043. This circa 1905 Greek Revival home is just a few blocks from Faulkner's Rowan Oak.

Puddin' Place, 1008 University Avenue; (662) 234–1250. Beautifully restored 1892 bed-and-breakfast. Short walk to the Courthouse Square, Ole Miss, and Rowan Oak.

Smitty's, 208 S. Lamar Boulevard, south of the square; (662) 234–9111. The menu here announces: "If'n You Need Anything That Ain't on Here, Holler at the Cook." And it's all good.

Spahn House, 401 College Street, Senatobia; (662) 562–9853. This delightful fifteen-room bed-and-breakfast, circa 1904, is about 45 minutes from Oxford but well worth the extra driving time. Proprietress Daughn Spahn makes Southern breakfasts to die for (forget your diet; don't even bother) and puts books in every room for her visitors. Some rooms have Jacuzzi baths.

Natchez

Natchez, perched on the Mississippi River in the southwestern part of the state, is home to the Linden estate, whose front door played an important role in the movie version of *Gone With the Wind*. The Federal-style home's front doorway was copied for Tara. *Gone With the Wind*, incidentally, was shot entirely on studio lots in California.

What is now an imposing mansion grew from a two-story cottage that was built around 1792. In 1818, Thomas Reed, Mississippi's first U.S. senator, bought the house and started the expansion that now includes a white-columned front gallery stretching more than a hundred feet across the front of the house.

Natchez was also the birthplace, in 1908, of writer Richard Wright, whose works include the classic *Native Son* and the autobiography, *Black Boy*. Wright protégé James Baldwin called *Native Son* "the most powerful and celebrated statement we have yet had of what it means to be a Negro in America." Wright's family moved around a lot, and he also spent a good deal of time in Memphis, Tennessee, and Jackson, Mississippi, during his formative years.

They weren't happy ones, by all accounts. Wright lived fifty-two years; he spent thirty-three of them outside the South. *Native Son* is set entirely in the North, and Wright's ashes rest in Pere Lachaise Cemetery in Paris, which became his second home.

Literary Lures and Southern Sights

Linden, 1 Linden Place; (601) 445–5472 or (800) 2–LINDEN. Open 10 A.M. to 3 P.M. daily, April through September. Admission fee for those not staying overnight.

Monmouth Plantation, 36 Melrose Avenue; (601) 442–5852 or (800) 828–4531. This huge, historic inn, circa 1818, has become the state's unofficial "Hollywood connection." In the mid-1990s, actors and crew stayed there while in Natchez filming John Grisham's *A Time to Kill*. The immaculate grounds, twenty-six acres' worth, are lush, as are the home's decorative fixtures. This is the only property in Mississippi that's one of the National Trust's Historic Hotels of America, and it's also a National Historic Landmark.

Natchez Convention and Visitors Bureau, P.O. Box 1485, Natchez, MS 39121–1485; (601) 446–6345 or (800) 647–6724; www2.bkbank. com/ncvb.

Natchez Historic City Tours, 508 Orleans Street; (601) 445–9300 or (800) 647–6724. Features more than fifty antebellum homes and churches on an hourlong tour. Hourly tours from 9 A.M. to 4 P.M. Mondays through Saturdays. Fee.

Natchez in Historic Photographs, 405 State Street; (601) 442–4741 or (800) 647–6724. More than 300 photographs, displayed in the Statton Chapel of the First Presbyterian Church in downtown Natchez. Collection includes some of the finest photographs ever taken of early Mississippi River life.

Natchez Literary and Cinema Celebration, annually; (601) 446–6345 or (800) 647–6724. Held at Copiah-Lincoln Community College, this conference is devoted to area literature, history, and culture. Themes vary from year to year; the 1998 theme was "The South: Its Land and Its Literature."

ACCOMMODATIONS AND RESTAURANTS

Aunt Pitty Pat's, 306 S. Rankin Street; book through Natchez Pilgrimage Homes; (601) 446–6631 or (800) 647–6742. Bed-and-breakfast named for Scarlett's flighty, elderly aunt in *Gone With the Wind*. Built in 1886, on the National Register.

The Briars Bed and Breakfast, 31 Irving Lane; (601) 446–9654 or (800) 634–1818. This National Register landmark, circa 1814, was the site of Jefferson Davis's wedding to Varina Howell in 1845.

The Burn, 712 N. Union Street; (601) 442–1344. Three-story Greek Revival mansion now a bed-and-breakfast, with a striking semispiral staircase and unusual gardens. Built in 1834.

Cedar Grove Plantation, 617 Kingston Road; (601) 445–0585. This circa 1830 country estate of 150 acres was once part of a cotton plantation and now includes a bed-and-breakfast.

Coyle House, 307 S. Wall Street; (601) 445–8679. One of the oldest accommodations in Natchez, this historic preservation award–winner was built in 1793 and 1794.

Dunleith Plantation, 84 Homochitto; (601) 446–8500 or (800) 433–2445. This circa-1856 Greek Revival inn is often used for movies, such as the 1993 version of *The Adventures of Huckleberry Finn*.

Governor Holmes House, 207 S. Wall Street; (601) 442–2366 or (800) 647–6742. Circa 1794, this is one of the oldest and most historic homes in Natchez's old Spanish Quarter. Now a lovely bed-and-breakfast.

King's Tavern, 619 Jefferson Street; (601) 446–8845.

Linden, 1 Linden Place; (601) 445–5472 or (800) 2–LINDEN. Built around 1800, this inn's front door was used as the model for Tara's entryway in *Gone With the Wind*.

Local Color, 201 N. Pearl Street; (601) 442–1054.

Magnolia Grill, 49 Silver Street; (601) 446–7670.

Mammy's Cupboard, 555 Highway 61 South; (601) 445–8957.

Mark Twain Guest House, 25 Silver Street; (601) 446–8023. Features rooms overlooking the Mississippi River. Circa 1830.

Monmouth Plantation, 36 Melrose Avenue; (601) 442–5852 or (800) 828–4531. One of the most romantic of Natchez's inns.

Ole Railroad Cafe, 207 State Street; (601) 446–6456.

The Wharf-Master's House, 57 Silver Street, Under-the-Hill; (601) 445–6025.

Greenville

The Mississippi River town of Greenville, northwest of Jackson, has spawned writers of diverse talents, such as Shelby Foote, best known for his Civil War narrative, and Walker Percy, who won the National Book Award for his first novel, *The Moviegoer*, which is set in New Orleans.

Foote, who now lives in Memphis, was born in Greenville in 1916; his family also lived for short times in Mobile, Alabama; Vicksburg, Mississippi; and Pensacola, Florida. In 1922, Shelby's father died, and he and his mother moved back to Greenville to live with his aunt and uncle. He entered seventh grade there and was eventually appointed editor of *The Pica*, his high school newspaper. Walker Percy, who would become his lifelong friend, was the paper's gossip columnist.

Although Foote's Civil War chronicles have secured his place in America's literary stratosphere, he has also written half-a-dozen novels about characters in mythical Jordan County, Mississippi—creating his own universe, much as Faulkner did with Yoknapatawpha County. Also like Faulkner, Foote seems well tuned to the quirkiness of Southern life. Welcoming an interviewer to his Memphis home, he apologized for the garden's unkempt status. The writer pooh-poohed Foote's apologies, saying surely the gardener would eventually return. "I don't think so," Foote replied calmly. "I believe he shot a man."

Percy, born in Birmingham, Alabama, in 1916, went to live with his father's cousin, William Alexander Percy, after both his parents died. Walker attended Greenville High School, where he met Foote. Writer Jay Tolson's 1997 book, *The Correspondence of Shelby Foote and Walker Percy*, gives some keen insight into the men's relationship, including strong evidence that they were at least partially responsible for each other's becoming writers.

Foote told the editors of the anthology *Growing Up Southern* that "it was Walker's and my friendship with each other that led us to do some very advanced reading for kids. I remember in 1934, I guess it was, I was a sophomore or junior in high school. I heard somewhere, probably from Mr. Will, that the three big novels of the twentieth century so far were probably Joyce's *Ulysses*, Proust's *Remembrance of Things Past* and Thomas Mann's *Magic Mountain*. So that summer I read all three of those books. That is the kind of reading we did."

The first novel Foote remembers reading, however, was by fellow Mississippian William Faulkner. "The first modern novel I ever read was about 1932. Faulkner's *Light in August* had just come out," Foote recalled for *Growing Up Southern*. "That is a helluva first novel to read. It practically knocked me off my feet. Here was somebody writing about my homeland and enabling me to see it better than I had ever seen it before." Foote's first encounter with Faulkner came at age sixteen.

As they grew up, Percy and Foote weren't without their squabbles. That first summer they were friends, a running argument started. "Walker was a Tolstoy fan and I was a Dostoevsky fan," Foote says. "I kept claiming that Tolstoy was the greatest slick writer who ever lived. About thirty-five or forty years later Walker and I were driving across Lake Pontchatrain (in New Orleans) and he suddenly said, 'You know, Shelby, you were right on that.'"

LITERARY LURES AND SOUTHERN SIGHTS

The Great Wall of Mississippi, downtown waterfront. This levee was
built by the U.S. Army Corps of Engineers after the April 1927 flood
that devastated Greenville, destroying thousands of acres of rich Delta
farmland. The flood and its aftermath—and the prominent Percy
family's reaction and response—are vividly described in John M. Barry's
terrific 1997 book, *Rising Tide: The Great Mississippi Flood of 1927 and
How It Changed America.*

Greenville Writers Exhibit, Washington County Library, 341 Main
Street; (662) 335–2331. Showcases works and artifacts of Greenville's
writers, including Shelby Foote, Ellen Douglas, Walker Percy, and Beverly Lowry. Open 8 A.M. to 5 P.M. Mondays through Fridays. Free.

Washington County Convention and Visitors Bureau, 401 Washington
Avenue, Greenville, 38701; (800) 467–3582; www.thedelta.org.

ACCOMMODATIONS

Azalea House Bed and Breakfast, 548 S. Washington Avenue; (662)
335–0507. Circa 1915 home on a shady, tree-lined street near downtown.

Cotton Country Inn, 1263 Highway 61 South, Hollandale; (662)
827–2277.

Colonial Inn, 1812 Highway 82 East; (662) 335–3337.

Clarksdale

Clarksdale, in the Delta heartland between Greenville and Memphis, was
the childhood home of playwright Tennessee Williams, who was born in
Columbus, in western Mississippi. Williams's grandfather served as rector
of St. George's Episcopal Church at First and Sharkey Streets for sixteen
years, and Williams spent many a day playing in the rectory there.

LITERARY LURES AND SOUTHERN SIGHTS

Coahoma County Chamber of Commerce and Tourism Commission,
1540 DeSoto Avenue (Highway 49); (662) 627–7337 or (800)
626–3764; www.clarksdale.com/chamber.

Tennessee Williams Festival, every October, Clarksdale Civic Auditorium; (662) 627–7337 or (800) 626–3764. Event includes discussions, plays, walking tours, music, and local cuisine. The 1998 festival featured a banquet at Uncle Henry's on Moon Lake, the Moon Lake Casino mentioned in Williams's *Summer and Smoke*.

ACCOMMODATIONS AND RESTAURANTS

Boss Hog's Barbecue, 1410 State Street; (662) 627–5264.
Chamoun's Rest Haven, 416 S. State Street; (662) 624–8601. Wonderful Lebanese fare, such as stuffed kibbie, stuffed cabbage and grape leaves, spinach pie, tabbouleh, and hummus.
Days Inn, 1910 N. State Street; (662) 624–4391.
Hampton Inn, 710 S. State Street; (662) 627–9292.
Sarah's Kitchen, 208 Sunflower; (662) 627–3239. Great meals at low prices—on the weekends, fried chicken plates or catfish strips are $4.
Southern Inn, Highway 61 North; (662) 624–6558.

Columbus

This Mississippi town, 160 miles southeast of Clarksdale and 150 miles northeast of Jackson, was the birthplace of Tennessee Williams.

LITERARY LURES AND SOUTHERN SIGHTS

Columbus/Lowndes Convention and Visitors Bureau, P.O. Box 789, Columbus, MS 39703; (662) 329–1191 or (800) 327–2686; www.columbus-ms.org.
Tennessee Williams Welcome Center, 300 Main Street; (662) 328–0222. Open daily from 8:30 A.M. to 5:30 P.M. Admission free. This Victorian house, built in 1878, was Williams's first home.

ACCOMMODATIONS AND RESTAURANTS

Amzi Love, 305 Seventh Street; (662) 328–5413. This 1848 Italian-style villa is in Columbus's historic district. The bed-and-breakfast has its original furnishings and scrapbooks of the families who lived there.

The Tennessee Williams birthplace in Columbus, Mississippi. (photo courtesy of the Columbus Convention and Visitors Bureau)

Barnhill's Country Buffet, 625 18th Avenue N.; (662) 328–4313.

Cartney-Hunt House, 408 S. Seventh Street; (662) 329–3856. This circa-1828 bed-and-breakfast is the oldest Federal-style brick house in northern Mississippi.

Gingham Gourmet, 224 Fifth Street S.; (662) 329–2144.

Liberty Hall, Armstrong Road; (662) 328–4110. Early nineteenth-century home, now a comfy bed-and-breakfast; artifacts include an old planter's diary and Civil War–era medical books.

Miz Lou's Barbecue, 903 Waterworks Road; (662) 327–2281.

Proffitt's Porch, Officer's Lake Road; (662) 327–4485.

3

Florida

On the distant horizon the great white clouds were mountains beneath a roofless and star-filled heaven. Ah, it never failed to take my breath away—this southern sky filled with azure light and drowsy relentless movement. . . . All of this is Miami, city of water, city of speed, city of tropical flowers, city of enormous skies. . . . There is a menace beneath the shining surface of Miami, there is desperation and a throbbing greed, there is the deep steady pulse of a great capital—the low grinding energy, the endless risk. It's never really dark in Miami. It's never really quiet.

—Anne Rice, *The Tale of the Body Thief*

Someone in Florida once remarked to me that it's the only place in America where you have to go north to hear a Southern accent. While that's not literally true—you'll hear plenty of the dulcet tones of Dixie while traveling the Sunshine State—it is true that Florida has a much more eclectic population and culture than the rest of the South. The north-to-central portion is more traditionally Southern, with plantation homes where Scarlett O'Hara would have felt right at home strolling beneath the moss-dripping oaks. The Southern sector, though, has a distinctly Caribbean feel and attitude, not unlike New Orleans.

Floridians north *and* south, however, seem to share an almost organized disdain for doing things in ways the rest of the county would consider normal. This could well be a holdover from frontier times. Texas and the Southwest have captured most of the Wild West attention, but Florida could easily have been dubbed the Wild Southeast. Peter Matthiessen's gorgeously written trilogy—beginning with *Killing Mister Watson*, then *Lost Man's River* and finally *Bone by Bone*—perfectly captures the lawlessness that characterized the state at the turn of the century. In grim and often gory detail, Matthiessen documents the savaging of Florida's ancient culture and once-thriving wildlife, telling of the slaughter of thousands of egrets and flamingos for their plumage and the plundering of Indian mounds for relics.

In *Bone by Bone*, the character Watson recalls killing alligators for their hides, "stripping the soft flats off the bellies and rolling them up by firelight. It was exciting for a while, because stacking flats at such a rate was like heaping up cash money. . . . It soon turned to a stink of putrefaction, as if the Everglades had rolled over and died."

Some authors, of course, have focused on the state's more pleasant aspects, of which there are many. On the northwest panhandle, for instance, the seaside town of Destin is known for its snow-white beaches and, to literary travelers, as the vacation getaway of Anne Rice's Mayfair family in her *Tales of the Mayfair Witches* series. Marjorie Kinnan Rawlings, author of *The Yearling*, lived in central Florida for decades and set her most famous books here.

West central Florida, known locally as the Suncoast, might well be the best-kept secret of the literary world; the barrier islands stretching from St. Petersburg to Port Charlotte have attracted dozens of writers, from mystery maestro John D. MacDonald to horror guru Stephen King.

Miami and the Atlantic coast also have their share of literary landmarks. Elmore Leonard wrote more than half a dozen novels set in South Florida, including *Gold Coast* and *Glitz*. There seems to be some odd compulsion among mystery writers to set mayhem amid paradise—Leonard's *Split Image* tells the altogether gruesome, but intriguing, tale of a Palm Beacher who murders a Haitian gardener just for the fun of it. Leonard lived for a time in the Old Port Cove section of North Palm Beach. One has to wonder about his luck in finding gardeners.

Despite the undeniable attractions of the rest of Florida, the prime destination for writers and book lovers visiting the state has been and remains Key West, which has beckoned the publishing world's luminaries for decades. Ernest Hemingway, Robert Frost, William Faulkner, Truman Capote, Tennessee Williams . . . they all visited here, and some stayed for decades. Writers still flock to Key West, as if to receive inspiration from simply breathing the air. Or maybe it's something in the water. Or the margaritas, if you believe Jimmy Buffett.

SOUTHERN SIGHTS

Florida Information; www.floridainfo.com; Tampa Bay-area information and links to other areas.
See Florida; www.see-florida.com; fabulous site operated by See Florida magazines.
South Florida tourism; www.floridagoldcoast.com.
Visit Florida; www.flausa.com; the most comprehensive Florida site, by far.
Inn Route of Florida; www.florida-inns.com; bed-and-breakfasts, small inns, and historic hotels, organized by region.

Cross Creek

Cross Creek, tucked between two central Florida lakes about ten miles southeast of Gainesville, was the setting for a much-beloved American classic, *The Yearling.* Author Marjorie Kinnan Rawlings lived in Florida for a quarter of a century, in both Cross Creek and St. Augustine. She wrote the Pulitzer Prize–winner *The Yearling* while living in central Florida, and her autobiographical *Cross Creek* recounts her years there. Rawlings begins *Cross Creek* with this description:

> Cross Creek is a bend in a country road, by land, and the flowing of the Lochloosa Lake into Orange Lake, by water. We are four miles west of the small village of Island Grove, nine miles east of a turpentine still and on the other sides we do not count distance at all, for the two lakes and the broad marshes create an infinite space between us and the horizon. We are five white families; "Old Boss" Brice, the Glissons, the Mackays and the Bernie Basses; and two colored families, Henry Woodward and the Mickenses. People in Island Grove consider us just a little biggety and more than a little queer.

The Yearling, one of those "required reading" books that children actually enjoy, was written on an old wooden table on the screened front

Marjorie Kinnan Rawlings wrote *The Yearling* while living in this house in rural Cross Creek, Florida. (photo courtesy of the Alachua County Visitors and Convention Bureau)

porch of Rawlings's Cross Creek home. Her rusty typewriter now stands watch on that screened porch, or lanai. The lanai is a Florida necessity since, as locals often joke, the mosquito is the state bird. The book tells in vivid detail the story of a young boy's coming-of-age in the big scrub country that is now the Ocala National Forest. Rawlings's home was set plop in the middle of a citrus grove, surrounded by bright tropical birds and deep, mysterious swampland. When she died in 1953 in St. Augustine, she was brought back to Cross Creek and buried in nearby Antioch Cemetery.

Like Thomas Wolfe, who alienated the entire city of Asheville, North Carolina, with *Look Homeward, Angel*, Rawlings ticked off a few neighbors with her all-too-accurate descriptions in *Cross Creek*. One of the friends Rawlings described in the book, Zelma Cason, took huffy exception to her portrayal in the book as "an ageless spinster, resembling an angry and efficient canary." Cason sued Rawlings in what became known as the Cross Creek Trial, and the incident inspired a book, *Invasion of Privacy*, by Patricia Nassif Acton. In 1999, a play by the same name by Larry Parr premiered in Sarasota.

Rawlings, for her part, clearly adored the local residents—at least the nonhuman variety. In *Cross Creek*, for example, she pens a charming love letter to the humble lizard:

> I find lizards altogether ingratiating. . . . The small gray lizards have a catholic taste in dwelling places. Every abandoned house is full of them; they live in the woods; they live comfortably in your home with you, wondering what you are doing there, but tolerant on the whole of your intrusion. They are the color of old cypress shingles, with bellies of rich cobalt blue, and there is nothing more impudent unless it is a mockingbird.
>
> The little chameleons are definitely friendlier. Yet they are detached, like friends with their minds on other matters. They are partial to a warm bed that a human has slept in and expects to sleep in again that night. They have to be lifted by the tail, which surprises you by breaking off in your fingers. They clamber slowly, gracefully, up and down screens. They watch you for hours with bright small eyes. They enjoy being brought into the house on a bunch of roses, to serve on the dining table for ornament, shading obligingly from their favorite sage-green through taupe or a pinkish mauve, according to their passage over leaf or stem or blossom.

After the publication of *The Yearling*, Rawlings moved from Cross Creek to the Crescent Beach area of St. Augustine, America's oldest settlement, on Florida's northern Atlantic coast. The home she purchased at 6600 S. Broward Street, with money from *The Yearling*, was Rawlings's primary residence for the last decade of her life. She was a major supporter of the St. Augustine Library Society, especially during World War II, when she served as the group's president. One of her short stories, *The Pelican's Shadow*, is set at the home in St. Augustine, which also served as a de facto literary salon. Guests who visited included Zora Neale Hurston, Dylan Thomas, and Ernest Hemingway.

LITERARY LURES AND SOUTHERN SIGHTS

Book Gallery West, 4121 N.W. Sixteenth Boulevard, Gainesville; (352) 371-1234. Great Florida section, and many first editions as well as new stock.

Books Inc., 505 N.W. Thirteenth Street, Gainesville; (352) 374–4241. General literature, science fiction, modern firsts.

Omni Books, 99 S.W. Thirty-Fourth Street, Gainesville; (352) 375–3755. Good selection of Florida specialties and first editions.

Gainesville Area Chamber of Commerce, 300 E. University Avenue; (352) 334–7100; www.gainesvillechamber.com.

Marjorie Kinnan Rawlings State Historic Site, South County Road 325, Cross Creek. Write to Route 3, Box 92, Hawthorne, FL 32640, or call (904) 466–3672 for information. Open from 9 A.M. to 5 P.M. daily, with tours on the hour, except at noon, from 10 A.M. to 4 P.M. Tours not offered in August, September, or on major holidays. Admission fee. The site has been listed on the National Register of Historic Places since 1970, and is seen as a rare, pristine microcosm of rural Florida life that has all but vanished.

ACCOMMODATIONS AND RESTAURANTS

Brasserie, 101 S.E. Second Place, Sun Center, Gainesville; (352) 375–6612. Tapas bar and Mediterranean fare.

Daniela's, 10110 Martin Luther King Highway; (904) 418–3077, Alachua.

Herlong Mansion Bed-and-Breakfast, 402 N.E. Cholokka Boulevard, Micanopy; (352) 466–3322. Close to the Cross Creek home of Marjorie Kinnan Rawlings.

Ivey's Grill, 3303 W. University Avenue; (352) 371–4839. Billed as "fine dining in Gatorland."

The Magnolia Plantation, 309 S.E. Seventh Street, Gainesville; (352) 375–6653 or (800) 201–2379; www.magnoliabnb.com. 1885 French Second Empire Victorian home, now an elegant inn.

Pura Vida Coffee House and Restaurant, 12 S.W. First Avenue, Gainesville; (352) 378–3398.

Shady Oak Bed-and-Breakfast, 203 Cholokka Boulevard, Micanopy; (352) 466–3476.

Sweetwater Branch Inn, 625 E. University Avenue, Gainesville; (352) 373–6760 or (800) 595–7760.

Wild Flowers Cafe, 201 N.E. Highway 441; (352) 466–4330, Micanopy.

Wise's Drug Store, 239 W. University Avenue, Gainesville; (352) 372–4371. Operating since 1938, this old-fashioned drugstore has a soda fountain and the best sandwiches in town.

Eatonville

Eatonville, population 2,200, is just north of Orlando in Walt Disney country. The town is small, especially compared to Disney Central a few miles south, but holds a precious place in the literary world as the home of Zora Neale Hurston, one of the country's foremost African-American authors. Eatonville, where she lived as a child, bestowed on Hurston an early, deeply held knowledge of her roots, something many black authors had to find later in life.

"I was born in a Negro town. I do not mean by that the black back-side of an average town—Eatonville, Florida, is a pure Negro town—charter, mayor, council, town marshal and all," she writes in her 1942 autobiography, *Dust Tracks on a Road*. "It was not the first Negro community in America, but it was the first to be inclusive, the first attempt at organized self-government on the part of Negroes in America."

While her recollection of the town is accurate, her statement that she was born there isn't. Hurston was born dirt poor in 1891 in the east-central Alabama hamlet of Notasulga; in addition to transplanting her birthplace, she habitually shaved at least ten years off her life and often claimed her year of birth as 1901, 1902, or 1903. Her reputation for embellishment in the name of a good story was well known. In 1999, Kristy Andersen, an independent filmmaker working on a documentary about Hurston, told Y'all.com that "Zora was a really great liar. She is a very unreliable narrator. You have to assume everything she says is a lie and go from there."

Even fellow Southern doyenne Maya Angelou, a native of Arkansas, has questioned Hurston's account of her own life. In an introduction to the fiftieth-anniversary edition of *Dust Tracks on a Road*, Angelou writes: "It is difficult, if not impossible, to find and touch the real Zora Neale Hurston."

The house where Hurston lived in Eatonville is long gone, but visitors can see the block where it sat, bounded by West, Lime, People, and Lemon Streets. Both *Dust Tracks on a Road* and *Their Eyes Were Watching God* bring Hurston's years in Florida to vivid, and sometimes disturbing, life. Despite the hardships her family encountered, though, Hurston rarely touched on racism, an apparently deliberate oversight that infuriated some critics, black and white alike.

But Hurston was adamant in her opposition to dwelling on race. "From what I had read and heard, Negroes were supposed to write about the race problem," she laments in *Dust Tracks*. "I was and am thoroughly sick of the problem. My interest lies in what makes a man or a woman do such-and-such, regardless of his color."

In addition to Eatonville, Hurston lived in much larger Fort Pierce, a city of several thousand in St. Lucie County on the central Atlantic coast. Buried at Fort Pierce's Garden of the Heavenly Rest, Hurston's remains lay ignored in an unmarked grave for decades. But in 1973, author Alice Walker came searching for Hurston's grave. Walker was aghast that one of America's most important black authors had seemingly been forgotten in death.

"We are a people. A people do not throw their geniuses away," Walker writes in "Looking for Zora," the article she eventually wrote about her Florida pilgrimage. "And if they are thrown away, it is our duty as artists, and as witnesses for the future, to collect them again for the sake of our children, and, if necessary, bone by bone."

Walker did just that, seeing to the placement of a stone on Hurston's grave, and honoring the author's preferred (if inaccurate) year of birth. The engraving reads:

Zora Neale Hurston
"A Genius of the South"
1901–1960
Novelist, Folklorist, Anthropologist

Walker took the line "A Genius of the South" from a poem by Jean Toomer.

Today, Hurston remains a compelling influence on a new generation of writers, such as Florida resident Connie May Fowler, who has lived in St. Augustine and now makes her home in Alligator Point. She named the character of Miss Zora, an eccentric healer and recluse, after Hurston in her novel *Before Women Had Wings*. Oprah Winfrey has bought movie rights to the book and plans to play Miss Zora in the film.

LITERARY LURES AND SOUTHERN SIGHTS

Brandywine Books, 114 S. Park Avenue, Suite E, Winter Park; (407) 644–1711. General, Floridiana, history.

Garden of the Heavenly Rest Cemetery, North Seventeenth Street at Avenue S., Fort Pierce.

Zora Neale Hurston Festival of the Arts and Humanities, 227 E. Kennedy Boulevard, Eatonville; (407) 647–3307; www.zoranealehurston.cc. Festival each January spotlighting local music, dance, drama, visual arts, folk arts, and ethnic cuisine. More than 85,000 people turned out for the festival in 2000.

Zora Neale Hurston Home, 1734 School Court Street, Fort Pierce. Not open to the public, but you can take a "good hard squint" at it, as they say around here.

ACCOMMODATIONS AND RESTAURANTS

The Courtyard at Lake Lucerne, 211 N. Lucerne Circle E., Orlando; (407) 648–5188 or (800) 444–5259.

Calico Jack's Oyster Bar and Seafood House, 5601 S. Semoran Boulevard, Orlando; (407) 281–9464.

Darst Victorian Manor Bed-and-Breakfast, 495 W. Old Highway 441, Mount Dora; (352) 383–4050 or (888) 533–2778.

Dinner Bell Diner, 1125 S. Semoran Boulevard, Casselberry; (407) 281–0422.

Dock Side Grill, 5494 Central Florida Parkway, Orlando; (407) 239–8552.

Easy Street Cafe and Delicatessen, 2500 S. Semoran Boulevard, Orlando; (407) 380–9520.

The Emerald Hill Inn, 27751 Lake Jem Road, Mount Dora; (352) 383–2777 or (800) 366–9387. Near the Ocala National Forest that inspired Marjorie Kinnan Rawlings's writings.

Froggers Oyster Bar and Grill, 4459 N. Pine Hills Road, Orlando; (407) 293–3199.

The Higgins House, 420 S. Oak Avenue, Sanford; (407) 324–9238 or (800) 584–0014. Victorian bed-and-breakfast, circa 1894.

Judy's Diner, 5220 Old Winter Garden Road, Orlando; (407) 295–9532.
Meadow Marsh Bed and Breakfast, 940 Tildenville School Road, Winter
   Garden; (407) 656–2064 or (888) 656–2064.
Perri House Bed and Breakfast, 10417 Centurion Court, Orlando; (407)
   876–4830 or (800) 780–4830.
Princeton Diner, 3310 Edgewater Driver, Orlando; (407) 425–5046.
Rick's Oyster Bar, 5621 Old Winter Garden Road, Orlando; (407)
   293–3587.
Thurston House Bed and Breakfast, 851 Lake Avenue, Maitland; (407)
   539–1911 or (800) 843–2721.

St. Petersburg and Sarasota

One of the least-known, but most interesting, literary connections in this
west central Florida area concerns "beat poet" Jack Kerouac, author of
the classic *On the Road*. He, his wife, and his mother originally moved to
Florida because his mother hated the cold winters in their hometown of
Lowell, Massachusetts. Jack apparently wasn't ecstatic about moving to
Florida; at a party shortly before the move, he reportedly told fellow
guests, "St. Petersburg is a place where old ladies walk all by themselves
at midnight, talking to themselves on the sidewalk."

Kerouac never got the chance to be one of the corresponding old
men; he died in St. Petersburg in 1969 at age forty-seven. Oddly, to this
day the house at 5169 Tenth Avenue N. remains unoccupied most of the
year, and Kerouac is still listed in the local phone book. The estate passed
to his mother after his death; she, in turn, left everything to Stella, Jack's
widow, who left it to her brothers and sisters.

In January 1999, a writer for *Tampa Bay* magazine asked Jack Sampas,
Stella's youngest brother, about the St. Petersburg house. "He told me
that family members still come down to St. Petersburg and stay in the
house," says writer Sherry Babbitt. "As for the phone listing, they didn't
see any reason to change it."

Considerable rancor has plagued the family over the estate's succes-
sion; Kerouac's daughter Jan wanted to turn the home into a memorial
for her father but died in 1996 with that wish unfulfilled. As if respond-
ing to his family's incivility, many believe the ghost of Jack Kerouac shuns
his former home and instead haunts Haslam's Book Store in St. Peters-

burg. One of the owners told *Tampa Bay* that following Kerouac's death, strange things started happening—typical ghostly maneuvers such as books falling off the shelves and unexplainable cold spots. A local TV station investigating the story hired a psychic, who claims that indeed, Kerouac's restless spirit is present at Haslam's. Roy Hinst, one of the bookstore's owners, told the magazine writer that Kerouac is welcome to stay "as long as he behaves himself."

Not likely, given his reputation for wandering outside the bounds of politically acceptable behavior—even at that bookstore. Kerouac often visited Haslam's and was frequently seen moving his books to more prominent positions on the shelves. He'd no doubt enjoy the ghostly rumors; they can't hurt sales of his books, after all.

Other authors who have lived on the Suncoast include Rick Bragg, an Alabama native who now heads the *New York Times*'s Miami bureau. Bragg did a stint as a reporter at the *St. Petersburg Times*. In his autobiography, *All Over But the Shoutin'*, he describes St. Petersburg-Tampa:

> An odd place, in many ways. Pinellas County was paved from Tampa Bay to the beaches, pretty much, with all manner of people living elbow to elbow in little pastel tract houses, rambling brick ranchers and bayside mansions.
>
> To find the reasons we ever came here in the first place, you had to live at the edge of it, by that beautiful water, or drive inland, through the sugar cane, to the heart of it. I rented a small apartment near the bay that was perhaps the most peaceful place I had ever lived. At night, when the water in the inlet I lived on was smooth as glass, you could sit on the ground and watch the mullet jump, and egrets and other wading birds would take pieces of peeled orange out of your hands. I heard other reporters complain about how slow it was and dull it was, how life was just one big Early Bird Dinner Special, but I loved it.

Bragg also tells a hilarious story that perfectly crystallizes the often wacky interplay of man and nature in Florida:

> The highlight of my time there, at least in the first few months, was the story of Mopsy the chicken. The little bayside town of

Dunedin, north of Clearwater, had been the target of a serial killer. It seemed that a bobcat was, night after night, slaughtering the chickens of the retirees. The editor walked up to me, straight-faced, and told me that there had been a bobcat attack the night before but the chicken had miraculously survived, clawed but still clucking. The chicken's name, he told me, was Mopsy. I said something to the effect that he had to be kidding.

Twenty minutes later, I was motoring to the quiet and peaceful town of Dunedin. I was twenty-nine years old. I had won a whole wallful of journalism awards and risked my life in bad neighborhoods and prisons and hurricanes. I was going to interview a goddamn chicken. The lead on the story: "Mopsy has looked into the face of death, and it is whiskered." . . . The moral, I suppose, was this: Do not, on purpose, write a bunch of overwritten crap if it looks so much like the overwritten crap that you usually write that the editors think you have merely reached new heights in your craft.

Following the unfortunate Mopsy incident, Bragg graduated to covering southwest Florida, including the Everglades, where one of his assignments was writing about an alligator hunt.

Mystery writer John D. MacDonald's protagonist, Travis McGee, hangs his detective hat in Fort Lauderdale on that "other coast." Slip F18 at Bahia Mar has a special plaque designating it as the home of the *Busted Flush*, McGee's houseboat. But MacDonald himself lived in the place many of its residents call paradise on earth—Siesta Key, a lush little barrier island off Sarasota on the west coast, perched between Sarasota Bay and the Gulf of Mexico.

MacDonald moved to Florida in 1952 and rented a house on Casey Key, the island immediately south of Siesta. The two keys once were separated by the romantically named Midnight Pass, which is now closed but may eventually be reopened by Sarasota County for ecological reasons. For now, a sandbar connects Siesta and Casey, and adventurous or privacy-seeking beachcombers can walk from Turtle Beach at the south end of Siesta all the way to Palmer Point at the northern end of Casey.

After renting for a time, MacDonald bought a home on Point Crisp Road at the southern end of Siesta, not far from Turtle Beach but on the bay side of the island. MacDonald's home, in fact, faced Midnight Pass

John D. MacDonald lived on Point Crisp Road on idyllic
Siesta Key, near Sarasota on Florida's southwest coast.

when it was still navigable. His 1977 book *Condominium*, set on a fictitious island called Fiddler Key, tells a political firecracker of a story: Evil
condominium speculators throw safety to the winds with shoddy construction that can't stand up to a monster hurricane. With typical Mac-
Donald flair, he absolutely nails the allure of Siesta Key and its island
brethren, as well as the bemused disquiet of retirees who discover that
maybe island life isn't *completely* perfect:

> He hugged her and went into the living room and knelt and tried
> to figure out how the rain could come under the sliding doors. As
> he knelt there he had the grotesque feeling that he was part of

some mass ritual, that up and down this west coast of Florida, on all these narrow elongated offshore islands tucked close to the subtropic mainland and named Clearwater Beach and Anna Maria and Longboat, Siesta Key and Casey Key and Manasota Key and Seagrape Key and this one he was on, Fiddler Key, there were thousands of sixty-two-year-old retired chemists named Howard something, all living in these tall pale structures by the sea, all of them at this moment kneeling and facing their sliding glass doors and wondering how the rainwater managed to seep in and stain their pastel shags.

Face west, all you plump old men, and ponder your tropic fates.

MacDonald also succinctly explains how the islands formed:

A very long time ago Florida had been under the sea. As the seas receded and the land rose, great rivers had come roaring off the mainland into the Gulf of Mexico, fed by continuing cloudbursts. When the seas retreated further and the rivers shrank, these off-shore islands appeared, composed of the materials the rivers had carried down to the sea and deposited in their delta areas. Thus they were quite unlike the true Florida keys, from Key Largo down to Key West, a long huge dead reef, composed of the googols of skeletal remains of tiny dead sea creatures.

It's been several decades since a hurricane struck the west coast of Florida, and the experts say that sooner or later—perhaps much sooner, maybe even the hurricane season of 2001, predicted to be one of the worst ever—the Suncoast's luck will run out. Even a near miss could be deadly, burying the keys in a wall of water that would reconnect the gulf with the bays.

MacDonald mercilessly sums up the potential devastation:

The worst thing that could ever happen to the West Coast of Florida would be to have a major hurricane follow the coastline right from the Ten Thousand Islands up to Cedar Key, with the eye never coming ashore, with the eye staying five or ten miles offshore. It would scour the keys clean, like a big brush. With the state of readiness right now, it would take a month just to count the bodies.

Other writers who have lately discovered the delights of the Suncoast include horror legend Stephen King, whose home state of Maine has played host to virtually all of his tales. But in one of his most recent books, *The Girl Who Loved Tom Gordon*, he signs off the introduction with "Stephen King; Longboat Key, Florida; February 1999." Ah, the delicious anticipation—perhaps we'll soon see a King epic set amid the palms and pools of Longboat Key, with icky, creepy things crawling out from under the sand at midnight in search of fresh pink flesh. Well . . . perhaps slightly older pink flesh, given the average age of the populace.

The Sarasota mainland also has its share of attractions, and *Gone With the Wind* fans should visit the historic Sarasota Opera House, where the chandelier that hung at Twelve Oaks is on display in the lobby.

LITERARY LURES AND SOUTHERN SIGHTS

St. Petersburg

Attic Bookshop, 6601 First Avenue S.; (727) 344–2398. General stock and out-of-print books.

Cooper's Books, 4906 Fortieth Street S.; (727) 867–5369. Specializing in books by and about Hemingway, military conflicts, and the American West.

Florida Suncoast Writers' Conference, weekend conference every February, University of South Florida, St. Petersburg campus; (813) 974–1711. This conference packs more than fifty workshops into forty-eight hours, with an emphasis on fiction that sells in the popular market. The same organization hosts the Florida Suncoast Writers' Weekend Workshop in April, for those who prefer discussion in small-group settings.

Haslam's Book Store, 2025 Central Avenue; (727) 822–8616. General stock and Florida specialties. Reputedly haunted by the ghost of Jack Kerouac.

Jack Kerouac home, 5169 Tenth Avenue N., St. Petersburg, not open to the public.

Lighthouse Books, 1735 First Avenue N., St. Petersburg; (727) 822–3278. General stock emphasizing Florida and the Caribbean.

St. Petersburg and Clearwater Convention and Visitors Bureau; (727) 464–7200 or (800) 345–6710; www.floridasbeach.com.

Sarasota

Coral Cove Books, 7282 S. Tamiami Trail (just south of the Stickney Point bridge to Siesta Key); (941) 924–3848. Excellent general stock, first editions, and collectibles.

Christine's Books, 4391 Pasadena Circle; (941) 356–0586. Good selection of first editions and Floridiana.

Circle Books, 478 John Ringling Boulevard on St. Armands Circle; (941) 388–2850.

Historic Spanish Point, 337 N. Tamiami Trail, Osprey; (941) 966–5214. Open 9 A.M. to 5 P.M. Mondays through Saturdays; noon to 5 P.M. Sundays.

Ringling Museum of Art and Circus Museum, 5401 Bay Shore Road; (941) 359–5700.

Sarasota Convention and Visitors Bureau, 655 N. Tamiami Trail; (941) 957–1877; www.discoversarasota.com.

Sarasota Opera House, 61 N. Pineapple Avenue; (941) 366–8450.

ACCOMMODATIONS AND RESTAURANTS

St. Petersburg

Bay Gables Bed-and-Breakfast, 340 Rowland Court N.E.; (727) 822–8855.

Bayboro House Bed and Breakfast on Tampa Bay, 1719 Beach Drive S.E.; (813) 823–4955.

Bayboro Inn and Hunt Room, 357 Third Street South; (727) 823–0498.

Mansion House Bed and Breakfast, 105 Fifth Avenue N.E.; (727) 821–9391.

Sunset Bay Inn, 635 Bay Street NE; (727) 896–6701.

St. Petersburg Beach

The Inn on the Beach, 1401 Gulf Way; (727) 360–8844.

Island's End Resort, 1 Pass-a-Grille Way; (727) 360–5023.

Don Cesar Beach Resort and Spa, 3400 Gulf Boulevard; (727) 360–1881.

Sarasota

Bein's and Joffrey's, 1345 Main Street, downtown; (941) 906–9500.

Coquina on the Beach Resort, 1008 Benjamin Franklin Drive, Lido Key; (941) 388–2141 or (800) 833–2141.

The Cypress B&B Inn, 621 Gulfstream Avenue S., Longboat Key; (941) 955–4683.

Half Moon Beach Club, 2050 Benjamin Franklin Drive, Lido Key; (941) 388–3694.

Harley-Helmsley Sandcastle, 1540 Ben Franklin Drive, Lido Beach; (941) 388–2181.

Hemingway's, 325 John Ringling Boulevard, St. Armands Circle, St. Armands Key; (941) 388–3948.

Marina Jack, 2 Marina Plaza, Sarasota bayfront; (941) 365–4232.

Melting Pot Restaurant, 1055 S. Tamiami Trail, mainland; (941) 365–2628.

Michael's on East, 1212 East Avenue, mainland; (941) 366–0007. The most elegant mainland restaurant; superb food and service.

Sand Cay Beach Resort, 4725 Gulf of Mexico Drive, Longboat Key; (941) 383–5044.

Word of Mouth, 2164 Gulf Gate Drive, mainland near Siesta Key; (941) 925–2400. A terrific breakfast place near Siesta Key.

Siesta Key

Banana Bay Club, 8254 Midnight Pass Road; (941) 346–0113. On the quiet southern end of Siesta Key.

Blasé Cafe, 5263 Ocean Boulevard; (941) 349–9822.

Bob's Boathouse, 1310 Old Stickney Point Road; (941) 312–9111. If your party has six or more people, reserve the upstairs boat, where you'll actually sit *in* a vessel while dining.

The Broken Egg, 210 Avenida Madera; (941) 346–2750. Great breakfast place in Siesta Village.

Captain Curt's Crab and Oyster Bar, 1200 Old Stickney Point Road; (941) 349–3885. Only here can you get a T-shirt proclaiming that you got the crabs at Captain Curt's.

Crescent House Bed-and-Breakfast, 459 Beach Road; (941) 346–0857.

Fandango Cafe, 5148 Ocean Boulevard; (941) 346–1711.

Lynmar Cottage, 445 Beach Road; (941) 923–6604.

Midnight Pass Pub, 8865 Midnight Pass Road; (941) 349–2280. Just across the street from the entrance to Turtle Beach, at the quiet end of the island.

Ophelia's on the Bay, 9105 Midnight Pass Road; (941) 349–2212. My favorite restaurant in the world. Exquisite view, perfect food, and unsurpassed service.

The Summerhouse, 6101 Midnight Pass Road; (941) 349–1100.

Turtle Beach House, 9008 Midnight Pass Road; (941) 346–1774.

Turtle Beach Resort, 9049 Midnight Pass Road; (941) 349–4554.

Turtle's Restaurant on Little Sarasota Bay, 8875 Midnight Pass Road; (941) 346–2207. Fabulous Sunday brunch.

Sanibel and Captiva Islands

These sun-drenched islands, scoured clean by the Gulf of Mexico and less crowded than other resorts, are off the west coast near Cape Coral and Fort Meyers. Sanibel Island hosts the International Hemingway Festival, officially sanctioned by his family, each June. Past conferences have hosted Pulitzer Prize–winners, Hemingway family members, and other literary luminaries such as Michael Tolkin, playwright-screenwriter of *The Player*. Foremost Hemingway scholar Dr. James Nagel is also a frequent speaker. It's not known whether Papa Hemingway ever visited Sanibel, but his family did, as documented in photos and letters. In deference to the Hemingway family's wishes, the festival is strictly nonprofit, with proceeds benefiting the American Diabetes Foundation, the Bay Pines V.A. Hospital in St. Petersburg, the J. N. "Ding" Darling National Wildlife Refuge, and Sanibel's CROW (Care and Rehabilitation of Wildlife).

In 1998, the festival included an Ernest Hemingway Exhibit, hosted by the BIG Arts Complex and featuring a huge collection of Hemingway papers—the largest array of Hemingway memorabilia outside the Kennedy Library in Boston. More than 350 family letters, original manuscript pages, telegrams, articles and photos from all over the world were featured.

Another author with local ties, who definitely did visit this part of Florida, was Anne Morrow Lindbergh, who lived on Captiva for some time. Lindbergh's bestselling and still popular book of reflections, *Gifts From the Sea*, was in part inspired by shelling expeditions on Captiva, whose east-to-west beaches are usually festooned with beautiful shell specimens. Current shell-lovers be warned, though: Strict shelling restrictions apply on both Sanibel and Captiva, with limits of two live shells per species per day, including sand dollars, sea stars, starfish, and urchins. Maximum fines are stiff: $500 and sixty days in jail for first-time offenders.

LITERARY LURES AND SOUTHERN SIGHTS

J. N. "Ding" Darling Wildlife Refuge, 1 Wildlife Drive, Sanibel; (941) 472–1100. Nearly 5,000 acres sheltering more than 290 species of birds, thirty-two kinds of mammals, and fifty types of amphibians and reptiles. Admission fee.

International Hemingway Festival; (800) 916–9727; www.hemingway festival.com. A three-day weekend every June of family-oriented literary and artistic workshops, contests, and sporting events. One nice touch for young Hemingway wannabes, a youth writing contest. If you can't make it in person, the Web site features a full selection of Hemingway-themed stuff, including T-shirts, fishing hats, and tote bags.

Sanibel-Captiva Islands Chamber of Commerce, 155 Causeway Road, Sanibel; (941) 472–1080; www.sanibel-captiva.org.

Sanibel Island Visitors Internet; www.sanibelisland.com.

ACCOMMODATIONS AND RESTAURANTS

Barney's Incredible Edibles, 2330 Palm Ridge Road, Sanibel; (941) 472–2555.

Captiva Island Inn, 11509 Andy Rosse Lane, Captiva; (941) 395–0882.

Lazy Flamingo, 1036 Periwinkle Way, Sanibel; (941) 472–6939.

North Captiva Island Club Resort, 4421 Bartlett Parkway, Captiva; (941) 395–1001.

Reservation Central, Inc., both islands; (941) 395–3682 or (800) 290–6920.

Sanibel's Song of the Sea, 863 E. Gulf Drive, Sanibel; (941) 472–2220 or (800) 231–1045.

'Tween Waters Inn, 15951 Captiva Road, Captiva; (800) 223–5865.

Windows on the Water, 1451 Middle Gulf Drive, Sanibel; (941) 395–6014.

Miami

"Some places you exist. You live and die in Miami," says Rick Bragg in his autobiography.

> In one month, when I was covering the place: a sixth-grader shot a homeless man over a slice of pizza; an Eckerd pharmacist shot and killed another pharmacist in the store; a trash hauler was shot in the spine when he refused to stop for a robber; a homeless man was doused with gasoline and set on fire; assorted tourists perished . . .
>
> You could whiz by it all, of course, with your windows rolled up tight, and whip into your gated community and pretend to be in Sarasota. Most people did. It was irrelevant that they lived in a city where the corpses [in the morgue] had bar codes on their toes, to keep up with them. I could have lived in Coral Gables with them, I guess, but that would be like tasting food without taking the Saran Wrap off.

Despite its heat and the attendant hotheaded violence, however, Miami retains a druglike, danger-tinged fascination for many writers. Bragg, in fact, recently moved back, becoming in 1999 the Miami bureau chief for the *New York Times*.

One of America's best-loved poets, Robert Frost, appeared to be firmly rooted in the North, but spent his later years in Miami. Frost wintered at Key West and Gainesville for several years before finally, in the 1940s, succumbing to Florida's lure full-time. He bought a place at 8101 S.W. Fifty-third Avenue in South Miami, which originally was called Larkin. The home, Pencil Pines, is listed on the National Register of Historic Places. Frost told friends in a letter that he was living in a place "with a yard full of fruit trees, avocados, and mango."

Legendary crime reporter Edna Buchanan, who worked for years on the police beat for the *Miami Herald*, sets her mystery series starring Britt Montero amid Miami's less-respectable neighborhoods, and fellow mystery writer Carl Hiassen also sets his darkly hilarious mysteries in south Florida.

In his 1986 book *Tourist Season*, Hiassen shares one of Miami's lesser-known advantages:

It was Dr. Allen who had determined that Greater Miami had more mutilation-homicides per capita than any other American city, a fact he attributed to the terrific climate. In warm weather, Allen noted, there were no outdoor elements to deter a lunatic from spending six, seven, eight hours hacking away at a victim; try that in Buffalo and you'd freeze your ass off.

The city does have its more pleasant aspects, including the funky Art Deco District of Miami Beach, one of the Vampire Lestat's favorite haunts in Anne Rice's *The Vampire Chronicles* series. In *The Tale of the Body Thief*, Monsieur Lestat stays at the "swanky little Park Central Hotel on Ocean Drive," he tells us, "every now and then letting my preternatural hearing sweep the chambers around me in which the rich tourists enjoyed that premium brand of solitude—complete privacy only steps from the flashy street—my Champs-Elysées of the moment, my Via Veneto."

Miami Beach started as desolate swampland, emerged as the nation's most glamorous resort for much of the twentieth century, then went into decline before a turn-of-the-millennium spurt of renewal. Back in the early 1980s, those prehistoric, pre–*Miami Vice* days, hoteliers along South Beach routinely hawked their accommodations at five dollars a night. Not anymore. Now South Beach is the epitome of hip, with fashion shoots and scores of European tourists. It's also one of Florida's most diverse communities, with yuppie couples sharing apartment buildings with hasidic Jews and Hispanics who moved in before the turnaround. The pastel buildings of Ocean Drive have been cleaned up and now sparkle with their former glamour.

Lestat describes the revamping, so to speak:

Old stucco hostelries, once the middling shelters of the aged, were now reborn in smart pastel colors, sporting their new names in elegant neon script. Candles flickered on the white-draped tables of the open-porch restaurants. Big shiny American cars pushed their way slowly along the avenue as drivers and passengers viewed the dazzling human parade, lazy pedestrians here and there blocking the thoroughfare.

The Park Central Hotel in Miami's Art Deco District is
the favorite coastal haunt of Anne Rice's Vampire Lestat.
(photo courtesy of the Park Central Hotel)

Pulitzer Prize–winning columnist Dave Barry takes a lighter view of
the city, often skewering local politics and quaint customs—such as the
devil-may-care avoidance of any known traffic laws—in his newspaper
pieces and books.

LITERARY LURES AND SOUTHERN SIGHTS

Art Deco District Welcome Center, Tenth Street at Ocean Drive, Miami
   Beach; (305) 672–2014. The beautifully restored district stretches
   along Ocean Drive west to Washington Avenue and between Fifth and
   Sixteenth Streets.

Greater Miami and the Beaches Tourism; (305) 539–3000 or (800) 933–8448; www.miamiandbeaches.com.

South Beach magazine, very cool Web site; www.southbeach.com.

ACCOMMODATIONS AND RESTAURANTS (MIAMI BEACH)

Beacon Hotel, 720 Ocean Drive; (305) 674–5200.

The Big Pink, 157 Collins Avenue; (305) 532–4700. Funky diner in the heart of the Art Deco District.

Casa Grande Hotel, 834 Ocean Drive; (305) 672–7003. Thirty-four suites in a classic Art Deco setting. Exotic decor, including antique lobby columns from Rajasthan. Mezzaluna Restaurant is on-site.

Cavalier Hotel, 1320 Ocean Drive; (305) 604–5000. Reasonable Art Deco hotel built in 1936, a short walk from the beach.

Century Hotel, 140 Ocean Drive; (305) 674–8855. An Art Deco jewel near the best part of the beach. The Joia Restaurant is next door.

Clevelander Hotel, 1020 Ocean Drive; (305) 672–7388. Very cool outdoor bar for people-watching.

The Delano, 1685 Collins Avenue; (305) 673–2900. Named for President Franklin Delano Roosevelt, who often stayed here with his family. Today the most celebrated guest is Madonna, who usually keeps the penthouse reserved. She owns the Blue Door Restaurant that's part of the hotel.

Eleventh Street Diner, 1065 Washington Avenue; (305) 534–6373.

Fountainebleu Hilton, 4441 Collins Avenue; (505) 538–2000. Favored by celebrities, this was the Miami hangout of Old Blue Eyes, Frank Sinatra.

Hotel Astor, 956 Washington Avenue; (305) 531–8081. Hip. Way hip.

Hotel Leon, 841 Collins Avenue; (305) 673–3767. Mediterranean ambience a block from the beach.

Joia Restaurant, 150 Ocean Drive; (305) 674–8871. Consistently named one of Miami's best, with many of the Tuscan specialties prepared at the table.

Marlin Hotel, 1200 Collins Avenue; (305) 604–5000. This twelve-room hotel, built in 1939 and renovated in 1997, has its own on-site recording studio.

News Cafe, 800 Ocean Drive; (305) 538–6397. Ever-trendy, great for people-watching and indulging in decadent desserts.

Osteria Del Teatro, 1443 Washington Avenue; (305) 538–7850. Northern Italian fare in a delightful setting.

Park Central Hotel, 640 Ocean Drive; (305) 538–1611. The Vampire
   Lestat's favorite Miami Beach pad boasts a beautiful Art Deco style
   with everything in shades of off-white, baby blue, and lilac.
Raleigh Miami Beach Hotel, 1775 Collins Avenue; (305) 534–6300.
   With possibly the most beautiful pool area on the Gulf Coast, this
   hotel was used for dozens of episodes of MTV's *The Grind.*
Tantra Restaurant, 1445 Pennsylvania Avenue; (305) 672–4765. Late-
   night fare and hip music.
The Tides Hotel, 1220 Ocean Drive; (305) 604–5000. This is where to
   stay if you're in the mood to splurge and be thoroughly pampered—but
   bring your savings. Interesting touches include telescopes that are stan-
   dard equipment in every room. The management diplomatically
   declines suggested subjects for close-up viewing, but one gets the idea
   that as many lenses are pointed *down* as *up.* Who needs constellations
   when you've got dazzling Ocean Drive?
Yuca Restaurant, 501 Lincoln Road; (305) 532–9822. New Wave Cuban
   cuisine and atmosphere.

Key West

The list of one-time visitors and residents of this, the two-mile by four-
mile island at the southernmost tip of the United States (less than ninety
miles from Cuba, but 150 from Miami), reads like a roll call of literary
stars: Robert Frost, Tennessee Williams, Carl Sandburg, Hunter S.
Thompson, Truman Capote, Alison Lurie, Judy Blume, Thomas
McGuane, David Kaufelt . . . and, of course, the Old Man: Ernest Hemingway. Eight Key Westers have won the Pulitzer Prize: Hemingway,
Williams, Lurie, Elizabeth Bishop, John Hersey, Joseph Lash, James Merrill, and Richard Wilbur. Beloved children's poet Shel Silverstein, author
of *Where the Sidewalk Ends* and *A Light in the Attic,* lived on Key West
until his death in early 1999.

   Today, more than a hundred writers live in Key West either full- or
part-time, and the key's literary and party reputation draws more than a
million visitors each year. During high season, tourists outnumber the
key's 30,000 year-round residents two to one.

   The island boasts—and I do mean *boasts*—a somewhat unsavory past.
Its early wealth was primarily derived from salvaging wrecks that crashed

into the deadly reefs that make up the island. During the mid-1800s, between one hundred and 150 vessels passed Key West every day on their way in and out of the Gulf of Mexico, and nighttime passages frequently didn't make it. The citizenry blatantly exploited this moneymaking situation. As one resident put it, "A wreck was the most wished for and thoroughly enjoyed thing that could happen." That . . . er, happy era dribbled to an end in the years following 1846, when a lighthouse was erected to alert ships to the dangers ahead.

Joy Williams, who has written several excellent guidebooks to Key West, puts the town's contrary nature thus:

> This peculiar and unlikely town does have a mind quite of her own with attitudes and habits which can either charm or exasperate, seduce or dismay the new acquaintance. The traveler seldom wants to see what he sees, he wants to see something else. And in many respects, Key West, which is so singular in its architecture and attitude, its posturing and fancifulness, its zany eclecticism, its seedy tropicality, is a town come upon unseen, unexpected, the something else almost felt. . . . It's odd. Actually odd. It is a rather dirty town and has very little dignity, but it has style.

Williams makes her point by relating the tale of a former mayor who, in the 1980s, when the military was for the most part deserting Key West, water-skied to Cuba to give the Florida brass an idea of how close the island is to vulnerable American shores. The water-skiing jaunt took the mayor six hours and ten minutes. "Key West, being Key West, didn't even think it a particularly strange thing to do," Williams notes.

In 1982, Key West revolted and formed the Conch Republic, in reaction to roadblocks erected by the border patrol near Florida City, ostensibly to watch for drug traffickers. The roadblocks irritated the tourists, which threatened the economy, which irritated the Conchs. "Conch," by the by, is the nickname for anyone born on the island or who's lived here awhile; it's pronounced *konks* and is taken from the tasty mollusk that's served in every seafood restaurant in town. For a mollusk, these critters are big, feisty, and a bit tough—an apt analogy for the local attitude. The name is so ingrained into local lore that the high school cheerleaders are called the Conchettes.

The secession—actually just a stunningly good excuse for a party—was accompanied by the ceremonial hurling of a stale loaf of Cuban bread into the air—a token shot declaring war against the mainland. Then the Conchs quickly surrendered and asked for $1 million in foreign aid from the state of Florida. The roadblocks came down, but they're still waiting for the cash.

This brief, albeit festive, rally for independence is now celebrated every April with Conch Republic Days, when the Conch Republic flag proudly waves and Conch Republic passports are issued. Activities include a bed race, in which teams of five people decorate beds on wheels and race them down Duval Street. In the immortal words of Miami columnist Dave Barry, I am *not* making this up.

An aura of lawlessness and a sense that anything, literally *anything*, might happen here hang over Key West like mid-afternoon haze. As Alison Lurie puts it in *The Last Resort:*

> "It's so pleasant in Key West," she sighed. "It doesn't seem as if anything really awful could ever happen here."
> "I know," Lee replied. "That's what I used to think, too."

Undeniably the biggest tourist attraction, aside from the island's reputation itself, is the Hemingway House Museum on Whitehead Street. The home, built in 1851, served as Ernest Hemingway's home in the 1930s. In his pool-house office adjacent to the Spanish Colonial house, the future Nobel Prize–winner wrote *For Whom the Bell Tolls*, *Death in the Afternoon*, *The Green Hills of Africa*, and *To Have and Have Not*. The latter, his only Key West novel, brilliantly captures the seedy life of islanders during the Depression. Hemingway's 1954 novel *The Old Man and the Sea*, written in Havana after his divorce from his second wife, Pauline, brought him his greatest critical acclaim and won the Pulitzer Prize.

The lemony-green (sort of the color of key lime pie, actually) house, a National Historic Landmark since 1968, remains virtually identical to the way Hemingway left it (he owned it for thirty years, from 1931 to 1961). His books still sit on the shelves, his collection of furniture from Spain, Africa, and Cuba looks as though it's just waiting for Papa to sit a spell, and clippings from interviews are preserved under glass. One newspaper article jauntily notes that Hemingway "never did anything he enjoyed that was legal."

Visitors love to spot the famous six-toed cats at Hemingway House in Key West. (photo courtesy of the Florida Keys Tourist Development Council)

The sense of Hemingway's presence lingers, too, in the extra-tall kitchen sink, oversize bed and other changes made to accommodate his height. And his feline heirs, the famous six-toed Hemingway cats, loll all over the place, giving the distinct impression that they're just *allowing* you to enter their domain. At last count, more than fifty of the friendly fur-balls populated the house and grounds, with their eating quarters tucked in every nook and cranny. Be careful on the home tour, or you might end up with sandal *à la* Meow Mix. The cats supposedly descend from a six-toed tomcat given to Hemingway by a ship's captain, but rumors strongly suggest that the house has become a local dumping ground for unwanted kitties. No one seems to have the nerve to check the toes and settle the matter, or perhaps they just don't want to spoil the story.

The money to purchase the Key West house—a whopping $8,000 at the height of the Depression—was given to Hemingway and Pauline by her wealthy uncle. The couple and their sons, Patrick and Gregory, moved into the home a week before Christmas, in 1931, with plasterers and painters and various other renovators still cluttering the rooms and hallways. The place was such a mess when the Hemingways bought it, a piece of plaster fell down from the ceiling and lodged in Pauline's eye, spurring her to dub it "that damned house."

Outside by the pool lies a reminder of the Old Man and his temper: Pauline had the pool built—actually painstakingly dug by pick and shovel—in 1937 as a gift for Hemingway; it was the first freshwater swimming pool on the key. But Hemingway wasn't exactly thrilled with the gesture. When he found out the pool's cost—$20,000, something like spending $225,000 on a pool today—he tossed a penny in the wet cement, saying, "You may as well take my last penny, too." That penny's still there, preserved under glass.

Pauline also converted an existing building into a pool house, with a writing studio on the second floor, and it was there that Hemingway did some of his best work. Today, Hemingway's old Royal typewriter—a sheet of paper poised in its steely grip—stands vigil in the office.

As with many homes of the rich and famous, completely unsubstantiated rumors claim that the previous owner haunts the place. Whispers about the Key West house began shortly after Hemingway shot himself in 1961. He hadn't actually lived in the house since 1940, but by all accounts spent his happiest days there. Some witnesses say they've seen Papa restlessly wandering and that they've heard the distinctive clickety-clack of his typewriter; others have said his ghost sometimes stares out a second-story window and occasionally waves at passersby.

Fans of James Bond might enjoy knowing that the home was used for the filming of *License to Kill*, the second in the series starring Timothy Dalton as Agent 007. In one scene, Bond's license gets revoked on the second-floor verandah of the house, and M demands that he turn over

Hemingway House, where the Old Man lived in the 1930s. (photo courtesy of the Florida Keys Tourist Development Council)

his gun. The erudite, obviously well-read Bond replies, "I guess it's a farewell to arms."

Philip Caputo, author of *A Rumor of War*, lived on Key West from 1977 to 1988. Caputo described the writer-friendly ambience that attracted him, and, undoubtedly, Hemingway, in a 1999 interview with *Spirit* magazine:

Village America . . . if you needed groceries or to see the pharmacist, you could walk there. You knew everybody, and everybody knew you. People accepted you for the way you related to them, not because you were anything, whether a writer or a painter or some big shot. You got to know people from all walks of life.

There was a kind of unenforced democracy about it all, because you were in this small town whose smallness was emphasized by the fact that it was an island. It was kind of like everybody being on a ship together. You had better get along.

One who got along quite nicely was playwright Tennessee Williams, who arrived on Key West in the 1940s and wrote plays such as *Cat on a Hot Tin Roof* and *Night of the Iguana* while living in a cottage at 1431 Duncan Street. His escapades were not solely literary; Williams was also renowned locally for swimming nude at local beaches. He spent some thirty years, off and on, on Key West, and the local historic preservation board would like to eventually purchase this house and turn it into a visiting playwrights' residence and museum.

The house itself is teensy, brightened by a white gazebo that Williams added while living there. He also wrote *The Rose Tattoo* while living here, and the 1956 film version of that play, starring Burt Lancaster and Anna Magnani, was filmed on the island, including this house and the Casa Marina grounds. Williams's gently addled sister, Rose, the role model for Laura in *The Glass Menagerie*, often visited him here, and locals will tell you that she spent much of her time watering trees in the garden, tirelessly fetching glasses of water from the kitchen sink.

Williams adored Key West and wanted to be buried at sea between the island and Cuba, dropped, as he put it, "overboard in a clean white sack." But he died in 1983 in New York City, and his brother, with whom Tennessee had ongoing battles, saw to it that he was buried in St. Louis, a city he detested. If any ghost were going to haunt Key West in search of happier days, Tennessee Williams should head the list of suspects.

Author Truman Capote visited Key West in the 1970s, just before publication of his controversial *Answered Prayers*. He stayed "at that motel in Key West in a trailer out back, parked close to the water's edge," according to George Plimpton's 1998 biography. In that book, John Richardson, another Capote biographer, sums up both the seediness and the magnetic lure of *Answered Prayers* and, incidentally, Capote himself: "It was offensive—cafe society, gossip of the trashiest kind—but it was rather brilliantly done. Shit served up on a gold dish. Extremely disconcerting."

Like Williams, Capote earned quite the reputation for raunchy mischief during his island stay. Joy Williams tells a story in one of her books about a female fan coming up to Capote in a bar and asking for an autograph around her navel, with the letters of his name like the numbers on a clock. Capote obliged, infuriating her husband, who promptly charged across the room, unzipped, hauled out his . . . well, equipment . . . and asked if Capote would like to autograph *it*. Capote's reply, a vintage Trumanism: "Well, I don't know if I can autograph it, but perhaps I could initial it."

Robert Frost wintered on Key West for several seasons, from the 1940s through 1960, staying in a cottage at 410 Caroline Street that now houses the Heritage House Museum. Despite his longevity, he never wrote a word about the island and was distinctly unimpressed with certain aspects of the place, such as the size of the homes, which he once described as "not much larger than a family burial plot." In her book *More Postcards From Paradise*, contemporary author June Keith tells about a friend's son who offered an explanation as to why Frost never wrote a poem about the island: "'He was on vacation,' Mikey says. 'He wrote his New England poems, the ones that made him famous, in the summers when he was up North. He came down here to party.'"

Of the contemporary authors to chronicle the quirky appeal of Key West, Keith is one of the most charming and self-effacing. In *More Postcards From Paradise*, she writes:

> When my name recently appeared in a front-page newspaper story about topless dancing, a job from which I once eked my living on Key West, my editor said, "My wife was absolutely shocked to learn that you'd been a topless dancer. She thought you were a very respectable Key West lady."
>
> Actually, I think I *am* a very respectable Key West lady.

From her home, four doors down from the Hemingway House, Keith often plays impromptu tour guide, sending tourists down to Papa's former abode. However, she understands the inherent irony. "It's right there," she directed one frazzled tourist seeking the master. "Right behind this wall that Hemingway had built to keep away the tourists."

The red brick wall was built in 1935 by Toby Bruce, a childhood friend of Pauline Hemingway. Today, according to the site's tour guides, about six hundred tourists a day stroll past that wall and into Hemingway's legacy. One doubts he would have approved, and his ghost, if truly lingering, would probably rather be fishing.

LITERARY LURES AND SOUTHERN SIGHTS

Bargain Books and News Stand, 1028 Truman Avenue; (305) 294–7446. Great selection of used and out-of-print books about the island.

Elizabeth Bishop House, 624 White Street. Home of Pulitzer Prize-winning poet Elizabeth Bishop from 1938 to 1942. Two of her rare prose pieces, *Mercedes Hospital* and *Gregorio Valdes*, are about Key West. Not open to the public.

Blue Heron Books, 1018 Truman Avenue; (305) 296–3508. Specializes in Key West authors, new books, gay and lesbian literature.

Captain Tony's Saloon, the original Sloppy Joe's, 428 Greene Street; (305) 294–1838. A dark, cavernous place, this is where Hemingway met Martha Gellhorn, the journalist who would become Mrs. Hemingway III after the oh-so-busy Hemingway divorced Pauline, wife number two. Maybe he was still upset about that pool.

Conch Tour Train, boarding sites at Mallory Square and Roosevelt Boulevard; (305) 294–5161. The train, running since 1958, provides an easy introduction to the island's four hundred years of history, with stops at all the high points—Hemingway House, Sloppy Joe's, the Wrecker's Museum, and the Lighthouse Museum. Tours daily from 9 A.M. to 4:30 P.M. Admission fee.

Discover Key West; www.key-west.com.

Duval Street Wreckers' Museum—The Oldest House, 322 Duval Street; (305) 294–9502. The oldest home in Key West was built in 1831 and was the home of a wrecking captain. Decor includes ship models and paintings, wreckers' licenses, and the dreaded Black List of unscrupulous wreckers. Admission fee.

Flaming Maggie's, 830 Fleming Street; (305) 294–3931. Gifts, books, erotica, and fresh-brewed coffee.

Florida Keys and Key West Visitors Bureau; (800) FLA–KEYS; www.fla-keys.com.

Hemingway Days Festival, three days in mid-July every year (near the author's July 21 birthday), P.O. Box 4045, Key West, FL 33041; (305) 294–4440; www.hemingwaydays.com. Part serious tribute, part license to party, this festival draws hundreds every year. Particularly popular is the Hemingway Lookalike Contest at Sloppy Joe's Bar, where finalists arm-wrestle to a win. There's also a costume party where people come as Hemingway characters; the winner one year was a Portuguese man-of-war from *The Old Man and the Sea*. Okay, so the festival is unaccountably held during the hot, humid, stormy summer months—go figure. But it's still great fun, and the heat makes a perfect excuse to knock off early, grab a margarita, and hit the beach. Fiction writers Russell Banks, Peter Matthiessen, E. L. Doctorow, Joyce Carol Oates, Joseph Heller, and Jamaica Kincaid are among the literary lights who have been part of the conference. Workshops often take place in local bars and grills; Papa Hemingway would surely have approved. A short-story contest, open to all, bears a prize of $1,000 plus airfare.

Ernest Hemingway House Museum, 907 Whitehead Street, a block off Duval; (305) 294–1575; www.hemingwayhouse.com. Registered National Historic Landmark, open daily from 9 A.M. to 5 P.M. Admission fee.

Heritage House Museum and Robert Frost Cottage, 410 Caroline Street; (305) 296–3573. Former home of poet Robert Frost. Admission fee.

Key West Accommodation Finder; (305) 292–2688 or (888) 453–9937.

Key West Chamber of Commerce, 402 Wall Street; (305) 294–2587 or (800) LAST–KEY.

Key West Historic Tours; www.historictours.com/KeyWest.

Key West Innkeepers' Association; (888) 539–4667; www.keywestinns.com.

Key West Island Bookstore, 513 Fleming Street; (305) 294–2904. Right off of Duval Street, this store has a rare-book room and a big section devoted to island authors.

Key West Literary Seminar and Writers' Workshops, one week or weekend in January every year; (888) 293–9291. Timing-wise, this one beats the Hemingway Days Festival to hell and back (which is just what Florida feels like in July), and it has a much more serious tone. The 1999 conference focused on "The American Novel," with speakers including Philip Caputo, Joseph Heller, Jamaica Kincaid, Alison Lurie, Peter Matthiessen, Joyce Carol Oates, Amy Tan, and Kurt Vonnegut. A separate four-day writers' workshop precedes each year's seminar and

involves some of its speakers. Seminar fee; workshop fee and pread-
mission writing samples required.

Key West Shipwreck Historeum, 1 Whitehead Street, Mallory Square;
(305) 292–8990 or (800) TOUR–HTA. Re-creates the 1856 world of
a Key West wreckers' warehouse, using actors, films, laser technology,
and actual artifacts from the *Isaac Allerton*, which sank in 1856 and
was recently discovered. The view from Tift's Wreckers Lookout is one
of the best on the island.

Key West Welcome Center, 3840 N. Roosevelt Boulevard (U.S. Highway 1);
(305) 296–4444 or (800) 352–8538.

Key West Writers' Walk, tours every weekend, December 1 through May
30. Meets at 10:30 A.M. Saturdays at the Heritage House Museum, 410
Caroline Street between Duval and Whitehead, and at 10:30 A.M. Sundays at Hemingway House, 907 Whitehead Street. Tickets are $10 and
should be purchased in advance at the Heritage House Museum or Key
West Island Bookstore.

Lighthouse Museum, 938 Whitehead Street; (305) 294–0012. Admission
fee.

Little White House, 111 Front Street (Truman Annex); (305) 294–9911.
Where President Harry S. Truman spent his vacations; now a presidential museum. Admission fee.

Monroe County Tourist Development Council; (305) 852–1469 or (305)
296–1552.

Old Town Trolley Tours; (305) 296–6688. Stops at Mallory Square,
Angela Street Depot, Key West Welcome Center, Casa Marina Resort,
the Southernmost Point, Bahama Village Market, and the waterfront,
as well as at most major hotels. Narrated ninety-minute tour explains
interesting local lore, such as the fact that Key West once produced 90
percent of the sponges used in the United States, and how the wrecking era brought vast wealth to the area.

Sloppy Joe's Bar, 201 Duval Street; (305) 294–5717. This is where Hemingway spent hours getting drunk with owner Sloppy Joe Russell, who
was also his favorite fishing buddy. Fishing gear owned by Hemingway
decorates the walls, alongside newspaper accounts of his suicide. Henry
Morgan, the protagonist of *To Have and Have Not*—a novel whose
main cast consists of fishermen and smugglers—is not-so-loosely fash-
ioned after Russell. After Hemingway's death, original manuscripts and

The Conch Tour Train passes by Sloppy Joe's Bar, a favored Hemingway hangout in Key West. (photo courtesy of the Florida Keys Tourist Development Council)

notes were found in a locked back room of the bar, where Hemingway had left them in Sloppy Joe's care after he moved away. Local lore insists the two became friends when Sloppy Joe was the only person in town who'd cash the newcomer's check.

Tennessee Williams house, 1431 Duncan Street (corner of Leon). Not open to the public.

L. Valladares and Son, 1200 Duval Street; (305) 296–5032. You can get a copy of the *New York Times* or books from Hemingway to Lurie. The oldest newsstand on the island.

ACCOMMODATIONS AND RESTAURANTS

Angelina Guest House, 302 Angela Street; (305) 294–4480. Once a 1920s bordello and famed gambling spot, this is a good place to immerse yourself in Key West lore.

Authors Guest House, 725 White Street; (305) 294–7381 or (800) 898–6909. Each suite in this nine-room guest house is dedicated to literary figures who at some point lived in the keys, with memorabilia and reading material relating to the room's namesake. Two cottage suites are given over to the Big Two of Key West, Hemingway and Williams.

Blue Parrot Inn, 916 Elizabeth Street; (305) 296–0033 or (800) 231–2473. Restored 1884 Bahamian-style house in the heart of Old Town.

Brass Key Guesthouse, 412 Frances Street; (305) 296–4719 or (800) 932–9119. Like staying in a plantation guest house. Features a whirlpool spa, heated pool, and dozens of exotic plants and flowers inside the hedged compound.

Captain Tony's Saloon, 428 Greene Street; (305) 294–1838. The original Sloppy Joe's.

Chelsea House Pool and Gardens, 707 Truman Avenue; (305) 296–2211 or (800) 845–8859. Restored Victorian mansion.

Conch House Heritage Inn, 625 Truman Avenue; (305) 293–0020 or (800) 207–5806. An early, historic family estate.

The Curry Mansion Inn, 511 Caroline Street; (305) 294–5349 or (800) 253–3466. Snuggled up against the original 1899 Curry Mansion, surrounded by the estate's dense tropical foliage.

Eaton Lodge, 511 Eaton Street; (305) 292–2170 or (800) 294–2170. Historic 1880 Victorian Mansion in Old Town, just a few steps from Duval Street.

Eden House, 1015 Fleming Street; (305) 296–6868 or (800) 533–KEYS. Casual, funky 1924 Art Deco hotel.

The Gardens Hotel, 526 Angela Street; (305) 294–2661. Tropical feeling and very private in the midst of Old Town, this elegant little hotel occupies what once was the largest private estate in town.

Hilton Resort and Marina, 245 Front Street; (305) 294–4000. Luxurious major hotel for those who want more amenities than a bed-and-breakfast.

Kelly's Caribbean Bar, Grill and Brewery, 301 Whitehead Street; (305) 293–8484.

Key West Diner, 2811 N. Roosevelt Boulevard; (305) 292–8002. Locally owned family restaurant, affordable, with great food and service.

Marriott's Casa Marina Resort, 1500 Reynolds Street; (305) 296–3535. Three-star resort with full array of health and sporting amenities and a fabulous restaurant as well.

The Mermaid and the Alligator, 729 Truman Avenue; (305) 294–1894 or (800) 773–1894. Elegant guest house in the heart of Old Town.

Ocean Key House Suite Resort and Marina, Zero Duval Street; (305) 296–7701 or (800) 328–9815.

Paradise Inn, 819 Simonton Street; (305) 293–8007 or (800) 888–9648. Just a block from Duval Street and within easy walking distance of the Atlantic and Gulf beaches.

Pepe's Casa Cayo Hueso Cafe, 410 Wall Street, Mallory Square; (305) 295–2620. Said to be the oldest eatery in the Florida Keys. Cuban-Conch cuisine using local herbs and spices. Next door to Mi Abuela's Bodega ("My Grandmother's Store"), which has a great selection of unusual souvenirs—Cuban spices, gifts, and other items.

PT's Late Night Bar and Grill, 902 Caroline Street; (305) 296–4245. Like it says, "late night."

The Quay Restaurant and Lounge, 12 Duval Street; (305) 294–4446. Overlooks the Gulf of Mexico, in the heart of Old Town.

Sloppy Joe's Bar, 201 Duval Street; (305) 294–5717.

Southernmost Point Guest House, 1327 Duval Street; (305) 295–0715. Heavenly Victorian mansion built by cigar-maker E. H. Gato Jr. before the turn of the nineteenth century.

Whispers B&B at the Gideon Lowe House, 409 William Street; (305) 294–5969 or (800) 856–SHHH. Listed on the National Register of Historic Places, and *very, very, very* quiet.

William Anthony House, 613 Caroline Street; (305) 294–2887. Renovated historic inn in Old Town.

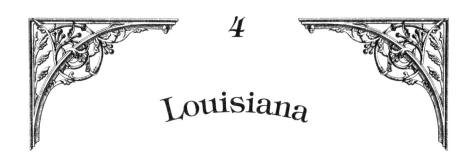

4

Louisiana

She was obsessed with New Orleans. Virginia was below the
Mason-Dixon line and Robert E. Lee would not have raised his
sword against it, but it lacked palm trees and a dilapidated air of
hopelessness. . . . The tropics induced mood swings—one minute
you are in ecstasy that the temperature is eighty degrees and there
are palm trees and that bemusing hopelessness—but of course the
next minute the hopelessness has gotten to you, or it is overcast
and depressing, or gets too hot to do anything, and you get a bad
mood swing in the opposite direction. You turn a corner and
suddenly you want to jump out of your skin, the weather changes
and suddenly you are demented.

—Nancy Lemann, *The Fiery Pantheon*

From Kate Chopin to Anne Rice, Tennessee Williams to Richard Ford, Louisiana has caught writers in its seductive web throughout its nearly three-hundred-year history. A book-loving traveler can start in the northwest region, in the Cane River Country where Chopin spent much of her life, and crisscross the state, stopping for literary nourishment along the way to New Orleans, the city that has perhaps drawn more writers than any other in the United States.

As country singer Pam Tillis sang in a hit song, "Read about you in a Faulkner novel, met you once in a Williams play." The tune, by

Michael Anderson, is called "Maybe It Was Memphis." Well, maybe. I'd bet it was New Orleans.

LITERARY LURES AND SOUTHERN SIGHTS

Louisiana Office of Tourism; (225) 342–8100 or (800) 677–4082; www.louisianatravel.com.
Louisiana Office of State Parks and Historic Sites; (225) 342–8111 or (888) 677–1400; www.crt.state.la.us/crt/parks.

New Orleans and River Road

Near where I live, there is the Lafayette Cemetery on Prytania Street. Anne Rice's Vampire Lestat lives in one of the tombs. A few decades later, a young poet, Everette Maddox, moved to New Orleans and rented [F. Scott] Fitzgerald's apartment. It's still available, cheap, like everything else in New Orleans. There is no memorial plaque. If New Orleans went into the memorial plaque business for all the writers who ever lived here, they would have to brass plate the whole town. There is a plaque on Pirate's Alley on the house where Faulkner lived, but there isn't any on Audubon's house.

—Andrei Codrescu, *The Muse Is Always Half-Dressed in New Orleans and Other Essays*

F. Scott Fitzgerald wrote his first book, *This Side of Paradise*, while living in the old-money Garden District, alongside Lafayette Cemetery, in an upstairs apartment at 2900 Prytania Street that overlooked the raised graves. "I can see him, coffee in hand, standing in his robe on the little balcony, wincing from last night's gin, looking down on the little houses of the dead, wishing he was in one of them," writes contemporary Garden District resident Andrei Codrescu, a novelist and National Public Radio commentator. "'It's not so great on *this* side of paradise,' he might have said, to no one in particular. No kidding. He hadn't even *met* Zelda yet."

F. Scott Fitzgerald lived in apartments overlooking New Orleans's spooky Lafayette Cemetery when he wrote *This Side of Paradise*.

Others who lived in the Garden District included Kate Chopin, who lived at 1413–15 Louisiana Avenue from 1876 to 1879, and Lillian Hellman, who lived at 1718 Prytania Street while writing *The Children's Hour*. Mark Twain was frequently a guest of George Washington Cable's home at 1313 Eighth Street, between Coliseum and Chestnut.

In *The Awakening*, published in 1899, Chopin put the Pontellier home not in the Garden District, however, but on the very edge of the Quarter:

The Pontelliers possessed a very charming home on Esplanade Street in New Orleans. It was a large, double cottage, with a broad front verandah, whose round, fluted columns supported the sloping roof. The house was painted a dazzling white; the outside shutters, or jalousies, were green. In the yard, which was kept scrupulously neat, were flowers and plants of every description which flourishes in South Louisiana.

Two writers with works inextricably linked to New Orleans are Walker Percy, whose *The Moviegoer* is set in New Orleans and Gentilly, across the lake, and John Kennedy Toole, whose posthumously published *A Confederacy of Dunces* resonates in equal parts with the city's hilarity and horrors.

Percy was born in Birmingham, Alabama, in 1916, and spent his youth in Greenville, Mississippi, where he lived with an older cousin, William Alexander Percy. The younger Percy majored in chemistry at the University of North Carolina at Chapel Hill, then went on to Columbia's College of Physicians and Surgeons, getting his medical degree in 1941. He practiced medicine for only a brief time before contracting tuberculosis and being forced to retire. Luckily for the literary world, he turned to his elder cousin's passions of reading and writing. What began as *Confessions of a Moviegoer* was written for himself, like Faulkner's *The Sound and the Fury*, but fortunately for readers an editor at Knopf recognized its brilliance and published it. *The Moviegoer* won the National Book Award in 1962.

Contemporary writers are no less adamant about Percy's talent and subsequent influence. Nancy Lemann, in *The Oxford American*, wrote about him in "My Actual Hero."

> It was strictly an epiphany, reading Walker Percy for the first time. The world stopped, you got off, and suddenly literature had a meaning far beyond anything it had ever achieved in your consciousness previously. He did what all great writers do: he put into words what you had always felt inchoately. Not only that, but in reading his works for the first time, literature suddenly acquired a strange, ardent new possibility, the possibility that you might follow it as your vocation.

The action in Percy's *The Moviegoer* spans just one hectic week in the life of the Big Easy, the seven days before Mardi Gras and, coincidentally, the week before the thirtieth birthday of the protagonist, Binx Bolling. Binx's reasons for living in Gentilly might have been Percy speaking about his decision to live in Covington, across Lake Pontchartrain, rather than in the ongoing insanity of New Orleans proper:

> For the past four years I have been living uneventfully in Gentilly, a middle-class suburb of New Orleans. Except for the banana plants in the patios and the curlicues of iron on the Walgreen drugstore one would never guess it was part of New Orleans. . . . I can't stand the old world atmosphere of the French Quarter or the genteel charm of the Garden District. I lived in the Quarter for two years, but in the end I got tired of Birmingham businessmen smirking around Bourbon Street and the homosexuals and patio connoisseurs on Royal Street.

Binx, like Percy, one suspects, ventures into the Quarter occasionally to see movies and, in this scene, glimpses a favorite actor:

> I alight at Esplanade in a smell of roasting coffee and creosote and walk up Royal Street. The lower Quarter is the best part. The ironwork on the balconies sags like rotten lace. Little French cottages hide behind high walls. Through deep sweating carriageways one catches glimpses of courtyards gone to jungle. Today I am in luck. Who should come out of Pirate's Alley half a block ahead of me but William Holden! Holden crosses Royal and turns toward Canal. As yet he is unnoticed. The tourists are either browsing along antique shops or snapping pictures. No doubt he is on his way to Galatoire's for lunch.

Spotting the occasional movie star is no rarity in New Orleans these days, either. Along that same stretch of Royal Street late one night, a friend and I spotted a tuxedo-clad Randy Quaid, on the way to or from some festivity, obviously in a very good mood.

Percy wrote one definitive New Orleans novel and helped bring another before the public. In 1976, when Percy was teaching at Loyola

University, John Kennedy Toole's mother sent him a manuscript, begging him to read the legacy of her only son, who had committed suicide in 1969 at the age of thirty-two. Percy sent it to an editor friend and eventually the book, A *Confederacy of Dunces*, won the Pulitzer Prize.

The opening of A *Confederacy of Dunces* grips the reader instantly in the force of personality that is Ignatius J. Reilly.

> In the shadow under the green visor of the cap Ignatius J. Reilly's supercilious blue and yellow eyes looked down upon the other people waiting under the clock at the D. H. Holmes department store, studying the crowd of people for signs of bad taste in dress. Several of the outfits, Ignatius noted, were new enough and expensive enough to be properly considered offenses against taste and decency. Possession of anything new or expensive only reflected a person's lack of theology and geometry; it could even cast doubts upon one's soul.

Toole gleefully sketches both the beauty of St. Charles Avenue and the slight seediness of the lower Garden District, where Reilly lives with his mother, through the character of Patrolman Mancuso.

> [He] inhaled the musty scent of the oaks and thought, in a romantic aside, that St. Charles Avenue must be the loveliest place in the world. From time to time he passed the slowly rocking streetcars that seemed to be leisurely moving toward no special destination, following their route through the old mansions on either side of the avenue. Everything looked so calm, so prosperous, so unsuspicious.
>
> At Constantinople Street, he turned toward the river, sputtering and growling through a declining neighborhood until he reached a block of houses built in the 1880s and '90s, wooden Gothic and Gilded Age relics that dripped carving and scrollwork, Boss Tweed suburban stereotypes separated by alleys so narrow that a yardstick could almost bridge them and fenced in by iron pikes and low walls of crumbling brick. . . . It was a neighborhood that had degenerated from Victorian to nothing in par-

ticular, a block that had moved into the twentieth century care-
lessly and uncaringly—and with very limited funds.

When Toole's mother, Thelma, died, she was living at 1016 Elysian
Fields in the Faubourg Marigny—not far from where Tennessee
Williams's Stanley and Stella Kowalski lived—just downriver of the
French Quarter. Mrs. Toole's will stipulated that her home be turned into
a museum for her son, which it wasn't. She also stipulated that *The Neon
Bible*, Toole's first novel, never be published. Of course, it was.

New Orleans has paid tribute to Toole, however. A bronze statue of
Ignatius J. Reilly, jointly commissioned by the Downtown Development
District and the Chateau Sonesta Hotel, stands watch under the restored
clock at the landmark D. H. Holmes building, now the Chateau Sonesta. And the wiener-shaped Lucky Dog hot-dog carts, inspiration for the
Paradise Vending carts Reilly wheels around in the book, remain ubiqui-
tous. Author Jerry E. Strahan, a Lucky Dog manager, chronicles the
funky company in *Managing Ignatius: The Lunacy of Lucky Dog and Life in
the Quarter*, an utterly hilarious tribute to the transient wiener hawkers
who might be, on any given day, drifters, drunks, or swindlers. You
haven't really been to New Orleans until you've had a Lucky Dog followed by coffee and a beignet at Cafe du Monde. Watch your wallet,
though, in both places.

The $23,000 Reilly sculpture—by Albany, Louisiana, artist William
Ludwig—shows Ignatius in the book's opening scene, standing patiently
beneath the clock awaiting his mother, watching the Canal Street
passersby. He clutches his Werlein's shopping bag and wears a hunting
cap, flannel shirt, and baggy pants.

The Pirate's Alley corridor described by Binx Bolling was the birthplace of William Faulkner's first book, published in 1925, *Soldier's Pay*.
Although Faulkner set his best-known novels in his native Mississippi,
Soldier's Pay was hatched while Faulkner lived in the Pirate's Alley building that now houses Faulkner's Book Shop.

Faulkner wrote about New Orleans in *Mosquitoes* (1927), a satiric
paean to the hip 1920s artsy set:

The violet dusk held in soft suspension lights slow as bellstrokes.
Jackson Square was now a green and quiet lake in which abode

Faulkner House, the middle building glimpsed through the trees in St. Anthony's Square on Pirate's Alley in New Orleans, is where William Faulkner lived when he wrote his first novel. It's now a cozy bookstore.

lights round as jellyfish, feathering with silver mimosa and pomegranate and hibiscus beneath which lantana and cannas bled and bled. Pontalba and cathedral were cut from black paper and pasted flat on a green sky; above them taller palms were fixed in black and soundless explosions. The street was empty, but from Royal Street there came the hum of a trolley that rose to a staggering clatter, passed on and away leaving an interval filled with the gracious sound of inflated rubber on asphalt, like a tearing of endless silk. Clasping his accursed bottle, feeling like a criminal, Mr. Talliaferro hurried on.

During the mid-1920s, Faulkner hosted an infamous party at Gala-toire's, paid for with the advance he received for *Mosquitoes*. At the dinner, he toasted many of the same New Orleans artsy types he then thoroughly skewered in the book. When it came out, they were una-mused; some never forgave him.

Connections to another Mississippian, Tennessee Williams, born Thomas Lanier Williams, can be found on just about every corner in New Orleans, whether it's a hotel or house he occupied for a few nights or months, or a bar where he partook of traditional Southern comfort. "If I can be said to have a home, it is in New Orleans," he once said, "which has provided me with more material than any other part of the country."

During his time in New Orleans, Williams lived in apartments at 722 Toulouse Street, on both the ground floor and third floor (the room with the gabled window), as well as at 431 Royal Street, 708 Toulouse, 538 Royal Street, and 632 St. Peter Street. He also had a cottage at 1014 Dumaine. Tennessee apparently took the local saying of *"Laissez les bon temps roulez!"* or, "Let the good times roll!" to heart—a party at 722 Toulouse so infuriated the landlady that she poured boiling water through the floorboards down onto his guests.

She was charged with malicious mischief, and Williams testified at her hearing. He immortalized that apartment, the mad landlady, and the boiling water, in *Vieux Carre*. "God, but I was ignorant when I came here!" the protagonist blurts to his landlady after an argument. "I ought to pay you tuition!"

The apartment at 632 St. Peter Street, between Jackson Square and Royal Street, is where Williams wrote a good portion of A *Streetcar Named Desire*, considered by many his masterpiece and the sole piece of literature that most evokes New Orleans. From his rooms above St. Peter, Williams could hear the rattletrap streetcar clanging a block away on Royal Street. He used the number 632 for Stanley and Stella Kowalski's address, at 632 Elysian Fields in the Faubourg Marigny, just downriver from the French Quarter.

Williams reportedly finished the final draft of *Streetcar* in Room 9 at the Maison de Ville Hotel at 727 Toulouse, just off Bourbon Street. The Maison was built as a private home, and its original slave quarters (includ-ing Room 9) date back to the 1740s and are thought to be among the oldest surviving buildings in the Quarter. One of the owners was phar-

Tennessee Williams lived in upstairs apartments at this house, 632 St. Peter in New Orleans, while writing *A Streetcar Named Desire*.

macist A. Peychaud, who, while experimenting with medicinal bitters one night, invented the potent Sazerac, one of the world's first cocktails.

In a book on Williams for the *Southern Writers* series, scholar Nancy M. Tischler of Pennsylvania State University summed up Williams's enormous contributions to the Southern gothic school of literature:

> It is clear that Williams' greatest talent lies in presenting a portion of the South, with Southern characters and Southern speech, which he endows with unusual meanings. It is also clear

632 Elysian Fields, the fictitious home of Stanley and Stella Kowalski in *A Streetcar Named Desire,* now houses a boarded-up barber shop.

that his natural form is tragedy, for his vision is essentially tragic. He sees no metaphysical hope to relieve the impending doom. He sees the horrible things that men do to one another and to themselves. He sees the corrupting influences of the American scene and especially of the American South.

He recognizes the frightening conflict between romance and reality, between man's aspirations and his actual accomplishments. He sees purity turned perverse and diseased, youth grown old and ugly, sensitivity trampled under the boots of the mighty. In the midst of this jungle-world, he also sees the heroism of which the human spirit is capable, the dignity with which man can rise briefly out of his own ashes, the joy he can know in his moment of bliss. His sympathy lies entirely with that man or woman who is sensitive enough to commit himself to deep feelings, who gambles with life, and who dies or fails beautifully.

Truman Capote, although more associated with Alabama and New York, where he spent most of his life, nonetheless was born in New Orleans and occasionally wandered back this way. He was born on September 30, 1924, at Touro Infirmary, in the Garden District, and then lived for a short time with his family at the Hotel Monteleone, in the Garden District. In the mid-1940s, he had an apartment at 711 Royal Street.

Lee Radziwill (Jaqueline Kennedy's sister) told George Plimpton for his Capote biography:

> New Orleans was perhaps the most at home I ever saw him. One wasn't worried in New Orleans, which I longed to go to since I'd never been and I couldn't think of anyone more marvelous to go with than Truman. The heat was overwhelming, nevertheless, in the evening he'd sit around with his scotches and talk late into the evening. He carried this little black doctor's bag like an ancient country doctor's—I'd never seen those except in old movies. It was stuffed with pills. He had a barrel of stuff in there to choose from. Something for everything from your big toe to your tummy, your ear. He'd want to crunch it all up for you. I'll never forget when he opened that bag at our hotel, the Maison d'Orleans!

William Burroughs, author of the frankly gloomy *Naked Lunch*, lived across the river from New Orleans, in Algiers, in the late 1940s. In 1949, he lived at 509 Wagner Street in Algiers and was visited there by his friend Jack Kerouac, who recounted the stay in his classic, *On the Road*. A commemorative plaque was placed on the house in August 1996. The easiest way to get to Algiers is via the Canal Street ferry, the best free ride in New Orleans.

Among contemporary authors, the one most closely identified with New Orleans is probably native Anne Rice, whose vampires and witches play, make love, and wreak havoc in the French Quarter and Garden District. In the Quarter, the Vampires Lestat, Louis, and Claudia had a townhouse in the 1100 block of Royal Street, based on the real-life historic Gallier House. The Old Ursuline Convent, Cafe du Monde, and Jackson Square all play significant parts in the *Vampire Chronicles*.

Rice's Mayfair Witches spend more time uptown and in the Garden District. Rice's own home, at 1239 First Street at Chestnut Street, is instantly recognizable to any *Witching Hour* fan as the ancestral home of the Mayfairs. Fans peeking through the thick cypress and crape myrtle trees along the First Street side can barely glimpse the porch—glassed-in in real life, screened in the book—where the ruined Deirdre Mayfair rocked out her last days. And on a dark night, with magnolia leaves fluttering by and the oaks whispering above you, it's easy to imagine that you see the shadow of Lasher lurking at Deirdre's side.

On the edge of the Garden District is the home of Triana, Anne Rice's alter ego in *Violin*, the Claiborne Cottage at 2524 St. Charles, in the same block as Our Lady of Perpetual Help Chapel, which faces Prytania Street and is also owned by Rice. Further uptown, at 3711 St. Charles, is the peach-and-white nineteenth-century house that was the home of the "Uptown Mayfairs." The 55,000-square-foot St. Elizabeth's, a nineteenth-century former convent at 1314 Napoleon Avenue, uptown, has been restored by Rice and houses her 800-piece doll collection, book-related memorabilia, and several art galleries. Rice's famous generosity to her fans is reflected in the tours given by Kith and Kin, her family company, of St. Elizabeth's. Donations are requested for the tours of St. Elizabeth's, with benefits given to St. Alphonsus and St. Mary's churches in the nearby Irish Channel. Both churches played significant roles in Rice's life and those of her characters.

Another contemporary writer, Shirley Ann Grau, author of *The House on Coliseum Street* and *The Keepers of the House*, which won the Pulitzer, was born in New Orleans and lived there and in Montgomery, Alabama, while growing up. She graduated from Ursuline Academy and Sophie Newcomb College in New Orleans. In *The House on Coliseum Street*, she illuminates the peculiar early-fall weather particular to hurricane country:

> September was ending in its usual way, with sharp gusts of wind and gray sheets of rain. On the porches, leaves were jammed through screens like vegetables in a sieve. There were the usual hurricanes in the Gulf, hurricanes heading for the Texas coast. Once one passed so close that the gigantic neon clock advertising Jax beer (on lower St. Charles Avenue) got ripped off like a top-heavy flower. Coming down, it squashed two or three people, happy drunks who had come out of a nearby bar and were watching to see it fall. Between the storms were periods of brilliant Caribbean sunlight. Where everything shone with a desperate hard brightness, and the frenzied autumn growth shot forward.

The golden-rain trees shook their hideous pink seed pods over the walks, and camphor trees dropped their greasy black berries. Some superstitious people still sneaked out when the moon was right and picked up the camphor berries and sewed them in a little plain cotton bag; they wore them pinned on their slips and undershirts as a sure sign against fevers.

Nancy Lemann, author of *The Fiery Pantheon* and *Lives of the Saints*, perfectly grasps New Orleans's ability to induce both bafflement and delight in visitors. Of one character in *The Fiery Pantheon*, she writes:

> Mrs. Stewart was not intrinsically a Southern matron. Mr. Stewart had brought her from her native Massachusetts to New Orleans, which it had taken her exactly thirty years to adjust to. Thus she was an outsider, and this explained her ability to penetrate in observation the society surrounding her: the South.
>
> When she first came to New Orleans she could not help but notice that at the cocktail hour the women changed into oriental housecoats, everyone drank heavily, they got in towering arguments about genealogy and who married who in 1910 and in general turned into a Tennessee Williams play—as Mrs. Stewart looked on incongruously with her tweed skirts and knee socks and high ideals from the north.

Conversely, another Lemann character adores the city:

> In New Orleans she stayed at hotels. She stayed at the Pontchartrain, she stayed in the French Quarter, she stayed at the faceless Hilton Hotel downtown. But even a faceless Hilton Hotel, if it was downtown in New Orleans, could hold the answer to the mystery. . . . In New Orleans, a hotel room was different. You knew there was something tragic and sleazy and pitiful out there, but it still held the answer to the mystery.

Another native of the city, Sheila Bosworth, brings her trenchant observations to *Slow Poison* and *Almost Innocent*. In the raucous, enchanting *Slow Poison*, the character Merrill Shackleford carefully navigates through New Orleans society.

Because he knew the caprices of his native city's ruling class, Merrill did not make the mistake of instantly assuming that a New Orleans girl named Aimee Desiree was a whore, working Esplanade Avenue to the river. Hadn't he danced at the Comus ball with a frozen-lipped debutante called Lola, a name for a hot-blooded barmaid. Didn't he share a box each season at the symphony with a pedigreed divorcee christened Royal like a jockey out at the fairgrounds. Once he'd gone to a funeral luncheon with a highborn, gilded widow called Evangeline, as if she were of a Cajun household.

In New Orleans, the chances were excellent that an "Aimee Desiree" was the last darling of some madcap French aristocrat's frail heart and his robust last will and testament.

And Bosworth knows something of the tenacity of New Orleans character—not surprising given that the city was scooped, soggy and humid, out of a suffocating bowl of swampland, and that its first residents were the criminals, prostitutes, and other rejects of France and Spain. "Royal Beer, brewed and bottled in New Orleans, made with the water from the filthy Mississippi River, was the most popular beer in the city," Bosworth writes in *Slow Poison*.

"The people of New Orleans weren't scared of Royal. They hadn't been scared of anything since reconstruction, except that it might rain on Mardi Gras."

Mark Twain wrote quite a bit about Louisiana and New Orleans, particularly in his memoir *Life on the Mississippi*. "They bury their dead in vaults, above the ground," Twain writes, describing a hygienic necessity in a city that lies six inches *below* sea level. Until the populace learned to bury in the European fashion, coffins buried in the sodden earth would sometimes float right back up to the surface. The early practice of burying corpses in the river levee ended after a few bad floods, when bones and decaying bodies washed into the city streets, borne along the tides of stinking Mississippi water.

The cemeteries, however, took on a macabre splendor. "Many of the cemeteries are beautiful, and are kept in perfect order," Twain continues. "When one goes from the levee or the business streets near it, to a ceme-

Mark Twain remarked on the beauty and meticulous care of New Orleans's cemeteries. This statue of a weeping angel tops a tomb in Metairie Cemetery.

tery, he observes to himself that if those people down there would live as neatly while they are alive as they do after they are dead, they would find many advantages in it."

Andrei Codrescu, the National Public Radio commentator who has adopted New Orleans as his home-away-from-Romania, paraphrased Faulkner's famous line—"The past is never dead. It's not even past."— when writing about the city's cemeteries. "In New Orleans, certainly, cemeteries tell all the great stories because there are so many of them. There are more dead than living people here, and the dead are not all that dead."

Twain also cherished the Southern drawl heard in the French Quarter and Garden District, so unlike the Midwestern twang he heard along most of the Mississippi River's route:

> I found the half-forgotten Southern intonations and elisions as pleasing to my ear as they had formerly been. A Southerner talks music. At least it is music to me, but then I was born in the South. The educated Southerner has no use for an *r*, except at the beginning of a word. He says "honah," and "dinnah," and "Gove'nuh" and "befo' the waw," and so on. The words may lack charm to the eye, in print, but they have it to the ear.

The New Orleans atmosphere oozes electricity—expectant, succulent, crackling with promise and a hint of danger. Andrei Codrescu, in *The Muse Is Always Half-Dressed in New Orleans*, declares: "Ghosts and pirates are thick as the morning fog on certain days in New Orleans. You open your notebook at some outdoor cafe in the Vieux Carre and find yourself holding intense congress with the shadows between the huge leaves of the palm or the fig above you. On certain afternoons light filters its arabesques through the grillwork of the balconies, and you dream without touching your coffee."

Ellen Gilchrist, who was born in Vicksburg, Mississippi, is best known for her sensuous New Orleans stories—"If it smells like sex, it grows here," she has written about the city—many starring the irrepressible Rhoda Manning. As described by Y'all.com in a story on Gilchrist, Rhoda epitomizes a certain breed of New Orleans girl: "sort of Becky Sharp on Dexadrine: compulsively talking, spoiled rotten, sex-obsessed, capricious and forever caught in a comic web that can only partly veil her loneliness and defeat."

In Gilchrist's short story *The President of the Louisiana Live Oak Society*, she captures the brilliance of spring in the Crescent City:

> It is the middle of the afternoon and under the low-hanging branches of the oak tree the air is quiet and cool and smells of all the gardens on the boulevard; confederate jasmine, honeysuckle, sweet alyssum, magnolia, every stereotyped Southern flower you can imagine has mingled its individual odor into an ardent, humid soup.

John Grisham also has a New Orleans connection; *The Client* and *The Pelican Brief* are both set partially in the Big Easy, and the movie versions of each book were shot here. And Julie Smith, although not a native, has become a local favorite with her detective series starring Skip Langdon. In *Jazz Funeral*, she writes, "The newcomer is told three things by the old New Orleans hand: don't walk on the lake side of the Quarter, don't drink the water, and always take a United Cab." New Orleans, Skip marvels at one point, "could teach you tricks of the heart you thought Tennessee Williams was just kidding about."

Even writers who aren't from New Orleans and have no intention of writing about it live there, often in blessed anonymity. Richard Ford, originally from Montana, told Codrescu that he maintains his secrecy from his home in the 1100 block of Bourbon Street because, "I don't need to hang out with writers. These two streets by my house are enough." As Codrescu says, "People—not just writers—are attracted to New Orleans because it's full of stories and listeners who have nothing better to do than to listen to them."

Like New Orleans, the winding River Road between the city and Baton Rouge also has inspired many an author. Anne Rice plucked details for the keenly imagined dwellings of her supernatural protagonists from Destrehan Plantation, about twenty minutes north of New Orleans; Oak Alley, perhaps the most-photographed plantation in Louisiana; and Madewood Plantation House, farther north on the Bayou LaFourche.

Destrehan, built in 1787, was one of the inspirations for Pointe du Lac, the Vampire Louis's indigo plantation in *Interview With the Vampire*, and scenes from the movie version of the book were shot there. For a glimpse into what Louis's and Lestat's life on a Creole plantation would have been like, visit Laura Plantation, about an hour south of New Orleans in Vacherie. The tour guides here are marvelous, letting visitors in on highlights both savory and not-so of the Creole lifestyle. Also near Vacherie is Oak Alley, built in 1839 and boasting a double row of twenty-eight 300-year-old oaks leading to its front steps. Oak Alley is recognizable as Rice's inspiration for the country headquarters of the Talamasca in the *Mayfair Witches* books.

Madewood, located outside Napoleonville, inspired Rice to create Fontrevault, the Mayfair Witches' tumbledown mansion in the bayou country. The real Madewood is anything but dilapidated; it's a pristinely

Destrehan Plantation just outside New Orleans served as Anne Rice's inspiration for Pointe du Lac, Louis the vampire's indigo plantation.

preserved, formal twenty-one-room home that's now a gracious bed-and-breakfast. It's out of the way and doesn't get many tourists, and you really will feel like Scarlett O'Hara sleeping under a canopy bed or eating one of the sumptuous Madewood dinners (for which the owners kindly ask that you dress appropriately). Wine and cheese are served each evening, followed promptly with dinner by candlelight.

The Greek-Revival mansion, designed by Irish-American architect Henry Howard—who also created some of New Orleans's most gorgeous homes—was built in 1846 by Colonel Thomas Pugh, a sugarcane planter. Trees on the property were used to construct the house, hence its name, Madewood. The home was renovated in the mid-1960s by Naomi and Harold Marshall, and is owned today by their son, Keith Marshall. In 1993, the home was designated a National Historic Landmark. The feeling of stepping back in time is enhanced by the absence of telephones or televisions in the rooms. For those who want more informal accommodations, the Charlet House, an 1830s Greek-Revival cottage on the Madewood grounds, has three suites for bed-and-breakfast guests.

The double row of 300-year-old live oaks at Oak Alley Plantation were seen in *Interview With the Vampire*, covered in faux Spanish moss. Oak Alley inspired Anne Rice's setting for the country headquarters of the Talamasca in the Mayfair Witches series.

LITERARY LURES AND SOUTHERN SIGHTS

New Orleans

Beauregard-Keyes House, 1113 Chartres Street, in the French Quarter; (504) 523-7257. Admission fee. Nationally registered landmark, built in 1826 and once home to author Frances Parkinson-Keyes (rhymes with "eyes"). Also was home to General P. G. T. Beauregard, the Confederate army officer who ordered the first shots of the Civil War fired. Rumored to be haunted by Beauregard and his battleground cohorts, among them a mule with a cannon hole in its side.

Beckham's Bookshop, 228 Decatur Street, in the French Quarter; (504) 522-9875. Creaky, dusty, the perfect place to dig around for first editions and rare literary wonders.

Bienville Tours' Literary Walk; (504) 945-6789. Tours every Sunday with retired University of New Orleans professor Dr. Kenneth Holditch,

Beauregard-Keyes House, the supposedly haunted French Quarter home of author Frances Parkinson Keyes.

who's been giving this tour since 1974 and definitely knows his stuff. Bienville also sponsors tours on the Great Women of New Orleans, Jazz: Its Roots and Its Future, Multicultural Legacy, Gay Heritage, and Cycling the Crescent City. All great fun and well done.

Blaine Kern's Mardi Gras World, 233 Newton Street, in Algiers (across the river from the French Quarter); (504) 361–7821 or (800) 362–8213; www.mardigrasworld.com. Admission fee. If you can't go for Mardi Gras, this is the next best thing, with floats, costumes, and a video theater. The sequins are so bright, you gotta wear shades.

BookStar, 414 N. Peters Street, in the French Quarter; (504) 523–6411. If you're looking for regional authors, they'll have 'em, as well as a terrific section of guidebooks, all at a discount. And they're open late.

Crescent City Bookstore, 204 Chartres Street, in the French Quarter; (504) 524–4997. A good place to root around for used and rare literary treats. Kinda haunted, according to the owners and psychics brought in to investigate.

Faulkner House Books, 624 Pirate's Alley, in the French Quarter; (504) 524–2940; www.members.aol.com/FaulkHouse. In the apartment building where Faulkner wrote his first book, *Soldier's Pay*, along the atmospherically creepy Pirate's Alley. Specializes in works by Faulkner and other Southern authors. Also the host bookstore for Words and Music, an annual conference put on by the Pirate's Alley Faulkner Society that salutes a local author each year.

Gallier House Museum, 1118-1132 Royal Street; (504) 525–5661. The 1857 home of architect James Gallier Jr., this elegant townhouse was Anne Rice's inspiration for Louis, Lestat, and Claudia's Royal Street townhouse in the *Vampire* series. There's even a built-in doghouse in the courtyard that Mojo, Lestat's German shepherd, would certainly have coveted.

Garden District Book Shop, 2727 Prytania Street (the Rink), in the Garden District; (504) 895–2266. Owner Britton Trice and his friendly, knowledgeable staff will guide you to works by Southern favorites such as Anne Rice, Julie Smith, and others. This is Anne Rice's neighborhood bookstore; she often does signings of her books there, and Trice publishes gorgeous, pricey special editions of her books for especially fanatic fans.

Greater New Orleans Metropolitan Convention and Visitors Bureau; (504) 566–5011 or (800) 672–6124; www.nawlins.com.

Haunted History Tours; (504) 861–2727; www.hauntedhistorytours.com. They're campy, wacky, and some have called their research a tad suspect, but there's no denying the sheer *fun* of these folks' tours. Go if you're in the mood to have a great time and get more than a little bit spooked.

Hermann-Grima Historic House, 820 St. Louis Street; (504) 525–5661. One of the settings for Anne Rice's *The Feast of All Saints*, her historical novel of New Orleans's free people of color, the *gens de couleur libre*.

Historic New Orleans Walking Tours; (504) 947–2120; www.tournew orleans.com. Exceptionally well-done tours of the Garden District, cemeteries, and voodoo-related sites. Proprietor Robert Florence's guides are the best in town and have a sense of humor without being condescending (apparently a job requirement for some other tours). Recommended by Anne Rice's people as superior in pointing out sites related to her books.

Honey Island Swamp Tours; (504) 242–5877. If you want to get a look at the swamps north of New Orleans where Louis and Claudia ill-advisedly dumped the Vampire Lestat, these folks' tours are among the very best. Far from being gloomy or icky, however, the swamps are fresh,

In *Interview With the Vampire*, the vampires Louis and Claudia ill-advisedly dump their comrade Lestat in the swamps north of New Orleans.

clean, and rich in unexpected flashes of amazing beauty. Be nice, and the Cajun-patoied guides will even introduce you to El Whoppo, the sixteen-foot alligator whose favored perch is along the Pearl River.

Kith and Kin; (504) 899–6450; www.annerice.com. Anne Rice's dedicated, friendly family runs this company, which sells Rice-related merchandise and gives tours of St. Elizabeth's, a 55,000-square-foot former convent-orphanage located uptown. St. Elizabeth's was featured in *Memnoch the Devil* and was the site of the Memnoch Ball in 1995, a party for 8,000 of Anne's fans and closest friends. Her private home at 1239 First Street is the home of the Mayfairs in the Mayfair Witches series, and her home at 2524 St. Charles was the home of Triana in *Violin*. Tours of these homes are not available at this writing.

Madame John's Legacy, 632 Dumaine Street; (504) 568–6968 or (800) 568–6968. Reputedly built in 1727 and rebuilt by a sea captain in 1788, the home got its unusual name from a story by George Washington Cable. It plays a role in a scene in *Interview With the Vampire*, when coffins of Lestat's victims are viewed being taken from it and placed in horse-drawn hearses along Dumaine.

Magic Walking Tours; (504) 588–9693. Richard Rochester was the first to do "haunted New Orleans" tours, and his are still the best researched and enacted.

Maple Street Book Shop, 7523 Maple Street, uptown near Tulane University; (504) 866–4916. Owned by native Rhoda Faust, this is a little jewel of a bookstore with an excellent stock of local and regional works.

New Orleans *Times-Picayune Destination Guide;* www.neworleans.net.

Old Absinthe House, 240 Bourbon Street, in the French Quarter; (504) 523–3181. Established in 1807, this is said to be the oldest continually operating bar in the city. Authors who've tipped a few here include Walt Whitman, Oscar Wilde, O. Henry, and Mark Twain.

Pitot House, 1440 Moss Street, in New Orleans; (504) 482–0312. Open from 10 A.M. to 3 P.M. Wednesdays through Saturdays. Admission fee. Used for scenes in *Interview With the Vampire,* this classic West Indies–style house is reputedly quite haunted.

The Anne Rice Collection, 2727 Prytania Street (the Rink), in the Garden District; (504) 899–5996. The place for all things vampirian and witchy, including Lestat cologne and wine, T-shirts, candles, and prints depicting Rice's historic New Orleans homes.

Save Our Cemeteries; (504) 525–3377. Excellent tours of St. Louis No. 1 and Lafayette Cemeteries, heavily featured in the vampire and witch novels of New Orleans native Anne Rice.

St. Louis Cathedral, Jackson Square; (504) 525–9585. The cathedral is the site of a particularly brutal bloodletting in *Interview With the Vampire,* and James Lee Burke's Dave Robicheaux occasionally worships here. Cathedral store has a good selection of Gothic and Baroque items from the Vatican Library Collection.

Steamboat *Natchez;* (504) 586–8777 or (800) 233–2628. This is the steamboat glimpsed in the background as Rice's vampire family of Louis, Lestat, and Claudia stroll along the Mississippi River in the movie version of *Interview With the Vampire.*

Tennessee Williams New Orleans Literary Festival and French Quarter Literary Conference; (504) 524–0050 or (800) 479–8222. Annual March festival celebrating all things Tennesseean, including play readings, full productions, musical events, and a writing workshop. The 1999 festival featured authors Valerie Martin, Sheila Bosworth, Clyde Edgerton, Lee Smith, Shannon Ravenel, and Edmund White, as well as appearances by Kim Hunter, who played Stella in the original movie version of *A Street-*

The Old Absinthe House has played host to authors from Mark Twain to Oscar Wilde.

car *Named Desire*, and Tennessee Williams's brother, Dakin. An annual highlight of the event is the Stella and Stanley Shouting Contest, in which full-throated Kowalski wanna-bes hurl their best "Stellll-aaaaaaaaaa!" or "Stanleeeeeeeeeey!" from Jackson Square up to actors on a Pontalba Building balcony. And there's an undeniable magic to watching local professional actors perform *Streetcar* or other classics in Le Petit Theatre, just steps from where Williams lived and wrote.

Uptown Square Book Shop, 200 Broadway, Suite 101; (504) 865–8310. The official bookstore of the Tennessee Williams Literary Festival, well stocked and with a friendly, helpful, and well-versed staff.

The Witches' Closet, 521 St. Philip Street, in the French Quarter; (504) 593–9222. Dark, gloomy, and murky—just the place for buying a black

A stone angel adorns the entryway at St. Elizabeth's, a former convent now owned by Anne Rice and featured in her books.

candle or juju bags, used for warding off nasty spirits. Anne Rice's Mayfairs would feel right at home.

Zombie's House of Voodoo, 723 St. Peter Street; (504) 4-VOODOO (486-6366). Candles, spell books, gris-gris, whatever you might need. Look up as you walk inside—that iron gate hanging from the ceiling was used in filming *Interview With the Vampire*.

The River Road

Destrehan Plantation, on the River Road about twenty miles from New Orleans; (504) 764-9315; www.destrehanplantation.org.

A "faux tomb" (foreground) was constructed in Lafayette Cemetery for the filming of *Interview With the Vampire*, but has since been removed.

Laura: A Creole Plantation, near Vacherie, on the River Road; (225) 265–7690; www.lauraplantation.com. Built in 1805, this is a restoration-in-progress that gives a rare glimpse into nineteenth-century Creole life. The best tour on the River Road. Twelve of Laura's buildings are on the National Register of Historic Places, including the slave cabins where author Joel Chandler Harris originally recorded the Brer Rabbit tales.

Madewood Plantation House, 4250 Highway 308, two miles south of Napoleonville, on Bayou LaFourche; (504) 568–1988. Open for tours daily from 10 A.M. to 4:30 P.M. Admission fee.

Oak Alley Plantation, near Vacherie, on the River Road; (225) 265–2151 or (800) 463–7138; www.oakalleyplantation.com. Daily tours from 9 A.M. to 5 P.M. Admission fee.

ACCOMMODATIONS AND RESTAURANTS

New Orleans

Antoine's, 725 St. Louis Street, in the French Quarter; (504) 581–4422. Serving traditional Creole food since 1840. The setting for innumerable literary feasts, and where the locals still go for special occasions. In Ellen Gilchrist's short story "Indignities," she describes a scene unlikely in a fine restaurant in most cities, but perfectly plausible in New Orleans:

> Last night my mother took off her clothes in front of twenty-six invited guests in the King's Room at Antoine's. She took off her Calvin Klein evening jacket and her beige silk wrap-around blouse and her custom-made brassiere and walked around the table letting everyone look at the place where her breasts used to be . . . After mother took off her blouse the party really warmed up. Everyone stayed until the restaurant closed.

Arnaud's, 813 Bienville Street, in the French Quarter; (504) 523–5433. Another French Quarter tradition, dating from 1918.

Bed-and-Breakfast New Orleans Style, Garden District; (504) 897–9659.

Bienville House, 320 Decatur Street; (504) 529–2345 or (800) 535–7836. Intimate and romantic with eighty-three newly renovated rooms, close to the river.

Bourbon Orleans Hotel, 717 Orleans Street, in the French Quarter; (504) 523–2222; www.bourbonorleans.com. Historic ambience, once the site of the infamous quadroon balls. Rumored to be quite haunted; ask about Room 165 and the Ballroom Ghost.

Cafe du Monde, 800 Decatur Street, in the French Quarter; (504) 525–4544. Open twenty-four hours a day, with powdered-sugar-drenched beignets and chicory-laced coffee. Whatever you do, don't wear black.

Caribbean Room, Pontchartrain Hotel, 2031 St. Charles Avenue, in the Garden District; (504) 524–0581. Elegant Creole dining. Don't miss the Mile High Ice Cream Pie.

Central Grocery Store, 923 Decatur Street, in the French Quarter; (504) 523–1620. The best place in town for a muffuletta.

Chateau Sonesta Hotel, 800 Iberville Street (entrances on Iberville, Dauphine, and Canal Streets), downtown; (504) 586–0800 or (800) SONESTA. This 1849 landmark building, once the D. H. Holmes department store, became a literary landmark with John Kennedy Toole's *A Confederacy of Dunces*.

Clarion Historic French Market Inn, 501 Rue Decatur, in the French Quarter; (504) 561–5621 or (800) 827–5621. From here, you can have the same view Anne Rice's Vampire Lestat had from his quarters at Dumaine and Decatur.

Commander's Palace, 1402 Washington Avenue, in the Garden District; (504) 889–8221. The grande dame of the Brennan family restaurants and a popular dining spot for Anne Rice's Mayfair Witches (especially after family funerals at Lafayette Cemetery, across the street).

Cornstalk Hotel, 915 Royal Street, in the French Quarter; (504) 523–1515. A Victorian landmark along the stretch of Royal used for filming *Interview With the Vampire*.

Dauphine Orleans Hotel, 415 Dauphine Street, in the French Quarter; (504) 586–1800 or (800) 421–7111.

Emeril's, 800 Tchoupitoulas, in the Warehouse District; (504) 528–9393. Chef Emeril Lagasse's place, with homemade *everything*. Well worth the cab ride from the French Quarter or Garden District.

French Quarter Courtyard Hotel, 1101 N. Rampart Street, in the French Quarter; (504) 522–7333 or (800) 290–4BED. Near St. Louis No. 1 Cemetery, where Louis and Lestat had some memorable encounters in *Interview With the Vampire*.

Galatoire's, 209 Bourbon Street; (504) 525–2021. Don't even *think* about asking for reservations; they don't take them. And don't think about wearing jeans, either—they take "dress for dinner" seriously here.

Gumbo Shop, 630 St. Peter Street; (504) 525–1486. Casual setting with terrific shrimp Creole, red beans and rice, jambalaya, and, of course, gumbo.

Hotel St. Helene, 508 Chartres Street; (504) 522–5014 or (800) 348–3888. Small hotel just off Jackson Square and close to the river.

Hotel St. Pierre, 911 Burgundy Street, in the French Quarter; (504) 525–4401 or (800) 225–4040.

Andrew Jackson Hotel, 919 Royal Street, in the French Quarter; (504) 561–5881 or (800) 654–0224.

Lafitte Guest House, 1003 Bourbon Street, in the French Quarter; (504) 581–2678 or (800) 331–7971; www.lafitteguesthouse.com.

Le Meridien New Orleans, 614 Canal Street; (504) 525–6500; www.meridien hotel.com. Just across Canal from the French Quarter; truly elegant surroundings.

Maison DeVille and the Audubon Cottages, 727 Rue Toulouse, in the French Quarter; (504) 561–5858 or (800) 634–1600; www.mainson

deville.com. The buildings that make up this charming hotel are more than two hundred years old. The Bistro, the on-site restaurant, is a romantic dream. Tennessee Williams stayed in Room 9, reportedly finishing the final draft of *A Streetcar Named Desire* there.

Maison Dupuy, 1001 Rue Toulouse, in the French Quarter; (504) 586–8000 or (800) 535–9177.

Maison Esplanade Guest House, 1244 Esplanade Avenue, in the French Quarter; (504) 523–8080 or (800) 892–5529; www.neworleans.com/maison.

Maison St. Charles Quality Inn, 1319 St. Charles Avenue; (504) 522–0187 or (800) 831–1783; www.maisonstcharles.com. Lovely historic buildings, convenient to the Garden District and French Quarter by streetcar.

The McKendrick-Breaux House, on Magazine Street in the Lower Garden District; (504) 586–1700 or (888) 570–1700; www.mckendrick-breaux.com. Historic 1860 home, lovingly restored as a bed-and-breakfast in a resurgent area of the Lower Garden District.

Monteleone Hotel, 214 Rue Royal; (504) 523–3341 or (800) 535–9595. Another favorite spot for Rice's characters to take a break from supernatural matters, and one of the most elegant and gracious hotels in the city. This is the French Quarter's first "high-rise," newly renovated and sparkling like French champagne on a hot day. The infant Truman Capote lived with his family for a short time at the Monteleone.

Napoleon House, 500 Chartres Street; (504) 524–9752. Perfect Old New Orleans atmosphere, terrific drinks at the cozy bar while waiting for dinner (and you *will* wait; the place is usually packed).

Nola, 534 St. Louis Street, in the French Quarter; (504) 522–6652. Emeril Lagasse's French Quarter restaurant. Many discriminating diners believe Nola (as in New Orleans, *LA*) is superior to Chef Emeril's Warehouse District digs.

Omni Royal Orleans, 621 St. Louis Street, in the French Quarter; (504) 529–5333. Once the site of the nineteenth-century Saint Louis Hotel and a slave market. A portion of the original building can still be seen on the Royal Street side, and a painting of the Saint Louis hangs in the lobby.

Alex Patout's Louisiana Restaurant, 221 Royal Street, in the French Quarter; (504) 525–7788.

The Pontchartrain Hotel, 2031 St. Charles Avenue, in the Garden District; (504) 524–0581 or (800) 777–6193; www.grandheritage.com. The favored hostelry of Anne Rice's Mayfair Witches and the members of the mysterious Talamasca. Rice also keeps a suite there for writing getaways, and Walker Percy lived here for a time in the 1940s before renting a home on Calhoun Street.

Poppy's Grill, 717 St. Peter Street, in the French Quarter; (504) 524–3287. One of the few twenty-four-hour dining spots in New Orleans, surprisingly enough, Poppy's serves up tasty hamburgers and fries in a . . . well, let's call it stark . . . atmosphere devoid of decor, except for a little neon and a jukebox.

Provincial Hotel, 1024 Rue Chartres; (504) 581–4995 or (800) 493–2941; www.hotelprovincial.com. One hundred and five rooms constructed of various nineteenth-century buildings, reputedly extremely haunted. Close to the Old Ursuline Convent and the Gallier House, this is at Louis and Lestat's end of the French Quarter. The quiet-but-spooky end, that is.

Prytania Park Hotel, 1525 Prytania Street, in the Garden District; (504) 524–0427 or (800) 862–1984; www.prytaniaparkhotel.com.

Ritz-Carlton New Orleans, 921 Canal Street; (504) 524–1375 or (800) 241–3333.

Saint Louis Hotel, 730 Rue Bienville, in the French Quarter; (504) 581–7300; www.stlouishotel.com. One of the most luxurious hotels in the city, with a fabulous on-site restaurant, the Louis XIV.

Saint Ann Marie Antoinette Hotel, 717 Rue Conti, in the French Quarter; (504) 581–1881.

Southern Comforts Reservations; (800) 889–7859; www.southerncomforts. com.

Tujague's, 823 Decatur Street, in the French Quarter; (504) 525–8676. Old New Orleans ambience at a lower price than most of the French Creole restaurants in the Quarter. It's the city's second-oldest restaurant, after Antoine's, opening in 1856. It's pronounced "Two Jacks."

Windsor Court Hotel, 300 Gravier Street, in the Central Business District; (504) 523–6000 or (800) 262–2662. Absolutely luxurious, New Orleans–style Old World. Magnificent high tea served in the lobby restaurant, complete with finger sandwiches, petit fours and endless refills of the most exquisite teas on this side of the Atlantic.

Wisteria Inn, 2127 Esplanade Avenue, in the Esplanade Ridge District; (504) 943–8418.

The River Road

Madewood Plantation House, 4250 Highway 308, two miles south of
Napoleonville on Bayou LaFourche; (504) 568–1988. Open for tours
daily from 10 A.M. to 4:30 P.M. Seventy-five miles north of New
Orleans, forty-five miles south of Baton Rouge near the great River
Road's Sunshine Bridge over the Mississippi River. Five bedrooms in
the main house, three suites in the cottage. Absolutely worth the drive.
Oak Alley Plantation, Inn and Restaurant, 3645 Highway 18, near
Vacherie on the River Road; (225) 265–2151 or (800) 44–ALLEY;
www.oakalleyplantation.com. National Historic Landmark set amid a
quarter-mile row of ancient oaks. Bed-and-breakfast accommodations
are in turn-of-the-century Creole cottages on the grounds.

Iberia Parish

New Iberia, settled in 1779 by the Spanish, today lays claim as the only
permanent Spanish outpost in Louisiana. It's west of New Orleans and
south of Lafayette, with a cozy downtown area clustered around the
Bayou Teche. James Lee Burke, author of what many consider the most
literary series of mysteries ever written, has roots deep in New Iberia,
which is the setting for the adventures of Dave Robicheaux, his protagonist. Burke was born and raised in Houston, but both he and
Robicheaux claim Cajun country as their heart's home; when Burke visited family there as a youth, he could point out pirate Jean Lafitte's moor-
ings along the bayou. Burke returned to Cajun country for college,
attending the University of Southwestern Louisiana in Lafayette, and
recently built a home along the Bayou Teche.

Critics around the world have hailed Burke's work as not merely sur-
passing, but effortlessly bounding over, the constraints of the mystery
genre. Author Jim Harrison put it this way: "It has become apparent that
not since Raymond Chandler has anyone so thoroughly reinvented the
crime and mystery genre as James Lee Burke." Burke has won mystery's
highest honor, the Edgar Allan Poe Award, twice—in 1998 for *Cimarron
Rose* and in 1990 for *Black Cherry Blues*.

In one of the Robicheaux books, Dave describes the old poolroom in
a downtown New Iberia building: "The room smelled of draft beer and

gumbo and talcum, of whiskey and boiled crawfish and Virginia Extra tobacco, of pickled pig's feet and wine and Red Man. The owner's name was Tee Neg." Provost's, the downtown bar that was the model for Tee Neg's, closed in 1994. Also regretably gone is the Frederick Hotel, which made an appearance in *Sunset Limited*. It occupied the spot where the Main Street parking lot for the François Building now stands.

In *The Neon Rain*, Robicheaux describes the bayou country of New Iberia:

> Oak, cypress, and willow trees lined the two-lane roads; the mist still clung like torn cotton to the half-submerged dead tree trunks back in the marsh; the canebreaks were thick and green, shining in the light, and the lily pads clustered along the bayou's banks were bursting with flowers, audibly popping, their leaves covered with drops of quicksilver. The bream and bass were still feeding in the shadows close to the cypress roots; egrets were nesting in the sand where the sun had risen above the tree line, and occasionally a heron would lift from its feeding place on the edge of the cattails and glide on gilded wings down the long ribbon of brown water through a corridor of trees.
>
> Now these same bayous, canals, and marshlands where I had grown up were used by the Barataria pirates, [the modern-day drug smugglers nicknamed for French pirate Jean Lafitte's brigands and slavers].

The Burke family is completely entrenched in New Iberia, as recounted by the *Dallas Morning News* in 1998:

> "Everybody loves the Burkes," he [James Lee Burke] says one day as he watches bits of his family's history from the passenger seat of a car coursing through New Iberia at dusk. There is the street that bears his family name. There is his cousin P. R.'s house. There is where his ancestors once stayed, the ones who had escaped the Goliad massacre during the Texas War for Independence. "We were the masters of giving everything away. We were the masters of losing whatever we had."

Bill Minutaglio, the *Dallas Morning News* writer, capsulized Robicheaux's character and appeal:

> The Cajun lawman was an alcoholic, he prowled the bayou, tended to see the world divided into good and evil camps—and was constantly haunted by voices in the night, by some sort of deep-rooted sense of responsibility, by some sort of dogged determination to put one foot in front of the other even when he knew there were traps on the path.

The comparisons between Robicheaux and Burke himself are undeniable—the alcoholism, now under control, the soul-deep sense of righteousness. Burke even gave Robicheaux's adopted daughter the same name as his own daughter, Alafair. He told the *Morning News*:

> You know, Dave Robicheaux indicates that, in his view, there isn't one human family. There are a couple of them. There is one group that would like to make the Earth a truly awful place. And there is another group composed of people of good will. It's us against them. And I believe in that.
>
> The forces of greed, venality . . . they are always there, they are cunning and they are most successful during times of fear. They need to divide people and inculcate fear. They use race, gender, economics—that's their agenda.

His solution to living with those people? "Faith. The things that faith allows us to believe are usually not demonstrable . . . and that takes real guts. I once heard an Irish priest say that belief requires more courage than nonbelief because it imposes upon us introspection. It is like going out of the plane without a chute sometimes."

Burke apparently has fought his own demons with a potent weapon: laughter. Minutaglio summarizes it: "More often that not, when James Lee Burke finishes another one of his stories, he falls into one more laughing fit—a contagious, roaring clutch of laughter that causes him to slip his glasses off his face and grasp the sides of a table, a chair or even a tree as he walks down the road."

LITERARY LURES AND SOUTHERN SIGHTS

Books Along the Teche, 110 E. Main Street, New Iberia; (337)
367–7621. Touts itself as Dave Robicheaux's favorite bookstore, and it
probably is. Owner Howard Kingston is gracious about giving directions to local Robicheaux sites, and keeps a stock of Burke books and
caps, as well as T-shirts advertising "Robicheaux's Dock and Bait
Shop."
Episcopal Church of the Epiphany, 303 W. Main Street; (337) 369–9966.
Used as a hospital during the Civil War, this church was consecrated in
1848, and Dave Robicheaux sometimes worships here.
Greater Iberia Chamber of Commerce, 111 W. Main Street, New Iberia;
(337) 364–1836.
Iberia Parish Tourist Commission, 2704 Highway 14, New Iberia; (337)
365–1540 or (888) 9–IBERIA; www.iberiaparish.com.
Louisiana Sugar Cane Festival and Fair, City Park, Parkview Drive, New
Iberia; (337) 369–9323. Annual fall festival where everyone, locals and
visitors alike, gets inducted as a natural-born Cajun.
McIlhenny Tabasco Country Store and Visitor Center, south of New
Iberia on Avery Island; (337) 365–8173 or (800) 634–9599;
www.tabasco.com. Tabasco pepper sauce, a mainstay of Cajun cooking, calls this landmark factory home. The adjacent Jungle Gardens
give a lovely idea of what Louisiana would look like if man, hurricanes,
and other predators could be indefinitely held back. Admission fee.
Shadows-on-the-Teche Museum, 317 E. Main Street, New Iberia; (337)
369–6446. This coral-colored brick house was built from 1830 to 1834
by sugarcane planter David Weeks. The enormous moss-draped live
oaks surrounding the house gave it its name. David Weeks's great-
grandson began restoring the tumbledown place in the 1920s, then
bequeathed it to the National Trust for Historic Preservation in 1958.
Open 9 A.M. to 4:30 P.M. daily. Admission fee.
St. Peter's Catholic Church Cemetery, 108 E. St. Peter Street; (337)
369–3816, New Iberia. Where Burkes are buried and Dave Robicheaux
has laid to rest those closest to him. "We buried Annie in my family's
plot in the old cemetery by St. Peter's Church in New Iberia. The crypts
were made of brick and covered with white plaster, the oldest ones had
cracked and sunk into the earth and had become unwrapped with green
vines that rooted in the mortar," Dave says in *Heaven's Prisoners.*

Accommodations and Restaurants

Bon Creole Lunch Counter, 1409 E. St. Peter, New Iberia; (337) 367–6181. The town's best po'boys.

Cook's Garden at Rip Van Winkle Gardens, Jefferson Island, New Iberia; (337) 365–3332. Romantic bed-and-breakfast, with strolling peacocks and night-blooming jasmine amid fairytale gardens along the Teche.

The Inn at LeRosier, 314 E. Main Street, New Iberia; (337) 367–5306; www.lerosier.com. Haute cuisine and bed-and-breakfast accommodations.

Lagniappe Too Cafe, 204 E. Main Street, New Iberia; (337) 365–9419. Dave Robicheaux takes Megan to lunch here in *Sunset Limited*.

Teche Motel, 1830 E. Main Street, New Iberia; (337) 369–3756. Cabins straight out of a 1940s movie, shaded by giant oaks.

Victor's Cafeteria, 109 W. Main Street, New Iberia; (337) 369–9924. This hometown favorite has a sign out front that boasts, "Dave Robicheaux eats here." The cafe is mentioned in *Sunset Limited* and *Burning Angel*.

Lafayette Area

Lafayette is the home of the University of Southwestern Louisiana, where novelist Ernest J. Gaines has been a writer in residence. Gaines, author of *The Autobiography of Miss Jane Pittman* and *A Lesson Before Dying*, revitalized the annual Deep South Writers' Conference at the University of Southern Louisiana when he began teaching there in the 1980s. Gaines was born in south Louisiana's Cajun Country, but moved to San Francisco in the 1950s. By the mid-1960s, though, he was making frequent trips back to Louisiana.

"I wanted to smell that Louisiana earth, feel that Louisiana sun, sit under the shade of one of those Louisiana oaks . . . next to one of those Louisiana bayous," he wrote in a 1978 essay.

Northwest of Lafayette lies the little town of Sunset, population 2,200. The town is significant to literary travelers because of Chretien Point Plantation, whose stairway and the window above it were used as models for similar features at Tara, the O'Hara plantation, in the film version of *Gone With the Wind*. The tale of a Confederate lady of the house who shot a man on the front steps also was pirated for the movie, for the scene in which Scarlett shoots a Union soldier. Plantation guides will helpfully point out the step where the man was standing when he was felled by the Southern lady's bullet.

The house was built in 1831 of solid brick, with six round columns and double galleries across the front, for Hypolite Chretien II and his wife, Felicité. The home bears its Civil War significance proudly; it was central to a major battle, and a bullet hole still mars one of the front doors. Bed-and-breakfast guests can sleep in one of three upstairs rooms or the cozy downstairs suite, formerly the home's wine cellar. Racks that once held wine are now similarly stuffed with books.

LITERARY LURES AND SOUTHERN SIGHTS

Acadiana to Go, 619 Woodvale Avenue, Lafayette; (337) 981–3918. Multilingual tours.

Allons A Lafayette, 127 Baudoin, Lafayette; (337) 269–9607. Cajun Country tours; also offers dinner with Cajun delicacies, music, and dancers.

Cajun Country Store, 401 E. Cypress Street, Lafayette; (337) 233–7977 or (800) 252–9689; www.cajuncountrystore.com. Wonderful local arts and crafts, music, and food, housed in a 1930s warehouse.

Chretien Point Plantation, 665 Chretien Point Road, in Sunset, 10 miles north of Lafayette; (337) 662–5876 or (800) 880–7050. 1831 historic plantation, with tours and bed-and-breakfast accommodations. Admission fee.

Deep South Writers Conference, University of Southwestern Louisiana, Lafayette; (337) 482–5481; www.usl.edu/departments/English/index.html. Held annually in the fall, typically featuring well-known writers, agents, publishers, and teachers. Recent guests have included Tim O'Brien, Ernest Gaines, Luis Alberto Urrea, Tim Gautreaux, and screenwriter Steve Barancik (*The Last Seduction*).

Lafayette Convention and Visitors Commission, 1400 N.W. Evangeline Thruway, Lafayette; (337) 232–3737 or (800) 346–1958; www.lafayette travel.com.

ACCOMMODATIONS AND RESTAURANTS

Bayou Cabins, 100 Mills Avenue (Highway 94), Breaux Bridge; (337) 332–6158. Authentic Cajun cabins dating from the 1800s, along the Bayou Teche.

Bois des Chenes, 338 N. Sterling, Lafayette; (337) 233–7816. 1820 plantation house bed-and-breakfast, on the National Register of Historic Places.

Cafe Vermilionville, 1304 W. Pinhook Road, Lafayette; (337) 237–0100; www.cafev.com. Casual elegance in an 1800s Acadian inn.

Chretien Point Plantation, 665 Chretien Point Road, Sunset; (337) 662–5876 or (800) 880–7050. Five bed-and-breakfast rooms, swimming pool, full breakfast.

Country Oaks Cajun Cottages, 1138-A Lawless Tauzin Road, Breaux Bridge; (337) 332–3093 or (800) 318–2423. Acadian farmhouse, circa 1830, with guest cottages, a fishing lake, and walking trails on fourteen acres.

Loyd Hall Plantation, 292 Loyd Bridge Road, in Cheneyville, northwest of Lafayette; (318) 776–5641 or (800) 240–8135. Working cotton plantation of 640 acres, with ornate plaster ceilings, suspended staircases, and rare antiques. Charming bed-and-breakfast accommodations and tours.

Maison Mouton, 402 Garfield Street, Lafayette; (337) 234–4661. A downtown inn with twelve antiques-filled rooms.

Prejean's Restaurant, 3480 Interstate 49 North, Lafayette; (337) 896–3247; www.prejeans.com. Award-winning Cajun cuisine and live music every night.

Grand Isle

The island getaway south of New Orleans where Edna Pontellier, Kate Chopin's heroine in *The Awakening*, begins her odyssey toward psychological and physical independence. The island's appearance has changed considerably since Chopin visited there, mostly at the hands of a vicious hurricane in 1893, but it still boasts considerable bucolic allure.

LITERARY LURES AND SOUTHERN SIGHTS

Grand Isle Tourist Commission, Highway 1, Grand Isle; (504) 787–2997; www.sportsmans-paradise.com/grandisle.html.

Grand Isle State Park, Grand Isle; (504) 787–2559 or (888) 787–2559.

ACCOMMODATIONS AND RESTAURANTS

H and M Cabins and Fishing Charters, Highway 1 at Pine Street; (504) 787–3753.

Sun and Sand Cabins, Highway 1; (504) 787–2456. Fully furnished cabins with patios.

Natchitoches and Cloutierville

As any local will somehow work into the conversation within five minutes of meeting you, Natchitoches is the oldest settlement in Louisiana, founded in 1714, older than New Orleans by four years. Despite that distinction, however, prior to 1988 the town was mostly known for its all-out Christmas festivities and lights along Cane River Lake and the thirty-three-block historic district. That year, however, Hollywood descended to make the film version of *Steel Magnolias*, by local playwright Robert Harling.

More than a decade later, tour guides still point out all the places used in the film and the hangouts of stars Julia Roberts, Sally Field, Dolly Parton, Daryl Hannah, Olympia Dukakis, Shirley MacLaine, and Dylan McDermott. Local filming sites included St. Augustine Catholic Church (Shelby's wedding), the American Cemetery (Shelby's funeral), and the Odalie-Lambre Gwinn House on Williams Avenue (Shelby and Jackson's house).

Kate Chopin, the "pre-feminism feminist" of the late nineteenth century, was born Kate O'Flaherty in St. Louis, Missouri, and cut her literary teeth in New Orleans, the same city where she smoked her first cigarette at seventeen, on a trip in 1869. In her journal from that trip, she wrote, "New Orleans I liked immensely; it is so clean—so white and green. Although in April, we had profusions of flowers, strawberries and even blackberries."

She married Oscar Chopin in 1870, and the couple settled in New Orleans. But in 1879, Chopin's cotton brokerage failed and they moved to his family estate on the southern tip of Cane River Lake, in the tiny northwest Louisiana village of Cloutierville, about fifteen miles southeast of Natchitoches (pronounced "Nak-uh-tish").

The Cloutierville home was built by slaves between 1806 and 1813, and now houses the Bayou Folk Museum. Typical of the time and place, it was built of handmade brick, cypress and pine, and *bousillage*, a country mixture of Spanish moss and river mud. The ground floor, in deference to floods, was used only for storage, while the family lived in the upper rooms. Original features, such as the French doors opening onto the front balcony, glass panes, and upstairs wainscoting, remain, and many of the home's furnishings were retrieved from the immediate Cane River area.

Kate and Oscar raised six children here, but Kate still managed to write her stories in the elegant living room. When Oscar died suddenly of swamp fever in 1882, Kate took over the running of the plantation and general store, but soon sold them and returned to St. Louis with her children. Prior to her groundbreaking *The Awakening*, she published another novel, *At Fault*, as well as a collection of short stories about the people of the Cane River country, *Bayou Folk*.

In *The Awakening*, Chopin made her mark as an early feminist with words like these, spoken by her heroine, Edna Pontellier: "I always feel so sorry for women who don't like to walk; they miss so much—so many rare little glimpses of life; and we women learn so little of life on the whole." In contrast to Edna's relatively sheltered life, Chopin gives us the life of Edna's friend Mademoiselle Reisz, whose small apartment near the river allows the sights, smells, and sounds of New Orleans to flood in unimpeded. But Edna, like her creator, eventually finds her own gentle way to a brand of independence. "I would give up the unessential," she says in *The Awakening*. "I would give my money, I would give my life for my children, but I wouldn't give myself."

The Awakening, which seems eminently tame by late twentieth-century standards, shocked Victorian America and was banned in Chopin's hometown of St. Louis and other cities.

LITERARY LURES AND SOUTHERN SIGHTS

Beau Fort Plantation, ten miles south of Natchitoches, in Bermuda, down scenic Cane River Lake; (318) 352–9580. Open from 1 P.M. to 4 P.M. daily, except major holidays. Admission fee. This working 256-acre cotton plantation was named after historic Fort Charles, which stood there in the 1760s.

Kate Chopin Home and Bayou Folk Museum, 243 Highway 495, Cloutierville; (318) 379–2233. Open from 10 A.M. to 5 P.M. Mondays through Saturdays, 1 P.M. to 5 P.M. Sundays year-round except for major holidays. Admission fee.

Fort St. Jean Baptiste, Morrow at Jefferson Streets in Natchitoches; (318) 357–3101. Reproduction of the outpost that stood nearby in 1716. Open from 9 A.M. to 5 P.M. daily. Admission fee.

Little Eva Plantation, 5 miles south of Cloutierville; (318) 379–2382. The plantation got its current name from persistent tales that it was the inspiration for Harriet Beecher Stowe's *Uncle Tom's Cabin*, which was set on nearby Red River. Admission fee.

Melrose Plantation, on Cane River Lake, south of Natchitoches; (318) 379–0055. Melrose was the home of self-taught artist Clementine Hunter, known as the black Grandma Moses. The owner of Melrose was a freed black slave who began construction on the seven buildings in 1796. Since the early 1900s, the home has served as a literary and artistic haven, hosting the likes of Erskine Caldwell and Lyle Saxon.

Natchitoches Parish Tourist Commission, 781 Front Street, in Natchitoches; (318) 352–8072 or (800) 259–1714; www.natchitoches.net. Open 8 A.M. to 6 P.M. weekdays, 9 A.M. to 5 P.M. Saturdays and 10 A.M. to 3 P.M. Sundays.

Old Town Book Merchant, 512 Front Street, in Natchitoches; (318) 357–8900. Strong selection of regional history and fiction.

ACCOMMODATIONS AND RESTAURANTS

Beau Fort Plantation, ten miles south of Natchitoches, in Bermuda, down scenic Cane River Lake; (318) 352–9580. This working 256-acre cotton plantation was named after historic Fort Charles, which stood there in the 1760s. Offers tours as well as bed-and-breakfast accommodations.

Breazeale House Bed-and-Breakfast, 926 Washington Street, Natchitoches; (318) 352–5630 or (800) 352–5631. Kate Chopin was the sister-in-law of Congressman Phanor Breazeale, for whom the house was built, and she spent time here.

Cloutier Townhouse, 8 Ducournau Square, Front Street, Natchitoches, overlooking Cane River Lake; (318) 352–5242. Elegant three-story townhouse with two bed-and-breakfast rooms.

Fleur-de-Lis, 336 Second Street, Natchitoches; (318) 352–6621 or (800) 489–6621. Unpretentious five-room bed-and-breakfast in a beautiful

Queen Anne Victorian, with an in-house golden retriever named Moose, for those experiencing fur withdrawal, as well as a roomy front-porch swing and comfy family room.

Jefferson House, 229 Jefferson Street, Natchitoches; (318) 352–5756. Bed-and-breakfast near the historic district; verandah has comfy rocking chairs and a lake view.

The Landing, 530 Front Street, Natchitoches; (318) 352–1579. Big, noisy, very popular restaurant, with fabulous bread pudding and other local favorites. If you're yearning for a little blackened alligator, this is the place.

Lasyone's Meat Pie Kitchen and Restaurant, 622 Second Street, Natchitoches; (318) 352–3353.

5

Georgia

More than any other Northern general, Sherman loved the South because he understood both its pride and its contradictions, but that knowledge did not keep him from moving through its mountains and river valleys with a cold and unstinting fury. . . . From Chickamauga to the Atlantic, he rode out the seasons . . . and wrote his name in fire and blood across the sacrificial body of Georgia. . . . Sherman's name became the vilest two-syllable word in the South. Beautiful women with the manners of countesses spat in the dirt after pronouncing his name aloud.

—Pat Conroy, *Beach Music*

$\mathcal{S}$ ay "Georgia" and "book" in the same breath and the first image that popped into many minds, at least until recently, was Margaret Mitchell's unconquerable Scarlett O'Hara, holding her own through the devastating ravages of both romance and war. Scarlett got some serious competition, however, in 1994 with the publication of John Berendt's *Midnight in the Garden of Good and Evil*, a nonfiction firecracker that reads like fiction and effectively transports the epicenter of Georgian literary lore from Atlanta to Savannah.

Before Mitchell or Berendt, however, Georgia boasted literary lights such as Carson McCullers and Flannery O'Connor, and contemporary authors such as Alice Walker, Bailey White, Eugenia Price, and Anne Rivers Siddons have also called the state home.

SOUTHERN SIGHTS

Georgia Department of Tourism; (404) 656–3590 or (800) VISIT–GA; www.georgia.org.

Georgia Department of Natural Resources; (800) 864–PARK; www.ganet.org/dnr.

Great Inns of Georgia; (404) 843–0471 or (800) 501–7328; www.bbonline.com/ga/greatinns.

Atlanta and Commerce

The literary world can probably thank an errant equine for the timeless story of Scarlett O'Hara and her ruined South. In 1920, the already-frail Margaret Mitchell fell from a horse, beginning a series of physical mishaps that finally forced her retirement, in 1926, from her job as a newspaper reporter for the *Atlanta Journal*. According to Mitchell lore, she immersed herself every day in the books her husband, John Marsh, brought her from the Atlanta library, until one day he said, "I wish you would write one yourself." He next brought her a Remington typewriter and admonished, as good editors have since time immemorial, "Write what you know."

They were living in a dark, cramped Crescent Avenue apartment that Margaret had affectionately dubbed the Dump, and it was the hub of their circle of friends. So once the modest Mitchell got under way with the manuscript she called *Another Day*, she took great pains to hide the work-in-progress, secreting loose pages under the bed, beneath the sofa, or as props for wobbly table legs. When word leaked out that she had written a book, one friend said, "Well, I dare-say. Really, I wouldn't take you for the type to write a successful book. You don't take your life seriously enough to be a novelist."

Imagine Scarlett O'Hara's reaction to such a remark. Margaret "Peggy" Mitchell responded with much the same spunk: She gathered up the manuscript and hustled it down to Harold Latham, an editor for Macmillan who was staying at the Georgian Terrace Hotel while looking for new Southern writers. He'd just unwittingly tapped into the mother lode. Latham suggested a couple of changes—that the main character's name be changed from Pansy to Scarlett, and that the book's name be changed from its latest incarnation, *Tomorrow Is Another Day*, to *Gone With the Wind*. It was published in 1936.

"All the girls were busy reading," recalled Pulitzer Prize–winner George Goodwin, himself an Atlantan, of the ensuing furor. "You can't imagine how that thing swept Atlanta in the summer of 1936. There were just lots of stories of people who stayed up all night to read it. I finally got a copy of it and I can understand why. Damn hard to put down."

Comparisons between the book and real life are many. Fire, which played such a horrible role in both the book and film versions of *Gone With the Wind*, has many times devastated Atlanta, most often at the hands of man. In the wee hours of November 15, 1864, General William Tecumseh Sherman set fire to the entire city, destroying every single business and most homes. The hellish conflagration that Scarlett and Rhett race through on their late-night flight from the city actually happened: Only four hundred of the city's 4,500 buildings eluded Sherman's torches.

Treasures lost to fire in years since include the Loew's Grand Theatre, where *Gone With the Wind* had its world premiere, with Margaret Mitchell and stars Vivien Leigh and Clark Gable in attendance. The Georgia-Pacific Building now sits on the Loew's site; the movie theater burned in 1979. But despite the many blazes that have flickered nearby, the 1899 home where Mitchell wrote the book somehow managed to survive well into this century, possibly because it was made of brick— one of the first brick homes in the city.

The mansion-turned-apartment building was built for Cornelius J. Sheehan, a member of a prominent Atlanta family and owner of *Greer's Almanac*. The area was known as the Tight Squeeze because the houses were built so close together, on a section of Peachtree Street that looped around a thirty-foot-deep ravine.

In 1913, as local businesses encroached on the home's already-limited seclusion, it was literally picked up from its foundations and rolled back so that the Crescent Avenue facade became the main entrance. In 1919, it was converted into the ten-unit Crescent Apartments, and Mitchell and Marsh moved there following their July 4, 1925, wedding. The reception took place in the one-bedroom, ground-floor apartment that would be their home for the next seven years. In 1932, with *Gone With the Wind* virtually complete, they moved to another apartment on Seventeenth Street.

The apartment building on Crescent and Peachtree began to deteriorate after being abandoned and boarded up in 1977, and a group of preservationists unsuccessfully fought to save it. Then, in September 1994, someone set fire to the building, in what the Atlanta Fire Department called sophisticated arson. Rescue arrived from an unlikely source, the German industrial company Daimler-Benz, which bought and began restoration of the home in 1995. Just as renovations neared completion, the house caught fire again on the morning of Sunday, May 12, 1996. Again, investigators suspected arson.

Undeterred, Daimler-Benz decided tomorrow was another day; they financed the cleaning up and started renovating anew. Today the legacy of Margaret Munnerlyn Mitchell lives on in the Margaret Mitchell House, whose address is once again on Peachtree Street. Her fantasy couple of Scarlett and Rhett also lived on Peachtree Street, five blocks from Melanie and Ashley, whose home was on Ivy Street.

Mitchell's ancestry wasn't unlike that of her heroine's. She was born November 8, 1900, to descendants of Irish Catholics, Scotch-Irish, and French Huguenots. The family's military service included stints in the American Revolution and the Civil War, and young Margaret heard many Civil War tales directly from the source as a girl, riding her horse with Confederate veterans through the countryside around Atlanta and rural Jonesboro, where her great-aunts lived.

According to one bit of family lore, Margaret's mother, Maybelle, used the ravages of the war to lecture her wayward daughter on at least one occasion. When Margaret, an unexceptional student at a private school, announced that she couldn't do math and wasn't going back, Maybelle dragged her out to a rural road strung with plantation houses fallen to decay. "It's happened before and it will happen again," Maybelle told her daughter. "And when it does happen, everyone loses everything and everyone is equal. They all start again with nothing at all except the cunning of their brains and the strength of their hands." Margaret went back to school.

She debuted into Atlanta society in 1920, eliciting a scandal of which Miss O'Hara would've been proud by performing an "Apache dance"—all the rage in Paris—at the debutante ball with a male student from Georgia Tech. Peggy Mitchell had already insulted the society crowd by working as a teenage volunteer in the city's black clinics—one of the reasons she was rejected by the Junior League. She retaliated in true Mitchell style, declining their invitation to a *Gone With the Wind* costume ball the night the movie opened in Atlanta.

But Margaret Mitchell knew how to make an apology when she felt it was called for—for example, when Bishop Gerald O'Hara blessed and laid the cornerstone of Christ the King Cathedral on Peachtree Road. When she heard about Bishop O'Hara, Mitchell wrote him a personal note begging excuses for unintentionally naming Scarlett O'Hara's daddy after him. In a nice bit of literary coincidence, Bishop O'Hara laid his church's cornerstone the very year that Mitchell won the Pulitzer Prize for *Gone With the Wind*, in 1937.

In 1949, while crossing the intersection of Peachtree and Thirteenth Streets, just three blocks from the Dump where she penned her master-piece, Margaret Mitchell was struck by a speeding taxi. She died five days later at Grady Memorial Hospital, and her funeral took place at H. M. Patterson and Son's Spring Hill location at Spring and Tenth Streets. The funeral cortege followed the same route as the parade witnessed by more than 300,000 people during the world premiere of *Gone With the Wind*.

Both Mitchell and her husband, who died in 1952, are buried at his-toric Oakland Cemetery, a shaded, hilly Victorian treasure tucked under the skyscrapers of downtown. To find the Marsh plot, start at the west side of the white tower building at the center of the cemetery. Face the western wall, along Oakland Avenue, until you spot the obelisk of another Mitchell family at the end of a lane. Follow that lane about halfway to the cemetery's western wall; the Marsh-Mitchell plot is on the left surrounded by four conical shrubs.

Gone With the Wind was Mitchell's sole literary output; she never published another novel, although another manuscript was discovered in the 1990s and published as *Lost Laysen*. But the inevitable sequel to *Gone With the Wind* was written without Mitchell, by Alexandra Ripley. That book, *Scarlett*, did well with fans but was savaged by critics. In early 1999, South Carolina author Pat Conroy bowed out of negotiations to write a second sequel because of a dispute with the executors of Mitchell's estate. "I went through more negotiations with this *Gone With the Wind* than the Germans did in World War I with all the clauses at Versailles," Conroy told the *New York Times*.

Part of the problem in future sequels could be the restrictions imposed by the Mitchell estate—no miscegenation, no homosexuality, no dead Scarlett. Conroy was the second author approached; a manuscript by British writer Emma Tennant, who wrote two successful Jane Austen sequels, was rejected for not being Southern enough. After the Conroy debacle, the *Miami Herald* asked a few other Southern authors how they'd tackle the daunting task of continuing Scarlett's adventures.

Anne Rivers Siddons, an Atlantan by birth, said:

> I like the approach that Pat (Conroy) was going to take, telling the story from Rhett Butler's point of view. I would do that, or tell it from the perspective of a black person—maybe Prissy. The problem is that readers don't want Scarlett to change, and you can't write a novel in which the main character doesn't grow and change. It would be a wonderful thing to have her die. It's about the only thing she could do that would let us forgive her.

Jill McCorkle, author of *Carolina Moon*, said:

> Reunite Scarlett and Rhett after an appropriate period of suffering. Rhett would come home, and they would move to a downscaled, smaller house . . . Maybe they would become early civil rights activists, and maybe that poor old Suellen, who always got shafted and had her men stolen away, can take Ashley, and they can be boring and quiet together.

And my favorite, from Allan Gurganus, author of *Oldest Living Confederate Widow Tells All:*

> Mammy, with help from a small business loan and an advance from Rhett, refinances Tara, which is now a thriving bed-and-breakfast. The place's haggard, oft-divorced, much-lifted hostess is none other than a creaky yet indomitable Scarlett herself. She is an ill-tempered, dreadful employee who hates to give the tours again to "these washed-out Yankees." Sadly, Rhett died in an early Viagra experiment. Ashley Wilkes has finally "come out" and now manages a chic guest house in Key West called Twelve Palms.
>
> What fee do I expect for a new novel subtitled *Oldest Living Freed Slave Now Owns All?* Merely enough to guarantee that neither I nor any member of my family, so help me God, will ever go hungry again.

He gets my vote.

Flashing forward to the twentieth century, one of the best-known contemporary writers from the Atlanta area is the aforementioned Anne Rivers Siddons, who grew up in Fairburn, twenty miles away. Siddons's books include *Hills Town, King's Oak, Peachtree Road*, and *Homeplace*, all set in Georgia, as well as *Colony*, set in Maine but focusing on South Carolinian Maude Chambliss, and *Outer Banks*, about four Alabama sorority sisters who reminisce at a reunion in North Carolina.

In *Downtown* (1994), Siddons writes of Atlanta's last innocent era:

> Atlanta in the autumn of 1966 was a city being born, and the energy and promise of that lying-in sent out subterranean vibrations all over the just-stirring South, like underground shock waves—a call to those who could hear it best, the young. And they came, they came in droves, from small, sleeping towns and large, drowsing universities, from farms and industrial suburbs and backwaters so still that even the building firestorm of the civil rights movement had not yet rippled the surface.

Tom Wolfe set his acclaimed 1998 novel *A Man in Full* in Atlanta, depicting it, in the words of the *Oxford American*, as a "crass, money-grubbing kind of place." As Wolfe put it in the book, Atlanta is a place "where your 'honor' *is* the things you possess." The *Oxford American* makes the point, though, that:

> Atlanta really is the star of *A Man in Full*, and if Atlantans breathe deeply and think about it, they can't be unhappy with the way that Wolfe's bravura depiction of their city gives it almost mythic power. . . . Anyone who knows the place—and even Stuckey's cashiers go to conventions there—will see it with new eyes after reading Wolfe's descriptions of the palazzos, fitness centers, and trendy restaurants of Buckhead; the gleaming office towers of Midtown; the Southern-style slums of South Atlanta; the Asian quarter of Chamblee ("Chambodia"); even the seedy apartment complex of "Normandy Lea." The city's social landscape is also revealed in marvelous set pieces.
>
> Description like this just *has* to be good for any city—good for its soul, and maybe even for its pocketbook. As one percep-

tive booster told the *Journal-Constitution*, "If you look at what happened with Savannah and *Midnight in the Garden of Good and Evil*, the way it promoted tourism, . . . I think the same thing could happen here." Now *that's* the old Atlanta spirit!

Critics might also recall Scarlett O'Hara's feelings about the city:

> Let the older towns call Atlanta anything they pleased. Atlanta did not care. Scarlett had always liked Atlanta for the very same reasons that made Savannah, Augusta and Macon condemn it. Like herself, the town was a mixture of the old and new in Georgia, in which the old often came off second best in its conflicts with the self-willed and vigorous new.

Tiny Commerce, Georgia, northeast of Atlanta, is the setting for Olive Ann Burns's incredibly popular *Cold Sassy Tree* (1984) and *Leaving Cold Sassy*. In her acknowledgments to *Cold Sassy Tree*, Burns writes:

> Cold Sassy is a lot like Commerce, Georgia, at the turn of the century. I couldn't have understood small-town life in that era without the oft-told tales of my late father, William Arnold Burns. He grew up in Commerce, was fourteen in 1906, and, like Will Tweedy, could always make a good story better in the telling.

In the book, Burns elaborates:

> Cold Sassy is the kind of town where schoolteachers spend two months every fall drilling on Greek and Roman gods, the kings and queens of England, the Crusades, the Spanish Inquisition, Marco Polo, Magellan, Columbus, the first Thanksgiving, Oglethorpe settling Georgia, and how happy the slaves were before the War. A good teacher could cover the whole history of the world in two months and spend the rest of the school year on the War of the Sixties and how the Union ground its heel in our faces after it knocked us down. Seems like we never got much past the invasion of Yankee carpetbaggers before school let out for the year.
>   The Declaration of Independence and the Revolution were mentioned at school, of course, but just barely. In Cold Sassy,

nobody under forty had ever made or waved an American flag. Even today, in 1914, there's not but one United States flag in the whole town.

That preoccupation with the War of Northern Aggression may well have stemmed from boredom more than rampant Southern pride.

Cold Sassy never had been a whirlpool of excitement. If the preacher's wife's petticoat showed, the ladies could make that last a week as something to talk about. We had our share of cotton-gin fires, epidemics, storms and lawsuits, of course, but the only diversion we could count on was protracted meetings, recitals, ice cream socials, fish fries, and lectures.

LITERARY LURES AND SOUTHERN SIGHTS

Antebellum Jubilee, Stone Mountain Park every year in late March; (770) 498–5702. Practice your rebel yell for this raucus, slightly zany event.

Atlanta Convention and Visitors Bureau, 233 Peachtree Street N.E., Suite 2000; (404) 521–6600; www.acvb.com.

Atlanta Cyclorama, 800-C Cherokee Avenue S.E.; (404) 658–7625. The Battle of Atlanta in 1864 revolves around you, literally. Admission fee. Open daily from 9:20 A.M. to 4:30 P.M., Tuesday after Labor Day through May 31; open 9:20 A.M. till 5:30 P.M. June 1 through Labor Day. Completed in 1885, the Cyclorama is the world's largest diorama painting, measuring forty-two feet high and 356 feet around. Fictitious figures from *Gone With the Wind* were added to the depictions of real-life persona after visitors—and, reportedly, Clark Gable—kept asking for them. On a trip to see the Cyclorama during the premiere weekend of *Gone With the Wind*, Gable allegedly told Mayor William B. Hartsfield, "The only thing missing to make the Cyclorama perfect is Rhett Butler." Faster than you could say "Fiddle-dee-dee," Gable's face had replaced that of a fallen Union soldier. The South won that one, at least.

Atlanta-Fulton Central Library, 1 Margaret Mitchell Square; (404) 730–4636. Permanent Margaret Mitchell exhibit includes her typewriter, pages from the *Gone With the Wind* manuscript and movie script, her personal library, and other memorabilia.

Atlanta History Center, 130 W. Paces Ferry Road N.W.; (404) 814–4000. Tour includes the 1928 Swan House and the 1840s Tullie Smith Farm. Admission fee.

Atlanta Preservation Center, The Rufus House Hotel, 156 Seventh Street N.E.; (404) 876–2041; www.preserveatlanta.com. Offering a wide array of interesting, very good walking tours throughout Atlanta, including one focusing on "Miss Daisy's Druid Hills," the setting for *Driving Miss Daisy*.

Atlanta Visitors Information Bureaus:

231 Peachtree Street, Peachtree Center Mall, downtown.

3393 Peachtree Road, Lenox Square Shopping Center, Buckhead.

65 Upper Alabama Street, Underground Atlanta.

Chapter 11, 6237 Roswell Road; (404) 256–5518. Good all-around bookstore with local favorites, including many, many, many copies of *Gone With the Wind*.

Fox Theatre, 660 Peachtree Street N.E.; (404) 881–2100. A 1929 Moorish-Egyptian-Art Deco fantasy hosting a wide array of live performances and tours.

Martin Luther King Jr. National Historic Site, 450 Auburn Avenue N.E.; (404) 893–9882. The forty-two-acre compound includes the King Center and his birthplace at 501 Auburn Avenue.

Georgian Terrace, 659 Peachtree Street. Built in 1911 as an elegant Beaux Arts hotel, this building now houses luxury apartments and restaurants. Scarlett did sleep here; Vivien Leigh and the other stars of *Gone With the Wind* stayed here in 1939 when the film premiered at the long-since-demolished Loew's Theater. The Georgian Terrace also was the place where Margaret Mitchell delivered the book's manuscript to a New York editor.

Oxford Books at Buckhead, 360 Pharr Road; (404) 262–9975. Local institution with frequent signings by area authors.

Margaret Mitchell Childhood House, 1401 Peachtree Street. A historical marker on the site of a modern office building notes that the house that once stood here was Mitchell's childhood home, where she lived from 1912 to 1922.

Margaret Mitchell House, 990 Peachtree Street, corner of Tenth Street, in midtown Atlanta; (404) 249–7012 or (404) 249–7015; www.gwtw.org or www.scarlett.org/market/mmhouse.htm. For a virtual tour of the house, go to www.franklymydear.com/hotmedia.html. The house, vis-

ited by more than 50,000 fans annually, is open daily from
9 A.M. to 4 P.M., with the museum shop open till 5 P.M. Admission fee.
Adjacent to the Midtown MARTA subway station. In December 1999,
on the sixtieth anniversary of the movie's premiere, a new exhibit hall
opens, showcasing costumes and other memorabilia. In 2000, a special
celebration honored Mitchell's hundredth birthday, on November 8.
The house's Web site (www.gwtw.org) offers Margaret Mitchell souvenirs such as bookmarks, letter openers, and magnets depicting the
home's facade.

Moonlight and Magnolias Georgia Romance Writers Conference,
Atlanta; www.georgiaromancewriters.org. Three hundred romance writers descend on Atlanta every year, each and every one hoping to be
the next Margaret Mitchell or Alexandra Ripley. For readers, the Sat-
urday-afternoon Romance Book Fair features book signings with Southern romance writers.

Oakland Cemetery, 248 Oakland Avenue S.E. (main entrance at Oakland
Avenue and Martin Luther King Jr. Drive); (404) 658–6019. Free admission. Open daily from sunrise to 7 P.M. in summer, sunrise to 6 P.M. the
rest of the year. A Visitors Center, where you can obtain walking-tour
maps, is open from 9 A.M. to 5 P.M. weekdays. Margaret Mitchell and
members of her family are buried here, surrounded by thousands of Civil
War casualties, both Union and Confederate. The eighty-eight-acre Victorian cemetery was founded ten years before the Civil War.

Rhodes Hall, 1516 Peachtree Street N.W.; (404) 881–9980. One of the
last great mansions on Peachtree, this Romanesque Revival home was
completed in 1904 and boasts beautiful stained glass and mosaics.
Admission fee.

Stone Mountain Park, 6867 Memorial Drive, Stone Mountain; (770)
498–5600. Admission fee. Attractions include the *Scarlett O'Hara* paddle
wheeler, available for cruises on Stone Mountain Lake. The mountain's
monument to the Confederacy, a ninety-foot by 190-foot neoclassic
carving, is the world's largest sculpture, depicting Jefferson Davis, Robert
E. Lee, and Stonewall Jackson galloping on horseback into eternity. The
carving was begun in 1923 by Gutzon Borglum, who later carved Mount
Rushmore, and finished by Walter Kirtland Hancock and Roy Faulkner
in 1970. A nineteen-building antebellum plantation in the park contains the 1850 neoclassical, Tara-esque Dickey House.

Tall Tales, 2105 Lavista Road N.E.; (404) 636–2498. Terrific independent bookstore with a refreshingly literate staff.

Wren's Nest House Museum, 1050 Ralph David Abernathy Boulevard S.W.; (404) 753–7735. Victorian-era home of Joel Chandler Harris, author of the Uncle Remus and Brer Rabbit tales that originated in Louisiana. Admission fee.

Yesteryear Book Shop, 3201 Maple Drive N.E.; (404) 237–0163. Antiquarian bookstore specializing in military history and Georgiana.

ACCOMMODATIONS AND RESTAURANTS

Ansley Inn, 253 Fifteenth Street N.E.; (404) 872–9000. Twenty-two rooms and one duplex cottage in prestigious Ansley Park. Built as a private home in 1907 for a department store magnate, the Ansley has the feel of a quiet European inn. All rooms have Jacuzzis.

Atlanta Brewing Company, 1219 Williams Street N.W.; (404) 892–4436; www.atlantabrewing.com.

Atlanta Fish Market, 265 Pharr Road N.E.; (404) 262–3165.

Atlanta International Bed and Breakfast Reservations; (404) 875–2882.

Bed and Breakfast Atlanta; (404) 875–0525 or (800) 967–3224; www. bedandbreakfastatlanta.com.

Buckhead Diner, 3073 Piedmont Road; (404) 262–3336.

Blue Willow Inn, 294 N. Cherokee Road; (770) 464–2131 or (800) 552–8813; www.bluewillowinn.com. In the historic Social Circle area.

Canoe, 4199 Paces Ferry Road N.W.; (770) 432–2663. In the historic Vinings area, this lovely restaurant is situated directly on the Chattahoochee River.

Chops, 70 W. Paces Ferry Road; (404) 262–2675. Terrific steak and lobster.

Delectables, 1 Margaret Mitchell Square, Fairlie Street and Carnegie Way; (404) 681–2909. Near the Atlanta-Fulton Public Library. Helpful, courteous staff and terrific American fare.

1848 House Restaurant, 780 S. Cobb Drive, Marietta; (770) 428–1848. This National Historic Register plantation, north of Atlanta on thirteen landscaped acres, was the site of a Civil War battle.

1890 King-Keith House Bed-and-Breakfast, 889 Edgewood Avenue N.E.; (404) 688–7330.

Horseradish Grill, 4320 Powers Ferry Road; (404) 255–7277.

Hyatt Regency Atlanta, 265 Peachtree Street N.E.; (404) 577–1234 or (800) 233–1234.

Inn Scarlett's Footsteps Bed-and-Breakfast, 40 Old Flat Shoals Road, Concord; (770) 884–9012 or (800) 886–7355; www.gwtw.com. Ten rooms and two suites in a historic bed-and-breakfast north of Atlanta. The inn stages battle reenactments of the Recent Unpleasantness Between the States, as well as atmospheric carriage rides. The inn's brochure reads, "Dream of an eighteen-inch waist as you glide down the grand staircase." Sounds good to me.

Lily Creek Lodge, 2608 Araria Road, Dahlonega; (706) 864–6848 or (888) 844–2694.

Pittypat's Porch Restaurant, 25 International Boulevard between Peachtree and Spring Streets; (404) 525–8228. Southern cuisine in a charming restaurant named for Scarlett's fluttery Aunt Pittypat. "Twelve Oaks barbecued ribs" honor Ashley—Oh, Ashley—and the peach cobbler is worth whatever they decide to charge for it.

Renaissance Atlanta Hotel-Downtown, 590 W. Peachtree Street; (404) 881–6000.

Ritz-Carlton Atlanta, 181 Peachtree Street N.E.; (404) 659–0400.

Shellmont Bed and Breakfast, 821 Piedmont Avenue N.E.; (404) 872–9290.

Stone Mountain Park Inn, Jefferson Davis Road (U.S. Highway 78 East), Stone Mountain; (404) 469–3311 or (800) 227–0007. Low-rise neo-classic hotel built in 1965 inside the park boundaries, about sixteen miles east of Atlanta. Most bedrooms overlook the forest or inner courtyard. In-house restaurant, the Mountain View.

Sugar Magnolia Bed-and-Breakfast, 804 Edgewood Avenue N.E.; (404) 222–0226.

Woodruff Bed-and-Breakfast Inn, 223 Ponce de Leon Avenue N.E.; (404) 875–9449.

Milledgeville

Milledgeville, which has a population of about 18,000, was the birthplace and longtime home of Flannery O' Connor. She was born in Savannah in 1925, but after developing lupus in the early 1950s, stayed more or less permanently at Andalusia, the family farm near

Milledgeville. O'Connor graduated from Milledgeville's Georgia College for Women in 1945, and was a writer from day one, never holding any other full-time job. She never married, had no children, and died four months short of forty, in August 1964.

O'Connor's illness may have contributed to her absolute impatience with pussyfooting around any subject. Her wit and brevity were recalled by Celestine Sibley, a columnist with the *Atlanta Journal-Constitution*, who once sat with her on a panel discussion for aspiring writers at Emory University. "If ya'll are wanting to know about margins and what color ink to use, I don't want to fool with you," Sibley recalls O'Connor telling the students right off. That straightforwardness also applied to established authors: "Mr. Truman Capote," she said once, "makes me plumb sick."

The critics noticed that same blunt attitude in O'Connor's writing. "Highly unladylike . . . a brutal irony, a slam-bang humor, and a style of writing as balefully direct as a death sentence," declared *Time* magazine in a quote used for the cover of the second U.S. edition of *A Good Man Is Hard to Find*.

But manners clearly mattered to O'Connor in the right circumstances. "They had had a nice visitor yesterday, a young man selling Bibles," O'Connor writes in her short story *Good Country People*. "'Lord,' she said, 'he bored me to death but he was so sincere and genuine I couldn't be rude to him. He was just good country people, you know,' she said, 'just the salt of the earth.'" And although her characters were mostly . . . well, eccentric . . . Flannery O'Connor defended them staunchly. "My characters aren't grotesque," she told a gathering at the Iowa Writers' Workshop. "That's just the way people are in the South."

In *The South*, authors B. C. Hall and C. T. Wood put it this way:

> She wrote about people who had little or no control over their lives, people whose existence was always tinged with a strong sense of the absurd. Miss O'Connor pierced the veil and understood the Janus-faced nature of the Southern psyche. On display in her works were characters who were products of religious guilt gone berserk. Who else was Hazel Motes other than the personification of the South's rugged individualism forced to live in a homogenous community that condemned difference or change? Only madness in mythical, Oedipal proportion could be born of such parentage, and in her works O'Connor focused on the crit-

ical theme that abnormal response to the abnormal is normal, at least in the South.

Scholar Louise Y. Gossett has also written about the remarkable confluence of reality and fiction in O'Connor's world:

> There are the ramshackle stores, the kudzu-bordered roads, the religious and commercial billboards, the collapsing barns, the thin crops guarded by scarecrows, and the river baptisms that speak of the struggle by which O'Connor's characters live and die. Subsistence land and towns or cities indifferent to people challenge and baffle the characters. Sometimes beauty transfigures the scene: trees sparkle in hoarfrost or a peacock's tail shimmers like the Transfiguration.

Despite her obvious sympathy for the human species, O'Connor was well acquainted with the nastiness of human nature, brought home in this intense passage from her short story *Greenleaf*, in which death comes to a woman through blatant carelessness by her tenant farmer, who can't keep his bull penned in (read whatever you wish into *that*):

> She looked back and saw that the bull, his head lowered, was racing toward her. She remained perfectly still, not in fright, but in a freezing unbelief. She stared at the violent black streak bounding toward her as if she had no sense of distance, as if she could not decide at once what his intention was, and the bull had buried his head in her lap, like a wild tormented lover, before her expression changed. One of his horns sank until it pierced her heart and the other curved around her side and held her in an unbreakable grip.
>
> She continued to stare straight ahead but the entire scene in front of her had changed—the tree line was a dark wound in a world that was nothing but sky—and she had the look of a person whose sight has been suddenly restored but who finds the look unbearable.

Andalusia, the O'Connor dairy farm—with occasional deference to assorted peacocks, geese, and ducks—is set back from the Eatonville-to-Milledgeville highway about a half-mile, and is surrounded by traffic-buffering trees. Today No Trespassing signs dot the place, and there is no sign alerting the curious visitor that Mary Flannery O'Connor once lived here.

LITERARY LURES AND SOUTHERN SIGHTS

Milledgeville-Baldwin Convention and Visitors Bureau and Welcome Center, 200 W. Hancock Street; (912) 452–4687 or (800) 653–1804; www.milledgevillecvb.com.
Ina Dillard Russell Library, 231 W. Hancock Street; (912) 445–4047. Flannery O'Connor's home in Milledgeville is not open to the pubic, but the library has a memorial Flannery O'Connor Room.

ACCOMMODATIONS AND RESTAURANTS

Cafe South, 132 Hardwick Street S.E., Hardwick; (912) 452–3164. This little cafe is housed in what used to be the Old Hardwick Post Office and General Store, about a quarter-mile south of Milledgeville. Terrific Southern menu, and you can also buy paintings by the owner's brother, a respected local artist.
Cornbread Cafe, 1681 N. Columbia Street; (912) 452–4812. Comfortable, small-town setting for yummy breakfasts and cafeteria-style lunches.
Days Inn, 251 N. Columbia Street; (912) 453–8471. Two-story inn with seventy-five rooms and four suites.
Holiday Inn Milledgeville, 2627 N. Columbia Street; (912) 452–3502.

Jonesboro

Jonesboro, in Clayton County just southwest of Atlanta, was the site of Scarlett O'Hara's Tara and neighboring Twelve Oaks. In *Gone With the Wind*, Margaret Mitchell writes:

> Life in the north Georgia county of Clayton was still new, and according to the standards of Augusta, Savannah, and Charleston, a little crude. The more sedate and older sections of the South looked down their noses at the up-country Georgians, but here in

North Georgia, a lack of the niceties of classical education carried
no shame, provided a man was smart in the things that mattered.
And raising good cotton, riding well, shooting straight, dancing
lightly, squiring the ladies with elegance and carrying one's liquor
like a gentleman were the things that mattered.

Those were the things that mattered to the ladies, as well; *please*
don't bother them with talk of all that unpleasantness between the states.
"I'm mighty glad Georgia waited till after Christmas before it seceded or
it would have ruined the Christmas parties, too," Scarlett wails in the
opening chapter of *Gone With the Wind*. "If you say 'war' again, I'll go in
the house." And she does.

To the O'Haras, of course, the most important thing of all was the
land—terra, Tara:

> It was a savagely red land, blood-colored after rains, brick dust in
> droughts, the best cotton land in the world. It was a pleasant
> land of white houses, peaceful plowed fields and sluggish yellow
> rivers, but a land of contrasts, of brightest sun glare and densest
> shade. The plantation clearings and miles of cotton fields smiled
> up to a warm sun, placid, complacent. At their edge rose the
> virgin forests, dark and cool even in the hottest noons, mysteri-
> ous, a little sinister, the pines seeming to wait with an age-old
> patience, to threaten with soft sighs, "Be careful! Be careful! We
> had you once. We can take you back again."

LITERARY LURES AND SOUTHERN SIGHTS

Historical Jonesboro Clayton-Stately Oaks Historic House, 100 Carriage
   Lane; (770) 473–0197.

ACCOMMODATIONS AND RESTAURANTS

Buffalo's Cafe, 765 North Avenue; (770) 603–1300.
Econo Lodge, 340 Upper Riverdale Road; (770) 991–0069.
Holiday Inn South, 6288 Old Dixie Highway; (770) 968–4300.
Huddle House, 7326 Tara Boulevard; (770) 961–2690.
Scottish Inn, 599 Battlecreek Road; (770) 603–7300.
Shoney's Inn, 6358 Old Dixie Highway; (770) 968–5018.

Eatonton

Eatonton is the birthplace of Alice Walker, who won the Pulitzer Prize for *The Color Purple*.

LITERARY LURES AND SOUTHERN SITES

Eatonton-Putnam Chamber of Commerce, 105 Sumter Street; (706) 485–7701.

Savannah

Although Flannery O'Connor spent most of her life in Milledgeville, she was born in Savannah, at a home on Lafayette Square, in March 1925. The home dates from 1855, when it was actually built as two row houses, twenty feet wide. Literary programs now take place here throughout the year, including readings and lectures by and about other Southern authors. Also in the neighborhood is St. John the Baptist Cathedral, just across the square, where O'Connor was baptized, had her first communion, and was confirmed. Just east, on the site of the present-day Cathedral School, was St. Vincent's Grammar School, where little Mary Flannery O'Connor attended grades one through five.

Today, though, it's hard to find a tourist who even knows the O'Connor connection—they're all here to see the sights mentioned in what locals refer to as simply "the Book"—John Berendt's 1994 phenomenon, *Midnight in the Garden of Good and Evil*. A heady mixture of journalism and gossip, the book tells the sordid—and undeniably seductive—tale of an infamous murder, with elements of high society, homosexuality, money both old and new, and scene-stealing appearances by a local drag queen.

Savannah changed Berendt, and he responded in kind, wittingly or not. Local tourism has increased nearly 50 percent since the book's publication. After nearly five years on the bestseller lists, *Midnight* is still moving like wildfire, and it was summer 1999 before a paperback edition was issued. All the hoopla may have obscured the book's literary merit: It was one of three finalists for the Pulitzer Prize for general nonfiction, and won the 1994 Southern Book Award. Berendt took a few liberties with the book—he wasn't actually in town when the murder was committed, for instance—but Savannians and critics appear to have forgiven his transgressions.

Mercer House on Savannah's Montgomery Square, site of the infamous murder in *Midnight in the Garden of Good and Evil.*

Most of the places mentioned in the book aren't open to the public, but tour guides will obligingly point them out on jaunts devoted specifically to *Midnight.* It even merits its own store on Calhoun Square, where devotees can buy anything from a *Midnight* keychain to a miniature reproduction of Bird Girl, the enigmatic statue seen on the book's cover. The highlights of a tour about the Book:

> *Mercer House*, 429 Bull Street. Antiques dealer Jim Williams's historic abode, where he shot his house partner-lover, Danny Hansford. Williams himself also died there, in 1990. The red-brick Italianate mansion was once owned by the family of legendary songwriter Johnny Mercer, a Savannah native, but the Mercers never lived

there. Before Hansford's death—which Williams claimed was an accident, although the coroner shouted murder—Williams had transformed the once-dilapidated Mercer House into the site of *the* Christmas party every year in Savannah, for which Savannians would kill—perhaps literally—for an invitation. Mercer House is now occupied by Williams's sister, who wants no part of the publicity surrounding Hansford's death and the book, and has refused pleas to open it for tours.

Armstrong House, 447 Bull Street. Jim Williams lived and worked here before buying Mercer House. Then it was occupied by the law firm of Bouhan, Williams, and Levy, whose porter, Simon Glover, earned ten dollars a week for walking one of the owners' deceased dogs up and down the street. Yes, *deceased*. The ghostly pooch, lovingly documented in *Midnight*, apparently gets along fine with Uga, the real-life Georgia Bulldogs mascot that is kept by Frank Siler. Siler, Jim Williams's attorney, works in this same building. Confused yet? Join the club.

Bonaventure Cemetery, on Bonaventure Road, outside of town (drive out Wheaton Street east of downtown). The final resting place for Johnny Mercer, poet Conrad Aiken, and possible murder victim Danny Hansford. The Bird Girl statue was here when photographed for the cover of *Midnight*, but she's since been moved to Telfair Academy in town, for safekeeping. One of the book's most memorable scenes occurs at Bonaventure, when Berendt is escorted to the cemetery for martinis at sunset on the Savannah River. Only after the cocktails were consumed did Berendt's friend, Mary Harty, reveal that they were sipping martinis while sitting *on* Aiken's headstone—it's in the shape of a bench with the inscription: Cosmos Mariner, Destination Unknown. Aiken chose the epitaph from the description of a ship he once saw on the town's daily port register. Bonaventure Cemetery is certainly one of the most beautiful and surely haunted places in the South—the plantation home that once sat near the gates burned to the ground during a dinner party, and some say that after dark, clinking glasses and laughter can be heard amid the moss-curtained oaks. The place closes at sundown. Just as well.

Forsyth Park Apartments, Whitaker and Gwinnett Streets, southwest corner of Forsyth Park. Berendt lived here and put together most of *Midnight* in his fourth-floor apartment.

The *Bird Girl* statue featured on the cover of *Midnight* no longer rests in Bonaventure Cemetery, but many other statuary tributes remain in the supposedly haunted burial ground.

Lee Adler's Home, 425 Bull Street, just north of Mercer House. Adler, Jim Williams's main adversary in life and the book, restores historic Savannah properties from his home on Bull Street. In *Midnight,* Berendt recounts one operatically furious encounter between Adler and Williams, in which Adler's howling dogs inspired Williams to pour out an earsplitting version of Franck's *Pièce Heroïque* on his pipe organ. Adler retaliated by festooning his lawn with re-election signs for the district attorney who had prosecuted Williams—three times—for the murder of Danny Hansford before a fourth jury finally found Williams not guilty.

Clary's Cafe, where the *Midnight* crowd gathers for breakfast, lunch, and perhaps a peek at Luther Driggers.

Clary's Cafe, 404 Abercorn at Jones Streets. One of the few *Midnight* sites open to the public. Probably the most likely site for spotting Luther Driggers, a real-life book character who's rumored to possess a poison powerful enough to wipe out all of Savannah. Just don't leave your coffee unattended.

Club One, 1 Jefferson Street; (912) 232–0200. The infamous gay bar where *Midnight*'s Lady Chablis made such a strong impression. He . . . um, she . . . played herself in the movie, to rave reviews, and has written an autobiography, *Hiding My Candy*. When Chablis is in town, she still makes appearances at Club One, and while they've been toned down for the tourists, that doesn't mean toned *out*. It's a gay bar. Chablis is a drag queen. Live with that, or don't go.

In addition to its allure as a dementia-tinged murder mystery, *Midnight* also reveals Berendt's obvious love for the city on its own merits. Here, he describes his first glimpse of Savannah after driving in from Charleston:

> Abruptly, the trees gave way to an open panorama of marsh grass the color of wheat. Straight ahead, a tall bridge rose steeply out

of the plain. From the top of the bridge, I looked down on the Savannah River and, on the far side, a row of old brick buildings fronted by a narrow esplanade. Behind the buildings a mass of trees extended into the distance, punctuated by steeples, cornices, rooftops, and cupolas. As I descended from the bridge, I found myself plunging into a luxuriant green garden.

Walls of thick vegetation rose up on all sides and arched overhead in a lacy canopy that filtered the light to a soft shade. It had just rained; the air was hot and steamy. I felt enclosed in a semitropical terrarium, sealed off from a world that suddenly seemed a thousand miles away.

And in the precursor to the wonderful cemetery scene, Mary Harty adds her own take on the town and its personality:

"We may be standoffish," she said, "but we're not hostile. We're famously hospitable, in fact, even by southern standards. . . . That's because we've always been a party town. We love company. . . . We're not at all like the rest of Georgia. We have a saying: If you go to Atlanta, the first question people ask you is, 'What's your business?' In Macon they ask, 'Where do you go to church?' In Augusta they ask your grandmother's maiden name. But in Savannah the first question people ask you is 'What would you like to drink?'"

At the Colonial Park Inn, where I stayed on a visit, this was borne out by the presence of both a corkscrew and a shot glass in our room, and the proprietor's gracious, if practical, attitude. "Here's my card with my pager number," he told me and my friend on our arrival. "If you get thrown in jail, call me and I'll come get you." Thankfully, we didn't require his services, but I kept that card with me.

LITERARY LURES AND SOUTHERN SIGHTS

The Book Lady, 17 W. York Street; (912) 233–3628. Used and rare books in a quaint setting.

"The Book" Gift Shop, 127 E. Gorden Street; (912) 233–3867. Yes, an entire store on Calhoun Square devoted to *Midnight in the Garden of*

Good and Evil. You'll find everything from autographed copies of the book to *Midnight* afghans and cookie tins.

Carriage Tours of Savannah; (912) 236–6756. Tours focusing on historic Savannah, the Book, and ghost stories in comfy carriages for a dozen or so tourists. The Cobblestone Classic tour merits a private, romantic carriage for two.

Chippewa Square, Bull Street between Perry and Hull Streets. One of the twenty-two remaining squares that Savannah was built around, this is where most of *Forrest Gump*'s park scenes were shot. One town mayor wanted to install a bronze statue of Tom Hanks, as Forrest, on the bench eating his chocolates, in the square. But Savannians were outraged by the suggestion, noting that as delightful as Gump may be, he's hardly "real history" and therefore distinctly unworthy of sharing the square with the statue of Georgian hero General James Oglethorpe.

Clary's Cafe, 404 Abercorn at Jones Streets; (912) 233–0402. A local institution since 1903, more treasured than ever since its loving mention in *Midnight in the Garden.* Southern specialties include Savannah crab cakes, fried green tomatoes, and seafood pot pie. Inexpensive, atmospheric, and fun, and you can have your picture taken under the stained-glass window that recreates the cover art from *Midnight.*

Club One, 1 Jefferson Street; (912) 232–0200. The infamous gay bar where *Midnight*'s Lady Chablis made her . . . er, mark. If you've got sequins, this is the place to wear 'em, and the Lady still makes occasional appearances.

V. and J. Duncan, 12 E. Taylor Street; (912) 232–0338. Antique maps, prints, and books.

Hospitality Tours of Savannah, 141 Bull Street; (912) 233–0119 or (912) 233–4449. These folks did the first "By the Book" tour about *Midnight in the Garden of Good and Evil* sites, and still offer one of the best—a two-and-a-half hour *Midnight* odyssey that includes every site mentioned in the book. After-dark tours include Savannah Shadows Ghost Walk and the Haunted Pub Tour.

Flannery O'Connor Childhood Home, 207 E. Charlton Street, Lafayette Square, (912) 233–6014. Open 1 P.M. to 4 P.M. Saturdays, 1 P.M. to 5 P.M. Sundays. Donation requested.

Old Town Trolley Tours; (912) 233–0083.

Savannah Area Convention and Visitors Bureau, 101 E. Baystreet Avenue; (877) 728–2662; www.savannah-visit.com.

Savannah History Museum, 303 Martin Luther King Jr. Boulevard; (912) 238–1779. Includes everything from war and maritime memorabilia to props from the *Forrest Gump* movie. Open from 9 A.M. to 5 P.M. daily. Admission fee.

SavannahNOW, the *Savannah Morning News* local Web page; www.savannah now.com. Complete with a virtual *Midnight* tour.

Savannah Online; www.savannah-online.com.

Savannah Visitor Center, 301 Martin Luther King Jr. Boulevard; (912) 944–0455. Open from 8:30 A.M. to 5 P.M. weekdays, 9 A.M. to 5 P.M. weekends. A replica of Forrest Gump's bench is available for photos. Bring your own box of chocolates.

E. Shaver Bookseller, 326 Bull Street; (912) 234–7257. Twelve rooms chock-full of books, with a great regional section. Behind the DeSoto Hilton on Madison Square.

Southeastern Writers Workshop, St. Simons Island, south of Savannah; (912) 876–3118; www.southeasternwriters.com/conference. Annual June conference takes place at an antebellum plantation-turned-hotel called Epworth-by-the-Sea. Instructors include published authors and teachers who live in Georgia.

Southern Images Gallery, 132 E. Oglethorpe Avenue; (912) 234–6449. Featuring the exquisite photos of Savannah native Jack Leigh, who shot the strangely haunting cover photo for *Midnight*.

Telfair Museum of Art, 121 Barnard Street, on Telfair Square, (912) 232–1177. Open from 10 A.M. to 5 P.M. Tuesdays through Saturdays, 2 P.M. to 5 P.M. Sundays. If you're looking for the Bird Girl, the four-foot-high bronze statue on the cover of the book, she's been moved from Bonaventure Cemetery to this museum. Tourists at the cemetery were taking so many pictures with their arms wrapped around her that she was in danger of toppling. The Bird Girl, by the way, was never mentioned in the book, but Clint Eastwood gave her a cameo in his movie version starring Kevin Spacey and John Cusack. Well, actually Warner Bros. built a replica; go ahead and call it a stand-in. Like most of Savannah, it seems, Telfair is said to be haunted, with paranormal disturbances so powerful they sometimes set off the security alarms.

ACCOMMODATIONS AND RESTAURANTS

Ballastone Inn and Townhouse, 14 E. Oglethorpe Avenue; (912) 236–1484 or (800) 822–4553. Seventeen rooms with baths, fourteen suites.

Oglethorpe Park in Savannah has been seen in movies from *Midnight in the Garden of Good and Evil* to *Forrest Gump*.

City Market Cafe, 224 E. St. Julian Street, City Market; (912) 236–7133. Terrific fresh fish and homemade pizza in a restored 1790s warehouse.

Clary's Cafe, 404 Abercorn at Jones Streets, (912) 233–0402. Casual dining in true *Midnight* style.

Colonial Park Inn, 220 E. Liberty Street, (912) 232–3622 or (800) 799–3622. Renovated 1850 carriage house and garden suite, with true Southern hospitality delivered by the hosts.

Cotton Exchange Tavern, 201 E. River Street; (912) 232–7088. At the Abercorn Ramp on the Savannah River, in a restored 1790s cotton warehouse.

East Bay Inn, 225 E. Bay Street; (912) 238–1225 or (800) 500–1225.

Elizabeth on 37th, 105 E. Thirty-seventh Street; (912) 236–5547. Go for the Savannah Cream Cake.

Forsyth Park Inn, 102 W. Hall Street on Forsyth Park; (912) 233–6800.

Gaston Gallery Bed and Breakfast, 211 E. Gaston Street; (912) 238–3294 or (800) 671–0716.

Hamilton-Turner House and Ghost House, 330 Abercorn Street; (912) 233–4800. Mentioned in *Midnight*, this is the only Victorian house in town open to the public, and it's now a bed-and-breakfast. And—extra points!—it's said to be haunted.

Kehoe House, 123 Habersham Street, on Columbia Square; (912) 232–1020 or (800) 820–1020. Built by Irish immigrant William Kehoe, who became wealthy in the ironworks business, Kehoe is an 1892 Renaissance Revival house, with elements of Victorian and Italianate architecture. It opened in 1993 as an inn following a $1.4 million renovation. Tom Hanks stayed in Room 301 while filming *Forrest Gump*. Fifteen rooms, all with private baths.

Lion's Head Inn, 120 E. Gaston Street; (912) 232–4580.

Olde Harbour Inn, 508 E. Factors Walk; (912) 234–4100 or (800) 553–6533.

Nita's Place, 140 Abercorn Street; (912) 238–8233. Casual Southern fare in a no-frills atmosphere.

Oglethorpe Lodge, 117 E. Bay Street; (912) 234–8888.

Olde Harbour Inn, 508 E. Factors Walk; (912) 234–4100 or (800) 553–6533.

The Olde Pink House, 23 Abercorn Street; (912) 232–4286. Savannah's only remaining eighteenth-century mansion, circa 1771, an elegant setting for Southern dining. The Planters Tavern offers a more casual setting with the same superb food and service.

The Pirate's House, 20 E. Broad at Bay Streets, a block from the river; (912) 233–5757. Located in a building dating from 1734 that is reputedly haunted by Captain Flint, after whom Long John Silver named his parrot in *Treasure Island*. Upstairs from the Pirate's House is Hannah's East nightclub, where you're most likely to find Emma Kelly, the "lady of 6,000 songs" from *Midnight*.

Presidents' Quarters, 225 E. President Street; (912) 233–1600 or (800) 233–1776.

The Rail Pub Food and Spirits, 405 W. Congress Street, on Franklin Square; (912) 238–1311. Casual atmosphere in a historic 1880s bordello. Hey, history is history.

River Street Inn, 115 E. River Street; (912) 234–6400 or (800) 253–4229. Built in 1817, originally used to store, sample, grade, and export raw cotton.

Savannah Historic Inns; (877) 525–5638; www.historicinns-savannah.com.

Eliza Thompson House, 5 W. Jones Street; (912) 236–3620 or (800) 348–9378. Legend says that Eliza, one of Savannah's most celebrated hostesses, was the reason Sherman declined to burn the city during his march south.

Columbus

Columbus, a Chattahoochee River town of about 20,000 on the west-central Georgia border, was the birthplace of Carson McCullers. Born in 1917 as Lula Carson Smith, McCullers—who married would-be writer Reeves McCullers in 1937—was hailed as a literary wunderkind on the publication of her first novel, *The Heart Is a Lonely Hunter*, in 1940, when she was just twenty-three.

She spent the summer of 1946 on Nantucket Island with Tennessee Williams, who helped her adapt her second great success, *The Member of the Wedding*, into a play. It opened in January 1950 to glowing reviews and ran for 501 performances, winning the coveted New York Drama Critics Circle Award. Williams called her "the greatest living prose writer, and the greatest prose writer the South has ever produced."

LITERARY LURES AND SOUTHERN SIGHTS

Carson McCullers House, 1519 Stark Avenue (not open to the public). This is where Lula Carson Smith spent her formative years, ages ten to seventeen.

ACCOMMODATIONS

Rothschild-Pound House, 201 Seventh Street; (706) 322–4075 or (800) 585–4075. Near the restored downtown and Chattahoochee River-walk, this 1870 house was moved in 1993 to its current location in the historic district. Three double rooms in the main house, four double rooms in the adjacent cottage. Two rooms have whirlpool tubs.

6

North Carolina

If a man's from the mountains, he'll tell you. If he's not, why embarrass him by asking?

—Charles Kuralt, *North Carolina Is My Home*

We inhabit a fallen world where blind ignorance has replaced our early succulent innocence. The Southerner's history, whether cultural or personal, contains but one large incident: betrayal.

—Fred Chappell, interviewed for *Growing Up Southern*

Novelist/poet Fred Chappell, born in North Carolina in 1936, knows all about betrayal of that particularly Southern kind. Chappell, who grew up in Canton and now teaches at the University of North Carolina, at Greensboro, had a great-grandfather who lost a leg at Fredericksburg, and a great-grandmother who was robbed on her farm by Union soldiers. Chappell's childhood was invested with two things: the storytelling tradition and a deeply ingrained distrust of anyone who hailed from north of the Mason-Dixon. As Chappell noted in *Growing Up Southern*, "Graham Greene said that childhood is a writer's capital. I think I must have overspent mine two or three times now."

Fellow North Carolinian Lee Smith, one of the most beloved Southern authors, grew up in Grundy and teaches at University of North Carolina-Chapel Hill. She once told an interviewer that writers born in the South, no matter how seemingly modern, appear genetically to harbor a certain style that no Northern-born author can match.

"I might have a student who has grown up in the mall in Fayetteville and her parents have split up and she's lived a lot of places, but she writes a story which, though it doesn't take place in a small town, still has a voice that is thoroughly Southern," Smith said. "Southerners have a way of approaching facts and information and shaping them into a form that is a natural story."

Smith has incorporated many of her memories into her stories, such as this description of the grandmother in *Artists*—based on her own grandmother, Chloe Smith, and instantly recognizable to any Southern child who ever spent more than a day in the presence of a certain brand of elderly Southern matron:

> She wore hats and white gloves on every possible occasion. Her manner of dress had changed so little over the years that even I could recognize its eccentricity. She dressed up all the time. I never saw her in my life without her pale voile or silk or brocade dresses, without her stockings, without her feet crammed into elegant shoes at least two sizes too small for her, so that at the end her feet were actually crippled. I never saw her without her makeup or the flashing rhinestone earrings and brooches and bracelets that finally she came to believe—as I believed then—were real.

Doris Betts, who also teaches at University of North Carolina-Chapel Hill, was born on a farm outside Statesville, often called Greenway in her stories. Betts also has noticed the specific "Southern-ness" of her students. "One of the questions I ask my students is 'Where are you from?' They think that's a terribly Southern question," she said in *Growing Up Southern*. "But real Southerners understand that question immediately. Even if they have lived in four or five places, they know where they are from."

Another much-loved contemporary writer, Anne Tyler, was brought up in Raleigh and set her first three novels in North Carolina before moving her setting to Baltimore, where she and her family moved. And Gail Godwin, a native Ashevillian now living in New York, also set many of her works in North Carolina.

Sixty years after his death, though, Thomas Wolfe probably remains North Carolina's, and certainly Asheville's, most famous literary offspring. Wolfe is widely revered among Ashevillians, who named a plaza after him and offer tours of Wolfe sites. Hundreds of visitors come every year to see the Old Kentucky Home boardinghouse that was run by Wolfe's mother and was thinly disguised as Dixieland in his deeply autobiographical first novel, *Look Homeward, Angel*. But when that book first came out, the twenty-eight-year-old Wolfe became a town pariah, and it was years before he returned.

LITERARY LURES AND SOUTHERN SIGHTS

Carolina Culture Tours, Asheville; (888) 286–6272; www.culturetours. com. This wonderful company offers tours focusing on different aspects of Southern culture, such as storytelling, traditional music and dance, crafts, outdoor dramas, and "the Literary Carolinas."

ACCOMMODATIONS AND RESTAURANTS

North Carolina Bed and Breakfasts and Inns; (800) 849–5392; www.bbonline.com/nc/ncbbi.
North Carolina Division of Parks and Recreation; (919) 733–7275; www.ils.unc.edu/parkproject/ncparks.html.
North Carolina Travel and Tourism Division; (919) 733–8372 or (800) 847–4862; www.visitnc.com.

Asheville, Henderson, and Western North Carolina

Thomas Wolfe's autobiographical novels *Look Homeward, Angel* and *You Can't Go Home Again* earned him the lasting enmity of his Asheville neighbors. Now he's one of the town's primary tourist attractions, but he literally couldn't go home after the 1929 publication of *Angel*; Asheville society had turned pale and grim with righteous rage toward the man who so accurately depicted their every foible. The locals sniffed haughtily or feigned complete ignorance when "that book" was mentioned, and it was blacklisted by local libraries and bookstores as late as 1949. When Wolfe returned for a visit after the book came out, he received death threats.

Asheville's first skyscraper (on the left) is built on the site of Thomas Wolfe's father's monument shop.

Oddly enough, the book, in which Asheville was called Altamont, received respectable reviews from both local papers when it came out. On one visit back, Wolfe made apologies, of a sort, to the town. In an interview with the *Asheville Citizen*, he said, "If anything I have ever written has displeased anyone in Asheville, I hope that I will be able to write another book which will please them." For his part, Wolfe could be harsh regarding other writers' works—in a letter to a friend in 1937, he called *Gone With the Wind* "an immortal piece of bilge"—but typically reserved his strongest criticism for himself.

In a letter to editor Maxwell Perkins about *Look Homeward, Angel,* he lamented, "Although I am able to criticize wordiness and overabun-

The Old Kentucky Home, Julia Wolfe's boardinghouse,
which her son Thomas immortalized as "Dixieland" in
Look Homeward, Angel.

dance in others, I am not able practically to criticize it in myself. The
business of selection and revision is simply hell for me—my effort to cut
out 50,000 words may sometimes result in my adding 75,000."

The Old Kentucky Home, for which Wolfe bore deep and abiding
hatred, was torched by an unknown arsonist in July 1998 but is now
undergoing restoration. Sacreligious as it may sound to Wolfe fans, on
touring the home and hearing of Julia Wolfe's distinct lack of charity
toward her youngest son, a visitor gets the idea that Thomas Wolfe would
just as soon have let it burn.

Thankfully for his devotees, however, firefighters saved about 85 percent of the furniture and other Wolfe artifacts. Some of the most price-

less and irreplaceable pieces, including Wolfe's typewriter and desk, were housed in the nearby visitors center when the fire hit, thus sparing them. The main fire damage was confined to the dining room, one upstairs bedroom, the attic, and the roof. A $2.5 million restoration is under way and the Old Kentucky Home should reopen to visitors soon. Meanwhile, Wolfe pilgrims can still visit the adjacent Thomas Wolfe Memorial.

Wolfe's brilliance was well recognized by his fellow Southern writers. "He tried the hardest to say the most," William Faulkner once said of Wolfe. Fellow North Carolinian William Styron is quoted in an exhibit at the Wolfe Memorial with this backhanded compliment: "Wolfe wrote many a bad sentence, but never a dull one."

Some animosity—or at the very least, apathy—apparently remains toward Wolfe. At the local Chamber of Commerce in 1998, I overheard a Wolfe fan asking for directions to the bronze angel dedicated to the author. The elderly volunteer behind the counter didn't have a clue where to find Wolfe's angel and seemed disinclined to find out for the hapless tourist. For the record, the graceful angel stands in front of Pack Memorial Library on Pack Square.

South Carolinian Pat Conroy credits Wolfe with instigating his own literary career. In his novel *Beach Music*, Conroy writes:

> Taking out *Look Homeward, Angel*, I read the magnificent first page and remembered when I had been a sixteen-year-old boy and those same words had set me ablaze with the sheer inhuman beauty of the language as a cry for mercy, incantation, and a great river roaring through the darkness. "Hello, Eugene. Hello, Ben Gant," I said quietly, for I knew these characters as well as I knew anyone in the world. Literature was where the world made sense for me.

The Old Kentucky Home that Wolfe fictionalized as Dixieland in *Look Homeward, Angel*, and now transformed into something of a literary shrine, was a place where Wolfe found little happiness. In *Angel*, he refers to the "bleak horror of Dixieland" and says the boardinghouse had "all the comforts of a jail." His mother, the entrepreneurial Julia, took her youngest son with her when she moved from the family's comfortable Asheville home at 92 Woodfin Street (long since torn down) to run the boardinghouse. Wolfe's beloved father and his siblings were left behind on Woodfin. And from ages six to sixteen, while living at the boardinghouse, young Thomas

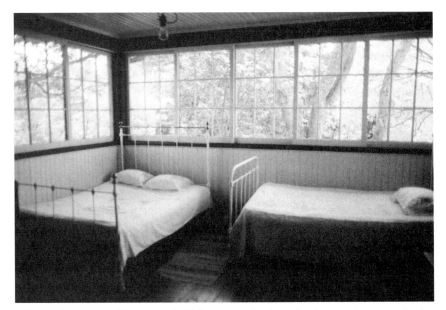

When Thomas Wolfe was a child living at the boardinghouse, he never had a room of his own, but instead took whatever space was unoccupied by paying customers.

never had his own room, shuffling instead each night to whatever room or bed or half-bed was unoccupied by paying patrons.

In *Angel*, he writes of his mother, fictionalized as Eliza Gant:

> By God, I shall spend the rest of my life getting my heart back, healing and forgetting every scar you put upon me when I was a child. The first move I ever made, after the cradle, was to crawl for the door, and every move I have made since has been an effort to escape.

It's reported that baby Thomas's first word was "moo." One wonders if he meant "move" (as in, "get the hell out of my way so I can get out of here").

Wolfe was born in October 1900 at the Woodfin Street house. All that remains of this site where Wolfe spent his early childhood is a wooden playhouse, which was saved and moved to the grounds of the Old Kentucky Home. His father, W. O. Wolfe, was a noted stonecutter who in 1869 created ornate trimmings for the South Carolina state capitol in Columbia; the original capitol decorations had been damaged in the Civil War. The elder Wolfe's monument shop stood at 22 S. Pack Square, Asheville's public square. A reproduction of his most famous work, that triumphant angel, now marks the site. The original angel statue marks a grave at the Hendersonville cemetery, south of Asheville.

Wolfe, who died of tuberculosis in 1937, is buried in the century-old, eighty-seven-acre Riverside Cemetery, which lies along the river in the historic Montford District of Asheville. The Old Kentucky Home finally had its revenge for Wolfe's portrayal of the place; doctors said he probably first contracted TB as a child from some transient boarder.

Fittingly, Wolfe wrote his own epitaphs. One of the two inscriptions on his tomb came from *Look Homeward, Angel:* "The last voyage, the longest, the best."

The other engraving, from *The Web and the Rock,* reads: "Death bent to touch his chosen son with mercy, love and pity, and put the seal of honor on him when he died." Asheville finally put the seal of honor on Thomas Wolfe, but it was decades after he died.

Greensboro-born short-story writer O. Henry (William Sydney Porter), master of the surprise ending, found his own ending at Riverside Cemetery as well, not far from Wolfe. And like Wolfe, O. Henry had an uneasy relationship with Asheville, once lamenting, "I could look at these mountains a hundred years and not get an inspiration—they depress me."

O. Henry was living in New York when he died, but his wife, an Asheville native, brought his remains back to North Carolina for burial. Surprise!

Asheville's joyously grand Grove Park Inn Resort—wittily described by a colleague of mine as "looking as if it was constructed of chocolate chips"—deserves its own literary license of some sort, having served as a home-away-from-home for, among others, F. Scott Fitzgerald, Charles Frazier, Jan Karon, and Allan Gurganus, not to mention innumerable movie stars, presidents, and others seeking its cool mountain air, majestic vistas, and unequaled Southern hospitality. The Grove Park staff strive in all ways to make their guests' visits worry-free, even providing handy little cards with directions to local sites such as Chimney Rock Park, Lake Lure, and Cold Mountain.

The inn opened July 12, 1913, chock-full of custom-built furniture and hammered copper lighting fixtures from the famed Roycrofters of New York. The hotel fell into disrepair in the 1930s and 1940s, but good

The Grove Park Inn, where F. Scott Fitzgerald stayed while waiting for Zelda's mental recuperation in a nearby hospital.

times returned when it was bought by Dallas entrepreneurs and philanthropists Charles and Elaine Sammons in 1955. The Sammonses tracked down and repurchased many of the original furnishings and fixtures, some of which had been sold off during the Depression, and set about restoring the hotel with extraordinary care and attention to detail. Now the Grove Park Inn is listed on the National Register of Historic Places and has seen expansion into two wings and a full-service spa.

Scott Fitzgerald stayed at the inn several times in 1936 and 1937 while Zelda recuperated from her intermittent breakdowns at nearby Highlands Hospital, a costly private sanitorium in the hills above the Grove Park. After Scott's death, Zelda lingered for several years but died in 1948 at Highlands, one of nine women patients killed in a fire. "Against all the rules, and for the hell of it, somebody had been smoking in bed," Allan Gurganus noted in an article about the Fitzgeralds. Strangely enough, one of Zelda's few friends while living in Asheville was Julia Wolfe, the mother Thomas Wolfe so savaged in his works.

While staying at the Grove Park, Scott Fitzgerald chose a room that did not overlook the mountains where he could have blown kisses across the valley to Zelda's hospital window. Instead, he picked Rooms 441 and

From the lawn of Grove Park Inn, Fitzgerald could see the mountains and a glimpse of the hospital where Zelda was trying to regain her sanity. He chose instead a room with a view of the front drive, with its ever-arriving debutantes.

443 facing the inn's circular driveway—decked with tall pines and lovely in its way, but hardly the mountain view that the other side of the inn offers. But those rooms apparently had precisely the view Fitzgerald preferred—of the Asheville debutantes stepping out of their chauffeured limousines. That way, he could make his evening's choice without being bothered to actually make small talk or other courting rituals. He saw what he wanted from his window, and that was that. Rare was the debutante who could resist a night with the charming Fitzgerald.

Room 441, where Fitzgerald stayed, has been painstakingly restored to the way it appeared during his residence—right down to a "reproduction" bullet hole in the ceiling where Fitzgerald fired a shot one night in a drunken swoon, apparently attempting suicide but having little control of his aim. The management, ever endeavoring for decorum, had the bullet hole repaired, but it has been put back, more or less in its original position. The bed boasts a simple cotton coverlet rather than the fluffy comforters found elsewhere at the Grove Park, and authentic, spare Arts and Crafts furnishings decorate the room—there are even the remnants of ink in the desk's built-in inkwell. The Arts and Crafts wastebasket is

Room 441 of the Grove Park Inn, where Scott Fitzgerald stayed in the 1930s.

unlined, as it would have been in 1936, the black 1920s dial phone works, and the hangers can actually be removed from the armoire's clothes bar, a sure sign that you've been transported back in time.

The Grove Park celebrates its Fitzgerald connection every September, with a festival honoring Scott's birthday. On the hundredth anniversary of his birth, in 1998, fellow Southern scribe Allan Gurganus wrote a special article for the occasion.

> I recently slept in Scott Fitzgerald's favorite rooms at the Grove Park. What haunting did I hope for? What vitamin fortification of my own prose? I really wanted to be waked by the ghostly sound of a typewriter, by the faded strains of Fats Wallers's jazz band downstairs. I could imagine the voice of some very young flapper in here, saying "Well, maybe just one more sip. Oooh but you are a caution, Mr. Fitzgerald, sir."

Alas, Gurganus received no such visitations.

> I longed, during my own stay there, to feel, what? Fitzgerald's tweedy itchy emanation, the swing band sway of his best Gatsby-

The desk in Room 441 at the Grove Park, where Fitzgerald stayed, still bears traces of ink in its built-in inkwell. Ya gotta wonder . . .

esque prose rhythms. I could imagine a great deal of pacing done here. But mainly I heard only the mountain breeze. . . . Scott Fitzgerald's rooms did not prove so haunted that they kept me awake. Nor did they drive me to drink more than my usual two Jack Daniels.

In an interview for this book, Gurganus said there was "something alive about that room [441] . . . They're so wise to keep it as it was. So many places would rush to gussy it up and they'd lose that magic."

The inn's magic extends to its fabulous lobby, which boasts its own literary links in the form of quotes written on the native stones of the massive fireplace. (The teensy elevator, still run by ever-so-polite, uniformed operators, is tucked into one corner of the fireplace.) The quotes offer good advice, simply stated: "Be not simply good—be good for something," Thoreau. "Take things always by their smooth handle," Thomas Jefferson. "Every book is a quotation: every house is a quotation out of all forests and mines and every man is a quotation from all his ancestors," Emerson.

Lately, the area's most celebrated novelist has been Charles Frazier, whose *Cold Mountain* was the 1997 National Book Award–winner. Frazier now lives in Raleigh, but grew up amid the ridges and valleys of western North Carolina, near Asheville. In the book, Inman is a Civil War deserter. His trek back to Cold Mountain and his lost love, Ada, propels the book's narrative. Here, Inman reminisces about his mountain home:

> There in the highlands, clear weather held for much of the time. The air lacked its usual haze, and the view stretched on and on across rows of blue mountains, each paler than the last until the final ranks were indistinguishable from the sky. It was if all the world might be composed of nothing but valley and ridge. . . . Swimmer had looked out at the land forms and said he believed Cold Mountain to be the chief mountain of the world. Inman asked how he knew that to be true, and Swimmer had swept his hand across the horizon to where Cold Mountain stood and said, Do you see a bigger'n?

Indeed, at 6,030 feet, Cold Mountain towers high above most of the neighboring Great Smoky Mountains. From Asheville, visitors can take the Blue Ridge Parkway west and see the mountain exactly as it looks on the book cover, rising up at sunset in a blue mist that lends it the quality of an Impressionist painting. The movie version of *Cold Mountain* will likely be shot in the area; director Anthony Minghella of *English Patient* fame is set to direct.

Near Asheville, twenty-six miles to the southeast, is the equally lovely East Flat Rock-Hendersonville area. Connemara, the early nineteenth-century home of two-time Pulitzer Prize–winner Carl Sandburg, is just outside Flat Rock. The 245-acre estate, named for the mountainous region in western Ireland, was Sandburg's home for much of his life, and he died here in 1990. The Sandburgs raised goats, and the goats remain—not unlike Hemingway's cats in Key West. More than 100,000 people visit

Connemara each year, and about half actually tour the house; the remainder content themselves with the grounds and an occasional goatly nudge.

Those who do venture inside will see Sandburg's personal library of more than 10,000 books, with stacks of yellowing newspapers and correspondence lying just where he left them when he died in 1967.

LITERARY LURES AND SOUTHERN SIGHTS

Asheville Area Chamber of Commerce and Visitors Center, 151 Haywood Street; (828) 258–6101 or (888) 247–9811; www.ashevillechamber.org. Open 8:30 A.M. to 5:30 P.M. weekdays, 9 A.M. to 5 P.M. weekends.

Captain's Bookshelf, 31 Page Avenue, Asheville; (828) 253–6631.

Chimney Rock Park, twenty-five miles southeast of Asheville; U.S. Highway 64-74; (828) 625–9611. Ticket office hours are 8:30 A.M. to 5:30 P.M., Memorial Day through Labor Day; 8:30 A.M. to 4:30 P.M., the rest of the year. This stunningly beautiful park, with lush meadows, looming mountains, and sparkling falls, was the site for the filming of *The Last of the Mohicans*, starring Daniel Day-Lewis. The buckskin-fringed duds worn by Day-Lewis as Natty Bumpo are on display, protected behind glass, in the Chimney Rock Park gift shop at the base of Chimney Rock. You'll ride in an elevator *inside* the mountain to get this far; any higher, and your own feet will have to take you.

Downtown Books and News, 67 N. Lexington Avenue, Asheville; (828) 253–8654.

Flat Rock Playhouse, Interstate 26, in Flat Rock; (828) 693–0731. Opened in 1952, this is the home of the North Carolina State Theater. The popular Vagabond Players present *The World of Carl Sandburg* annually on the grounds of Connemara.

Henderson County Travel and Tourism, 201 S. Main Street, Hendersonville; (828) 693–9708 or (800) 828–4244; www.historichendersonville.org.

Lake Lure Visitors Bureau, Lake Lure; (828) 625–2725. Twenty-seven miles long, this lake is where much of the movie *Dirty Dancing* was filmed. Lake Lure was also where Jack and Shyla McCall *didn't* spend their honeymoon in Pat Conroy's *Beach Music*, although that's what they told everyone when they eloped.

Malaprop's Bookstore-Cafe, 55 Haywood Street, Asheville; (828) 254–6734. Bookstore and coffee shop carrying local faves, such as

A display case at Chimney Rock Park contains the costume Daniel Day-Lewis wore in *The Last of the Mohicans*, which was filmed in the North Carolina park.

Thomas Wolfe, and contemporary Ashevillian authors, such as Gail Godwin.

Monument Corner, southeast corner of Pack Square, Asheville. The corner where W. O. Wolfe, Thomas Wolfe's father, had his stonecutting and tombstone shop. During the 1920s, real estate developer B. Jackson bought the property from Julia Westall Wolfe and built Asheville's first skyscraper, the Jackson Building, on the site. It opened in 1924.

Pack Memorial Public Library, 67 Haywood Street, Pack Square, Asheville; (828) 255-5203. The Thomas Wolfe Memorial Angel, donated by the

Lake Lure, visible in the distance from the top of Chimney Rock, stood in for an upstate New York resort in *Dirty Dancing*.

local chapter of the Daughters of the Confederacy, stands in front of the library, just doors away from the site of W. O. Wolfe's former stonecutting shop. The inscription beneath the bronze angel reads, "Whereon the pillars of this earth are founded, toward which the conscience of the world is tending—a wind is rising and the rivers flow," a quote from *You Can't Go Home Again*. The library that once banned Wolfe's works now holds an entire Thomas Wolfe Collection.

T. S. Morrison, "An Emporium of Useful Items," 39 N. Lexington Street; (828) 258–1891. Asheville's oldest store, it was around when the Wolfes lived here.

Oakdale Cemetery, U.S. Highway 74, Hendersonville; (828) 693–9708. The original angel statue from Wolfe's *Look Homeward, Angel* decorates a grave in this cemetery.

Riverside Cemetery, Pearson Drive at Birch Street, Asheville; (828) 258–8480. Open 8 A.M. to 6 P.M. November through March, 8 A.M. to 8 P.M. April through October. Office open 8 A.M. to 4:30 P.M. weekdays. The office has a brochure directing visitors to the grave sites of Thomas Wolfe and O. Henry.

Monument Corner, a memorial to the stonecutting
shop run by Thomas Wolfe's father in Asheville.

Carl Sandburg Home National Historic Site, Connemara, 1928 Little
River Road, Flat Rock; (828) 693–4178. Admission is free. Sandburg,
one of the great poets and authors of American history, spent his last
twenty-two years at Connemara, just outside Flat Rock. At the on-site
bookstore, you can buy Sandburg's works as well as books about one of
his favorite subjects, goats. One suspects he would have approved.

Thomas Wolfe Memorial, 52 Market Street; (828) 253–8304; www.home.
att.net/~WolfeMemorial/. Visitors center and museum, adjacent to the
home at 48 Spruce Street that was fictionalized as Dixieland in *Look
Homeward, Angel*. Admission fee. Sponsors the annual Thomas Wolfe

Festival, a four-day event built around his birthday on October 3. The festival highlights Wolfe's life and times with workshops, writing contests, tours, and theatrical presentations. The former boardinghouse was damaged by arson in 1998; renovations were still under way at this writing. The visitors center, which has an excellent exhibit on Wolfe and many artifacts, will remain open during renovations.

Wildacres Writers Workshop, in the Blue Ridge Mountains, about fifty miles northeast of Asheville; (800) 635–2049; www.wildacres.com. This annual May retreat takes place near Little Switzerland.

ACCOMMODATIONS AND RESTAURANTS

Abbington Green Bed-and-Breakfast Inn, 46 Cumberland Circle, Asheville; (828) 251–2454 or (800) 251–2454. Colonial Revival home built in 1908, in the heart of the historic district.

Acorn Cottage Bed-and-Breakfast, 25 St. Dunstons Circle, Asheville; (828) 253–0609 or (800) 699–0609. Arts and Crafts period home, circa 1922.

Albemarle Inn, 86 Edgemon Road, Asheville; (828) 225–0027 or (800) 621–7435; www.albemarleinn.com. Greek Revival mansion in a quiet residential area.

Asheville Bed and Breakfast Association; (828) 250–0200.

The Bier Garden, 46 Haywood Street, Asheville; (828) 285–0002.

Black Walnut Bed-and-Breakfast Inn, 288 Montford Avenue, Asheville; (828) 254–3878 or (800) 381–3878. Built in 1899 and restored in 1922.

Blue Moon Bakery, 60 Biltmore Avenue, Asheville; (828) 252–6063.

Cafe on the Square, One Biltmore Avenue, Asheville; (828) 251–5565.

Cairn Brae Mountain Retreat, 217 Patton Mountain Road, Asheville; (828) 252–9219. Tucked on a rocky hillside for which it's named, only minutes from downtown, but it gives a true mountain-hideaway experience.

Carolina Bed-and-Breakfast, 177 Cumberland Avenue, Asheville; (828) 254–3608 or (888) 254–3608.

Carolina Mornings Unique Accommodations; (800) 770–9055; www.carolinamornings.com. Bed-and-breakfasts, cabins, inns, and other accommodations in Asheville and western North Carolina.

Cedar Crest Victorian Inn, 674 Biltmore Avenue, Asheville; (828) 252–1389 or (800) 252–0310; www.CedarCrestVictorianInn.com. An 1890 Queen Anne delight.

The Claddagh Inn, 755 N. Main Street, Hendersonville; (828) 697–7778 or (800) 225–4700; www.CladdaghInn.com.

Depot Restaurant, 30 Lodge Street; (828) 277–7651. Casual dining in a restored 1896 railway station.

Dogwood Inn Bed-and-Breakfast, Highway 64-74A, Chinmey Rock; (828) 625–4403 or (800) 992–5557. An 1890s inn tucked in the Hickory Nut Gorge, on the banks of crystalline Rocky Broad River.

Flat Rock Inn Bed-and-Breakfast, 2810 Greenville Highway, Flat Rock; (828) 696–3273 or (800) 266–3996. Located on the National Register, this 1888 inn is near the Carl Sandburg home and Hendersonville.

The Grove Park Inn Resort, 290 Macon Avenue; (828) 252–2711 or (800) 438–5800; www.groveparkinn.com. Incredibly gorgeous setting, superb service, and you can sleep with the literary lions—according to your tastes in literature. Pick a room once occupied by F. Scott Fitzgerald (Main Inn 441 and 443), Charles Frazier (Main Inn 360, pre–*Cold Mountain*, right by the noisy Coke and ice machines; Sammons Wing 8037, post–*Cold Mountain*, no ice machine in sight), Sir Anthony Hopkins (Sammons 6041) or perhaps President Franklin Roosevelt (Main Inn 221) or singer John Denver (Vanderbilt Wing 5064). More than 500 rooms, including twelve suites. If you crave historic ambience, ask for a room in the Main Inn; otherwise, you can hobnob with contemporary celebrities in the lusher, more private Vanderbilt and Sammons Wings. Six on-site eating areas, including the elegant Horizons, the Blue Ridge Dining Room, and the spectacular outdoor Sunset Terrace.

Lake Lure Inn, 2771 Memorial Highway, Lake Lure; (828) 625–2525. Historic fifty-room inn nestled between the lake and the mountains. Great dining in the on-site Roosevelt Room.

The Lodge on Lake Lure, 361 Charlotte Drive, Lake Lure; (828) 625–2789 or (800) 733–2785. At the foot of Rumbling Bald Mountain on the lake. You'll expect Jennifer Grey and Patrick Swayze to stroll by any minute in a scene right out of *Dirty Dancing*—which, by the way, was almost entirely filmed nearby.

Melange Bed-and-Breakfast, 1230 Fifth Avenue West, Hendersonville; (828) 697–5253 or (800) 303–5253; www.circle.net/~melange. European-style bed-and-breakast with three rooms and a honeymoon suite.

Mountain Home Bed-and-Breakfast, 10 Courtland Boulevard, Mountain Home (between Asheville and Hendersonville); (828) 697–9090 or (800) 397–0066.

Mountain Smoke House, 20 S. Spruce Street, Asheville; (828) 253–4871. Great barbecue, mountain and bluegrass music, and clog dancers.

Old Teneriffe Inn, 2531 Little River Road, Hendersonville; (828) 698–8178 or (800) 617–6427. Circa-1850 Tudor mansion.

Owls Nest Inn at Engadine, 2630 Smokey Park Highway, Candler (just outside Asheville); (828) 665–8325 or (800) 665–8868; www.circle.net/owlsnest. A rustic mountain getaway, built in 1885.

Possum Trot Grill, Eight Wall Street, Asheville; (828) 254–0062.

Richmond Hill Inn, 87 Richmond Hill Drive, Asheville; (828) 252–7313 or (800) 545–9238; www.richmondhillinn.com. Circa-1899 mansion with rooms named for Thomas Wolfe, O. Henry, and F. Scott Fitzgerald. Scrumptious on-site dining at Gabrielle's or the Arbor Grille.

The Swag, 2300 Swag Road, Waynesville; (828) 926–0430. If you want to sleep in the shadow of Cold Mountain, this old-time retreat in the mist-curtained Smokies is the place. A sixteen-room lodge cobbled together from Appalachian log structures, homey and cozy.

23 Page Restaurant and the New French Bar, One Battery Park Avenue; (828) 252–3685.

Uptown Cafe, 22 Battery Park Avenue, Asheville; (828) 253–2158.

Waverly Inn, 783 N. Main Street, Hendersonville; (828) 693–9193 or (800) 537–8195; www.waverlyinn.com. The oldest inn in Hendersonville, a circa-1898 Victorian confection.

Wright Inn and Carriage House, 235 Pearson Drive, Asheville; (828) 251–0789 or (800) 552–5724; www.wrightinn.com.

Blowing Rock

Blowing Rock, a tiny hamlet northeast of Asheville, cradled beneath Grandfather Mountain about ten miles from the Tennessee border, will be familiar to millions of readers as the real-life counterpart for Mitford, the setting for Jan Karon's phenomenally successful five-book series starring Father Tim et al.

In the first book, *At Home in Mitford*, Karon describes the setting:

> The village of Mitford was set snugly into what would be called, in the west, a hanging valley. That is, the mountains rose steeply on either side, and then sloped into a hollow between the ridges,

rather like a cake that falls in the middle from too much opening of the oven door.

According to a walking parishioner of Lord's Chapel, Mitford's business district was precisely 342 paces from one end to the other. . . . Visitors who walked the two-block stretch of the main business district were always surprised to find the shops spaced so far apart, owing to the garden plots that flourished between the buildings. In the loamy, neatly edged beds were wooden signs:

- Garden courtesy of Joe's Barber Shop, upstairs to right
- Take Time to Smell the Roses, courtesy Oxford Antiques
- A Reader's Garden, courtesy Happy Endings Bookstore.

Karon, a native of the area, moved back from Raleigh in the mid-1990s after a successful career in advertising, and set about transforming the summer resort of Blowing Rock (population 1,500 in winter, 5,000 in summer) into her bucolic little town of Mitford. Karon was born in nearby Lenoir and raised by her grandparents in a rural spot a few miles outside of town. Her advertising days sometimes amusingly sneak their way into the Mitford series; readers, for instance, know livermush is one of the favored menu items at the town's Main Street Grill. Karon once wrote ad copy for Neese's Livermush, a North Carolina specialty. Visitors can munch on a livermush sandwich—it's sort of the Carolina version of Spam, a gloppy mixture of pork liver, cornmeal, and spices that's actually quite tasty—at Sonny's Grill in downtown Blowing Rock.

In an April 1999 interview with the *Atlanta Journal-Constitution*, Karon explained to a group of Atlanta fans that she wrote her first novel at age ten.

I wrote it on Blue Horse notebook paper. Do y'all remember Blue Horse notebook paper? I wrote this novel and it was very bad. It was set in the South. It had a house just like Tara and women with 14-inch waists. My sister found that book in my vanity. I though it was private. We lived with our grandmother, and Brenda came running in, "Mama, Mama, Janice wrote a book and it's got 'damn' in it!" The *Journal-Constitution* notes that Karon dragged the word out into two syllables, "Day-um!"

Her grandmother's response? "Go get me a switch." That's why, Karon says, "You won't find any cussing in my books today."

The Mitford series—*At Home in Mitford; A Light in the Window; These High, Green Hills; Out to Canaan;* and *A New Song*—began courtesy of the *Blowing Rocket*, the town's weekly newspaper. Editor Jerry Burns serialized the first book, paying Karon with a free copy of the ten-cent paper every week. He told the Atlanta paper:

> When people missed their papers, they got mad. It wasn't that they wanted the news. They wanted to know what happened to Father Tim and Cynthia and Barnabas and Dooley. Our circulation increased significantly—by 300 or 400. Another problem was, after the sixth or eighth week, we ran out of old copies for people who had just started it and wanted to catch up.

That little serialized novel has become an industry. Karon writes an Internet newsletter called *More From Mitford*, answering questions from readers about both Mitford and Blowing Rock. The town post office doesn't have home delivery, so Karon treks down daily to pick up the ever-growing bundles of fan mail. She's talking to TV executives about a series based on the books, and in July 1999 Hallmark was slated to launch a Mitford-inspired line of cards and gifts.

Karon told the Atlanta paper that, despite its association with Blowing Rock, Mitford is a state of mind, not place.

> You don't go to Blowing Rock or any small town and get Mitford. Here's what makes Mitford: You go to a community and start giving. You've got to participate. Mitford is an active verb. You've got to visit the nursing home, stop to speak to somebody on the street, pray for somebody you don't like—that's a good one—and brag on your kids. Mitford can happen in the middle of Manhattan. It can happen in Atlanta.

She told me much the same in a 1998 interview for this book. "I was born at the foot of the mountain on which I now live, and the spirit of this little town informed my books," Karon said. "These characters very much spring from this soil. But every place has that spirit, and I just drew on that. Mitford, the mythical Mitford, the Mitford where we all want to live, is my main character."

LITERARY LURES AND SOUTHERN SIGHTS

Appalachian Heritage Museum, 129 Mystery Hill Lane; (828) 264–2792. A living museum built in 1903.

Blowing Rock Chamber of Commerce, 1038 Main Street; (828) 295–7851 or (800) 295–7851; www.blowingrock.com.

Grandfather Mountain Visitors Center, 2050 Blowing Rock Highway, Linville; (828) 733–2013 or (800) 468–7325; www.grandfather.com.

Hemingway's Book and Gift Shop, 1203 S. Main Street; (828) 295–0666.

More From Mitford, newsletter about Mitford, Blowing Rock, and related interests; www.penguinputnam.com/mitford. Here you can get such yummy tidbits as the recipe for Esther's Orange-Marmalade Layer Cake.

ACCOMMODATIONS AND RESTAURANTS

Artist's Palate Restaurant, 711 Main Street; (828) 295–4300.

Azalea Garden Inn, 793 Main Street; (828) 295–3272.

Blowing Rock Cabins, 8332 Valley Boulevard; (828) 295–4272.

Blowing Rock Cafe, 349 Sunset Drive; (828) 295–9474.

Blowing Rock Inn, 788 Main Street; (828) 295–7921.

Brookside Inn, 7876 Valley Boulevard; (828) 295–3380.

Cliff Dwellers Inn, 116 Lakeview Drive; (828) 295–3121.

Crippen's Country Inn and Restaurant, 239 Sunset Drive; (828) 295–3487.

Dockside Ira's, 1143 Wonderland Trail; (828) 295–4008.

Gideon Ridge Inn, 202 Gideon Ridge Road; (828) 295–3644.

Green Park Inn, 9239 Valley Boulevard; (828) 295–3141.

Hemlock Inn and Suites, 134 Morris Street; (828) 295–7987.

The Inn at Ragged Gardens, 203 Sunset Drive; (828) 295–9703; www.ragged-gardens.com. In the quiet heart of the village.

Maple Lodge, 152 Sunset Drive; (828) 295–3331; www.maplelodge.net. An eleven-room historic lodge just a mile from the Blue Ridge Parkway.

Sonny's Grill, 1119 Main Street, (828) 295–7577. Livermush for everyone!

Rocky Mount

This northeastern North Carolina town is the birthplace and home of young writer Kaye Gibbons, and the surrounding Nash County area is the setting for many of her autobiographical novels. In *Sights Unseen* (1995), a riveting chronicle of the manic depression that Gibbons herself suffers from, she writes:

> My father was a gentleman farmer. Had we lived in town, my family would have owned the hardware store, the drugstore, the car dealership, an apartment building or two, and possibly a small department store. Had this been the mid-nineteenth century instead of the twentieth, our farm would have been called a plantation; the house, the Big House; the tenant farmers, slaves; and my mother, a classic nervous matriarch who suffered spells.

Despite the characters' similarities to her family, however, Gibbons, born in 1961, hardly had a plantation upbringing, or anything close to one. She grew up dirt poor in a four-room frame house where her mother committed suicide (Gibbons was ten at the time) and her father drank himself to death. After her parents' deaths, she was shuttled from foster home to foster home, a painful odyssey she wrote about in *Ellen Foster*. But Gibbons has never strayed far from home, attending North Carolina State University and University of North Carolina-Chapel Hill, and now living in Rocky Mount again with her second husband and their five children.

Gibbons's other books include *A Virtuous Woman, A Cure for Dreams, Charms for the Easy Life,* and *On the Occasion of My Last Afternoon,* the last a marvelously gritty Civil War story that Gibbons wrote under a cloud of manic-depressive energy. She deleted the first draft, all nine hundred pages, when she couldn't make it hang together, she told *Book* magazine in 1999, and then wrote a tighter, superior version in a burst of unhealthy productivity, once working sixty hours straight.

The 1928 mansion Gibbons and her husband, Raleigh attorney Frank Ward, now call home is "exactly where I want to be," she told Y'all.com in an early 1999 interview.

It's hard to go from living a hardscrabble life on Bend of the River Road to being on this street. It's a long way. When I was a child, it was very important that I grow up and live in a brick house because when I was a child, the children who lived in brick houses had responsible parents who didn't drink. They won the spelling bee, and they had nice lunchboxes—all those brick-house amenities. It was important when I grew up to live in a brick house.

Rocky Mount was also the home of fellow novelist Allan Gurganus, who, like Gibbons, graduated from Rocky Mount High School. "The odds of two novelists being from Rocky Mount are pretty slim," the author of *Oldest Living Confederate Widow Tells All* told Y'all.com. "Maybe it's something in the drinking water, or our appetite for revenge that pulled us out of there."

In a 1998 interview for this book, Gurganus said he grew up "taking Sunday drives where we'd drive around to amuse ourselves, riding past these houses that had been burned out and were just chimneys and shells. It was only ninety years after the Civil War, and Sherman's march was as close as yesterday to us." A pivotal scene in *Oldest Living Confederate Widow Tells All*, in which a piano falls through three floors of a ruined plantation, was hatched on those long-ago drives, Gurganus said. "People are amazed it took me seven years to write that book," he said with a laugh. "But I was really forty-five years writing it."

The sense of place and character, he said, are intrinsically joined and "essential to all Southern writing . . . the transformation of something mundane into something magical, all these middle-class people in middle-class towns keeping secrets better than anyone you've ever known."

LITERARY LURES AND SOUTHERN SIGHTS

Book Shoppe, 3006 Sunset Avenue; (252) 443–2808.

Lemstone Books, 1100 N. Wesleyan Boulevard, No. 198; (252) 977–6061.

Nash County-Rocky Mount Travel and Tourism, 116 S. Franklin Street; (252) 446–0323; www.rockymountchamber.org.

ACCOMMODATIONS AND RESTAURANTS

Acheson's Family Buffet, 2636 Sunset Avenue; (252) 443–3515.

Carleton House, 213 N. Church Street; (252) 977–6576.

Carolina Inn, 4350 S. Church Street; (252) 977–3661.

Bob Melton's Barbecue, 501 Old Mill Road; (252) 446–8513. The oldest sit-down barbecue restaurant in the state, with a wonderful view of the Tar River.

Sunset Inn Bed-and-Breakfast, 1210 Sunset Avenue; (252) 446–9524 or (800) SUNSET–N. Circa-1920 Georgian-style mansion with big bedrooms and Victorian family antiques.

Tarrytown Grill, 3612 Woodlawn Road; (252) 937–4745.

Thomas Street Seafood and Grill, 421 W. Thomas Street; (252) 442–9113.

Walnut Restaurant, 705 Walnut Street; (252) 446–0877.

Raleigh, Durham, and Chapel Hill

They call this the Research Triangle because of the world-renowned hospitals it contains, but it might as well be called the Literary Triangle—this area probably contains more published authors per capita than any other site in the United States, with the possible exception of New Orleans or Manhattan.

Raleigh-Durham is the home of Duke University, which, along with University of North Carolina-Chapel Hill, has scooped up most of the Southern crop of writers and teachers. Among those on staff here: the inimitable, priceless Reynolds Price.

The area also produced Clyde Edgerton, who was born in nearby Bethesda. Edgerton, author of the hilarious *Raney* and *Walking Across Egypt*, attended University of North Carolina-Chapel Hill. In *Raney*, Edgerton, like Reynolds Price, eerily manages to write in the unmistakable voice of a Southern woman. In this passage, he describes Raney's wedding night with Charles, a most suspicious type—a "liberal from Atlanta":

> Now, the honeymoon. I do not have the nerve to explain everything that happened on the first night there in the Holiday Inn.

We had talked about it some before—or Charles had talked about it. And we had, you know, necked the same as any engaged couple. And I had told Charles way back, of course, that I wanted my marriage consumed *after* I was married, not before.

One must assume Raney meant *consummated* rather than *consumed* . . . but on the other hand, maybe she meant exactly what she said. You can never be 100 percent sure with Southerners.

As for Chapel Hill, if you want to hit literary pay dirt, just set foot on this city's University of North Carolina campus, whose English faculty boasts some of the state's best talents—Lee Smith, Doris Betts, the list goes on and on. Among those who've attended UNC are Mississippi writer Shelby Foote, who talked his way in despite youthful insurgency that caused his high school principal to send a letter urging UNC not to admit him.

Asheville native Thomas Wolfe also was a UNC graduate. In *Look Homeward, Angel,* Wolfe, through the eyes of young Eugene Gant, describes UNC on graduation day:

> The college was charming, half-deserted. Most of the students, except the graduating class, had departed. The air was charged with the fresh sensual heat, the deep green shimmer of heavy foliage, a thousand spermy earth and flower-scents. The young men were touched with sadness, with groping excitement, with glory. . . . Eugene's face grew dark with pride and joy there in the lovely wilderness. He could not speak. There was a glory in the world: life was panting for his embrace.

Reynolds Price, author of the National Book Award–winner *Kate Vaiden,* as well as *Roxanna Slade, The Promise of Rest,* and more than two dozen other novels and books of poetry. He was born in the North Carolina hamlet of Macon, northeast of the Research Triangle near the Virginia border, and Macon-Warrenton and the Roanoke River provide the setting for many of his books.

With typical bluntness, he goes to the heart of Macon's character in *Roxanna Slade:*

In the kind of town where I grew up, few distinctions were made on account of money unless you were outright redheaded trash.

Truth was, you were either white or black. In those days we said colored if we meant to be courteous and not hurt people, and the color of your skin pretty much said all there was to say. The Bible forbade calling anybody common ... so even if they were the sorriest white skin ever conceived, the worst you could call them was ordinary.

LITERARY LURES AND SOUTHERN SIGHTS

Raleigh

Books at Stonehenge, 7414 Creedmore Road, Stonehenge Market; (919) 846–1404.

Greater Raleigh Convention and Visitors Bureau, 421 Fayetteville Street Mall, Suite 1505; (919) 834–5900 or (800) 849–8499; www.raleighcvb.org.

Quail Ridge Books, 3522 Wade Avenue, Ridgewood Shopping Center; (919) 828–1588.

State Library of North Carolina, 109 W. Jones Street; (919) 733–2570.

Durham

The Book Exchange, 107 W. Chapel Hill Street; (919) 682–4662. Terrific for hard-to-find books and out-of-print selections, especially those by university presses.

Duke University; (919) 684–8111; www.duke.edu. One of the most beautiful university campuses in the nation. Duke hosts an annual Writers Workshop on its west campus; (919) 684–5375. Held early in June every year since 1980, this exceptional writers' retreat welcomes both beginning and experienced writers, with teachers drawn primarily from North Carolina campuses (and their teachers, as noted, are no slouches).

Durham Convention and Visitors Bureau, 101 E. Morgan Street; (919) 687–0288 or (800) 446–8604; www.dcvb.durham.nc.us.

The Regulator Bookshop, 720 Ninth Street; (919) 286–2700.

Chapel Hill

Chapel Hill-Orange County Visitors Bureau, 501 W. Franklin Avenue; (888) 968–2060; www.chocvb.org.

University of North Carolina-Chapel Hill, Visitors Center at Morehead Planetarium, East Franklin Street; (919) 962–2211; www.unc.edu. The first state university in America, with a cornerstone laid on October 12, 1793. Hosts the annual North Carolina Literary Festival in April; www.sunsite.unc.edu/litfest/. More than 100 authors attend, with previous guests including John Grisham, Allan Gurganus, Annie Dillard, Elizabeth Forsythe Hailey, Clyde Edgerton, Doris Betts, Lee Smith, Ellen Douglas, Tony Horwitz, and dozens of others whose names you'd recognize.

Warrenton-Macon-Henderson

Henderson Book Company, 127 S. Garnett Street; (252) 438–3614. In Reynold Price's *Kate Vaiden*, the book-loving heroine laments that she'd have to go all the way to Henderson to find a newsstand or bookstore. She wasn't kidding.

ACCOMMODATIONS AND RESTAURANTS

Raleigh

401 Seafood Restaurant, 7735 Fayetteville Road; (919) 772–9409.

The Oakwood Inn Bed-and-Breakfast, 411 N. Bloodworth Street; (919) 832–9712 or (800) 267–9712; www.members.aol.com/oakwoodbb/. Nestled in the historic Oakwood District, rich with tree-lined lanes and restored homes.

The William Thomas House Bed and Breakfast, 530 N. Blount Street; (919) 755–9400 or (800) OLDE–INN; www.ntwrks.com/~wmthomasb+b. A Raleigh Historic Landmark, circa 1881.

Durham

Anotherthyme, 109 N. Gregson Street; (919) 682–5225. Vegetarian and seafood restaurant, casual and quite popular. Live jazz on Thursdays and Saturdays.

Arrowhead Inn Bed and Breakfast, 106 Mason Road; (919) 477–8430 or (800) 528–2207. Circa-1775 inn on four acres, with accommodations in the manor house, carriage house, and a two-room cabin.

Blooming Garden Inn, 513 Holloway Street; (919) 687–0801. Circa-1892 Queen Anne–style home in historic downtown.

Old North Durham Inn, 922 N. Mangum Street; (919) 683–1885; www.bbonline.com/nc/oldnorth. Early 1900s Colonial Revival home in a residential neighborhood.

Washington Duke Inn and Golf Club, 3001 Cameron Boulevard; (919) 490–0999 or (800) 443–3853. Grand four-star hotel on the Duke campus.

Chapel Hill

Carolina Inn, 211 Pittsboro Street; (919) 933–2001 or (800) 962–8519. Owned and operated by the University of North Carolina, this is a historic 1924 Colonial-style inn on the university campus, a block from the center of town.

Crook's Corner, 610 W. Franklin Street; (919) 929–7643. Excellent Southern fare lurking behind a funky facade.

Fearrington House Inn, 2000 Fearrington Village Center, Pittsboro; (919) 542–2121. Ten minutes south of Chapel Hill, this is a wonderful character-filled inn on sixty acres of beautifully landscaped grounds.

The Inn at Bingham School, 6720 Mebane Oaks Road; (919) 563–5583 or (800) 566–5583. Set on ten acres, this interesting inn is a combination of Greek and Federal styles.

Restaurant La Residence, 222 W. Rosemary Street; (919) 967–2506. Continental cuisine in a charming mid-twentieth-century house.

The Village Bed and Breakfast, 401 Parkside Circle; (919) 968–9984. Just a mile from UNC in Southern Village.

Warrenton-Macon-Henderson

Ann's Kountry Kitchen, Norlina Road, Warrenton; (252) 257–1180.

Burnside Plantation, 960 Burnside Road, Henderson; (252) 438–7688.

The Ivy Bed-and-Breakfast, 331 N. Main Street, Warrenton; (252) 257–9300 or (800) 919–9886.

Warren Restaurant, 139 S. Main Street, Warrenton; (252) 257–1306.

7

South Carolina

*Let me tell you the tale of Adams Run and how this Low Country
hamlet got its name. Some fool with a funny sense of geography
once mistook neighboring Edisto Island for the Garden of Eden—
and if you've ever seen its vine-tangled thickets and sweetgrass
marshes, you'll agree that's not such a stretch. So, naturally, when
Adam was cast out of paradise, he fled up the road to Charleston
and passed through here on the way. Hence, the biblical allusion.*

*I think of this yarn, handed down by one of my elderly Edisto
cousins, every spring when I return to ancestral haunts in the Low
Country, which stretches some 190 miles along the South Carolina
coast, roughly between Pawleys Island and the Savannah River. I
say roughly because it's difficult to define the area on a map. You'll
capture the Low Country's soul only after running barefoot down a
dock to watch a shrimp boat gliding out on the tide, riggers and
nets extended like a belle lifting her skirt out of the pluff mud. Or
while wandering through Charleston's back alleys, where the heady
fragrance of jasmine, as one of my great-aunts used to drawl, "is
like to make you swoon."*

—Shane Mitchell, *Travel and Leisure* magazine

*W*riters love extremes, and they're found in startling abundance in South Carolina—from the soul-numbing, energy-draining heat of summer, when you never really feel *dry* for more than a minute at a time, to the calculated chill that still overtakes a Charlestonian's heart when encountering even a hint of sympathy for the Yankees in "the War." You know the one, the only one that counts. The one that began at Fort Sumter, in Charleston Harbor, and has haunted this city ever since.

The Civil War damaged Charleston almost incalculably, turning it from an antebellum jewel box to a beaten-down, poverty-ridden embarrassment whose deflated residents responded to the war's ravages by encircling what was left of the city with a wall. Charleston remained walled off from the outside, licking its wounds from within, for more than a century after the Civil War ended.

Things got better, culminating in a renaissance of tourism and restoration in the early 1980s, with buildings once considered merely old and shabby refurbished and honored as historic treasures. But less than a decade later, a disaster even deadlier than General Sherman hit the city; this time its name was Hugo, and its winds blew in at more than 130 mph, causing a storm tide more than ten feet high. The September 1989 hurricane, the worst to hit the region in thirty-five years, engulfed historic Charleston and caused $7.1 billion in damages in the Carolinas alone.

But Hurricane Hugo had a silver lining: The insurance money helped rebuild and restore many of the historic buildings that had been languishing for centuries.

Literary Lures and Southern Sights

South Carolina Division of Tourism; (803) 734–1700 or (800) 734–0133; www.travelsc.com.

Accommodations and Restaurants

South Carolina Bed-and-Breakfast Association; (888) 599–1234; www.bbon line.com/sc/scbba.

Charleston, Beaufort, and The Low Country

In *Gone With the Wind*, a disillusioned Rhett tells Scarlett he's going back to his hometown of Charleston, "where there is still a little grace and charm left in the world." More than sixty years after Margaret Mitchell wrote those words, and a century and a half after Mr. Butler spoke them, that description still holds true.

Civility and concern for one's fellow travelers are paramount here, with courtesy something of a competitive sport. At our bed-and-breakfast, my friend and I were oh-so-graciously counseled by our hostess to make sure we were *very*, *very* quiet when coming in late at night—that'd be anytime after dark—so as not to disturb the other guests, who might be sleeping. We fully expected to see her don hoop skirts and start passing out mint juleps at any moment, and she actually hung up my clothes when we went outside to park the car.

Rhett begins and remains a scoundrel to the end, as described by Scarlett's sister in *Gone With the Wind*: "Oh, Scarlett, he has the most terrible

Charleston, the city to which Rhett Butler retreats at the end of *Gone With the Wind*, trying to regain a little of its "grace and charm."

Captaining his boat out of Charleston Harbor, Rhett Butler becomes one of the Confederacy's most successful gunrunners in *Gone With the Wind*.

reputation. His name is Rhett Butler and he's from Charleston and his folks are some of the finest people there, but they won't even speak to him." Maybe his parents never forgave him—but the ladies of Charleston did, at least in Margaret Mitchell's world, as the cynical Captain Butler became one of the Confederacy's most productive gunrunners.

"Everyone knew now that the fate of the Confederacy rested as much upon the skill of the blockade boats in eluding the Yankee fleet as it did upon the soldiers at the front," Mitchell writes in *Gone With the Wind*.

> Rumor had it that Captain Butler was one of the best pilots in the South and that he was reckless and utterly without nerves. Reared in Charleston, he knew every inlet, creek, shoal and rock of the Carolina coast near that port, and he was equally at home in the waters around Wilmington. He had never lost a boat or even been forced to dump a cargo. At the onset of the war, he had emerged from obscurity with enough money to buy a small swift boat and now, when blockaded goods realized two thousand percent on each cargo, he owned four boats.

He had good pilots and paid them well, and they slid out of Charleston and Wilmington on dark nights, bearing cotton for Nassau, England and Canada. The cotton mills of England were standing idle and the workers were starving, and any blockader who could outwit the Yankee fleet could command his own price in Liverpool. Rhett's boats were singularly lucky both in taking out cotton for the Confederacy and bringing in the war materials for which the South was desperate. Yes, the ladies felt they could forgive and forget a great many things for such a great man.

At least one Charleston institution has paid tribute to the *Gone With the Wind* connection, with drinks called the Gone With the Wind, a hardy confection of Southern Comfort, pineapple and orange juice, ginger ale, grenadine, and lime; the Scarlett O'Hara, with nectar de cassis, vodka, and lime; and the Frankly My Dear, I Don't Give a Damn, with Pusser's rum, peach schnapps, orange juice, grenadine, angostura bitters, and fresh lime. Yummy, all . . . just don't try more than one at a time.

Edgar Allan Poe visited Charleston several times and was apparently fascinated by the barrier islands; he set his 1843 *The Gold Bug* on Sullivans Island, the site of Fort Sumter National Monument. Poe, under the alias Edgar A. Perry, enlisted in the army at age eighteen, and his unit was sent to Fort Moultrie, where the monument is located. Fort Moultrie's active military history spans the years from the Revolutionary War to World War II.

Poe, who spent thirteen months on the island, described it thus: "This island is a very singular one. It consists of little else than sea sand, and is about three miles long. . . . It is separated from the mainland by a scarcely perceptible creek, oozing its way through a wilderness of reeds and slime, a favorite resort of the marsh-hen."

In true Poe fashion, he also concocted a shudder-inducing mystery for the place, built around still-pervasive rumors of buried pirate treasure.

> What are we to make of the skeletons found in the hole? This is a question I am no more able to answer than yourself. There seems, however, only one plausible way of accounting for them— and yet it is dreadful to believe in such atrocity as my suggestion would imply. It is clear that Kidd—if Kidd indeed secreted this

treasure, which I doubt not—it is clear that he must have had assistance in the labor. But this labor concluded, he may have thought it expedient to remove all participants in his secret. Perhaps a couple of blows with a mattock were sufficient, while his coadjutors were busy in the pit; perhaps it required a dozen—who shall tell?

In the wonderful book *Charleston: A Lowcountry Reader*, short story writer Harlan Greene describes the city's knotted-up relationship with history. In *Why He Never Danced the Charleston*, a story from that collection, he writes:

History haunted us all, especially those of us born in a sleepy old southern town that had Fort Sumter for a legacy. It rose up from our harbor to stain the sky. We could see it from our school in the mornings, red in the morning. We were used to it, the symbol of the city, its epitome. We'd stare at it in awe and reverence while we said our morning prayers, as if Sumter was the Olympus hovering over us. For God, we did not doubt, did dwell in Charleston; or the Lord of the lost cause did anyway. Savannah, we were taught, was not quite so bright a star in the constellation of southern cities. Charleston was the brightest.

For visitors from the north, Charleston's charms could never completely erase its past as the origin of a war that cost 600,000 American lives. "Filled as I am, in general, while there with the sadness and sorrow of the South," writes Henry James in *The American Scene*, "I never, at Charleston, look out at the old betrayed forts without feeling my heart harden again to steel."

Definitive South Carolinian Pat Conroy was actually born in Atlanta, in October 1945, but moved frequently due to his father's military career and eventually ended up in Charleston, where he enrolled at the Citadel. Conroy's *The Lords of Discipline* savagely relates his very unhappy days as a cadet there, and he made news in the mid-1990s with his public support of Shannon Faulkner, the first woman admitted to the military school. Faulkner won a court battle allowing her to attend the previously all-male school, but she dropped out after only a week on campus.

Horse-drawn carriages, palm trees, and lovingly preserved architecture make it easy to step back to Scarlett
O'Hara's time in Charleston.

Conroy's response: "They made sure that everyone in America saw
that that college hates women. They've made a blood sport of hating in
South Carolina."

After four very long years at the Citadel, Conroy moved to the Low
Country coastal town of Beaufort (pronounced *bew-fort*), where he taught
English, and has set all his books in this area—*The Water Is Wide*, *The
Prince of Tides*, *The Great Santini*, and *Beach Music*.

Conroy also taught underprivileged children in a one-room schoolhouse on Daufuskie Island near Hilton Head, and turned those experi-
ences into his first book, *The Water Is Wide*, in 1972. The island's

Cadets on parade at the Citadel, the setting for Pat Conroy's *Lords of Discipline*. (photo courtesy of the Charleston Area Convention and Visitors Bureau)

inhabitants, mostly the descendants of slaves, live on small farms among dilapidated churches, homes, and schools that have been deserted since antebellum times.

Dolphins can frequently be seen frolicking in the waters surrounding Beaufort—perhaps even Carolina Snow, the white dolphin Conroy tenderly describes in *The Prince of Tides*. In that same book, Conroy describes a typically stunning sunset in Beaufort, which he calls Colleton:

> The new gold of moon astonishing and ascendant, the depleted gold of sunset extinguishing itself in the long westward slide, it was the old dance of days in the Carolina marshes, the breathtaking death of days before the eyes of children, until the sun vanished, its final signature a ribbon of bullion strung across the tops of water oaks. The moon then rose quickly, rose like a bird from the water, from the trees, from the islands, and climbed straight-up, gold, then yellow, then pale yellow, pale silver, silverbright, then something miraculous, immaculate, and beyond silver, a color native only to southern nights.

The extent to which place determines personality is also explored by Conroy in *The Prince of Tides*:

> My wound is geography. It is also my anchorage, my port of call.
>
> To describe our growing up in the lowcountry of South Carolina, I would have to take you to the marsh on a spring day, flush the great blue heron from its silent occupation, scatter marsh hens as we sink to our knees in mud, open you an oyster with a pocketknife and feed it to you from the shell and say, "There. That taste. That's the taste of my childhood." I would say, "Breathe deeply," and you would breathe and remember that smell for the rest of your life, the bold, fecund aroma of the tidal marsh, exquisite and sensual, the smell of the South in heat, a smell like new milk, semen, and spilled wine, all perfumed with seawater.

In *Beach Music*, published in 1995, Conroy recalled his self-imposed exile from the South during the time he lived in Rome, Italy. His protagonist, Jack McCall, flees Waterford (another disguise for Beaufort) with his young daughter after his wife takes a suicidal dive off a Charleston bridge:

> And so in Rome we settled and began the long process of refusing to be Southern, even though my mother started a letter-writing campaign to coax me back home: "A Southerner in Rome? A low country boy in Italy? Ridiculous . . . You'll be back soon. The South's got a lot wrong with it. But it's permanent press and it doesn't wash out."
>
> Though my mother was onto something real, I stuck by my guns. I would tell American tourists who questioned me about my accent that I no longer checked the scores of the Atlanta Braves in the *Herald Tribune* and they could not get me to reread Faulkner or Miss Eudora at gunpoint. I did not realize or care that I was attempting to expunge all that was most authentic about me.

Jack even tries, overdoing it just a bit, to convince his daughter, Leah, that she'd *never* want to live in the horrid South. When Leah asks, "What's South Carolina like?" Jack responds:

Pat Conroy sets many of his works in the riverside town of Beaufort, South Carolina, where he spent much of his life.

Horrible. Very ugly and depressing to look at. It smells bad all the time and the ground's covered with rattlesnakes. It has laws making all children slaves from the time they're born until they're eighteen. The state doesn't allow ice cream or candy to be sold inside the state line and requires all kids to eat five pounds of Brussels sprouts a day. . . . All kittens and puppies are drowned as soon as they're born. Stuff like that. You never want to go there. Trust me.

Conroy's *The Great Santini*, published in 1976, made something of a local legend, if not necessarily a hero, of his father, Marine Colonel

Donald Conroy, who was depicted as a maniacally abusive despot in the novel. Pat's mother apparently thought the description accurate; when she filed for divorce, she presented the book to the judge as evidence.

In an essay in a 1998 issue of *Utne Reader*, Pat Conroy writes:

> As a father, Don Conroy carried a few shortcomings to the task of fathering, and I never thought he could tell the real difference between a sortie against the enemy and a family picnic. My parents taught me everything I needed to know about the dangers and attractions of the extreme. Even today, the purely outrageous to me feels completely normal. My novels reflect the absurdity and the exorbitance of a house in which the fully unexpected was our daily bread. My father once wiped out a dozen tanks working their way toward Marine lines in Korea, and my mother's hobby was collecting poisonous snakes. It's not my fault I was raised by Zeus and Hera, but my books mirror the odd, hothouse environment of my astonished childhood.
>
> All writers are both devotees and prisoners of their childhoods, and of the images that accrued during those early days when each of us played out the mystery of Adam and Eve in our own way. My mother's voice and my father's fists are the two bookends of my childhood, and they form the basis for my art. I came to the writing life because my father's warplanes took off against me, and my mother's hurt South longed for her special voice.

When Colonel Conroy died of colon cancer in 1998, the Book Shop in Beaufort displayed several editions of *The Great Santini* in its front windows with a sign forever naming Santini as "Col. Donald Conroy in our hearts." Although Pat Conroy painted his father as a brutal tyrant who regularly abused his children verbally and physically, outside the family the elder Conroy was widely adored as a larger-than-life Beaufort icon. With typical Conroy bravado, he had given himself the nickname of the Great Santini as a child, after seeing a magician with that name. After the book's publication, he frequently accompanied his son to book-signing events, and sometimes attracted more autograph seekers than Pat.

As for *The Great Santini*'s less flattering aspects, Colonel Conroy apparently dealt with the shame the book produced by making a complete turnabout, showering his adult children with affection that had been missing in their youth. And in a remarkable feat of familial diplomacy, he even managed to bind the gaping wounds created by Pat's book *The Prince of Tides* between the author and his sister Carol, on whom the suicidal character of Savannah Wingo was based. When he died, Pat Conroy described the once-loathed colonel as the perfect father.

Still, Don Conroy never actually asked his children's forgiveness for his earlier actions. As Pat Conroy put it after his father died, "Marines never apologize." The closest Don ever came to even acknowledging his violent past was after a 1979 screening of the movie version of *The Great Santini*, in which Robert Duvall portrayed his character. "If I'd beaten you more," Donald Conroy murmured to his son after seeing the film, "you'd be a better writer."

Beaufort's 300-acre historic district includes more than 170 public and private buildings. Tidalholm, at the very end of Hancock Street (the actual address is 1 Laurens Street), was featured in both *The Big Chill* and *The Great Santini*. The house, built in 1853 by James Fripp, was one of many local homes sold at auction by the federal government seven years later at the beginning of the Civil War, in 1860. A sympathetic Frenchman bought the house, however, and returned it to the Fripp family.

Tidalholm is privately owned, but visitors can get a glorious peek inside during the annual Historic Beaufort Foundation's Tour of Homes and Plantations in the fall. Tidalholm is always a star attraction.

Movies made in and around Beaufort include the movie adaptation of Conroy's *The Prince of Tides*, as well as *The Big Chill*, *Forrest Gump*, *Something to Talk About*, and *Midnight in the Garden of Good and Evil*. The Colonial-era Bay Street Inn, which served as an officers' club for the Union army after Beaufort fell to the Yankees during the Civil War, was used for several scenes in *The Prince of Tides*, which brought to town actress and director Barbra Streisand and Nick Nolte, who would win an Oscar nomination for his portrayal of Tom Wingo.

The Bay Street has had an unusually active military history for a seemingly benign inn; it began as a one-room dwelling in the late eighteenth century and was occupied by the British during the Revolution. It also faced bombardment during the War of 1812 and, in the 1850s, was completely rebuilt by a plantation family.

The Low Country also provides the setting for Padgett Powell's highly praised first novel, *Edisto* (1984), and the sequel, *Edisto Revisited*. In the first book, the South Carolina coast is seen through the eyes of twelve-year-old Simon Manigault, whose literary-minded mother desperately yearns for her son to be a poet. He disobligingly becomes an architect instead, but, like all Southern heroes, he must come home again, and for good measure has a dalliance with a heartsick cousin he describes as a "Piedmont horse–girl at large in the house, her genealogy preapproved."

In *Edisto Revisited*, Simon's irritation with what he calls the *Southern Living* boosterism of the South provokes him into wishing for a "napalm on malls, uncontrollable Pampers looting."

LITERARY LURES AND SOUTHERN SIGHTS

Charleston

Aiken-Rhett House, 48 Elizabeth Street; (843) 723–1159. Admission fee. The city's best-preserved antebellum museum and outbuildings.

Angel Oak, 3688 Angel Oak Road, Johns Island near Charleston; (843) 559–3496. A 1,400-year-old live oak believed to be among the oldest living creatures east of the Mississippi River. The tree, on busy little St. Johns Island, about thirty minutes from downtown Charleston, was named for Justis Angel, who owned the property it sits on in the early nineteenth century. The tree soars sixty-five feet, dwarfing its neighbors, and has a circumference of more than $25^1/_2$ feet, with limbs bowing and climbing and all but beckoning visitors to sit a spell.

Atlantic Books, 191 E. Bay Street; (843) 723–7654, and 310 King Street; (843) 723–4751. Terrific collection of Southern literature, history, and regional travel.

Boone Hall Plantation, 1234 Long Point Road; (843) 884–4371. Admission fee. Calls itself the most photographed plantation in the South, and it may well be. The 738-acre estate house is fronted by a magnificent row of moss-draped oaks, and Boone Hall's "Slave Street," with original cabins intact, is one of the few remaining in the country. Much of the TV drama *North and South* was filmed here, and the grounds were reportedly the inspiration for those at Tara in *Gone With the Wind*. The estate house was rebuilt in 1935, with attention paid to the original lines of the house, which was constructed in 1750. Breakfast and lunch are available in the Plantation Kitchen Restaurant.

Chapter Two Bookstore, 249 Meeting Street; (843) 722–4238 or (800) 722–4238. Excellent general bookstore, with frequent signings by Southern authors.

The Angel Oak outside of Charleston is one of the oldest living things east of the Mississippi.

Charleston Area Convention and Visitors Bureau, Visitors Center, 375 Meeting Street; (843) 724–7474 or (800) 774–0006; www.charleston cvb.com. Open from 8:30 A.M. to 5:30 P.M. daily, March through October; 8:30 A.M. to 5 P.M. daily, November through February. A well-done film, *Forever Charleston*, is shown every half hour.

Charleston Museum, 360 Meeting Street; (843) 722–2996. Open Mondays through Saturdays, 9 A.M. to 5 P.M.; Sundays 1 P.M. to 5 P.M. Founded in 1773, this is the oldest city museum in the United States. Now housed in a $6-million contemporary complex, it has an especially rich collection of South Carolina decorative arts—everything from Charleston silver to snuffboxes to eighteenth-century toys.

Charleston Strolls Walk With History; (843) 766–2080. Walking tours that take you from 1670 through the Civil War to the present.

CharlesTowne Landing 1670, 1500 Old Towne Road, Highway 61, between Interstate 26 and Highway 17; (843) 852–4200. Admission fee. The site of the first permanent English settlement in the state, this historic compound includes the commemorative sailing ship the *Adventure*, as well as a natural habitat zoo and "Settler's Life" replica village.

The Citadel Museum, 171 Moultrie Street, at Elmwood Avenue; (843) 953–6846. Admission is free. Open from 2 P.M. to 5 P.M. Sundays through Fridays; noon to 5 P.M. Saturdays. The Citadel's history from its founding in 1842 to the present.

Edmondston-Alston House, 21 E. Battery Street; (843) 722–7171; www.middletonplace.org. Museum house along Charleston's High Battery, built in 1825 by a Charleston merchant. Open for tours seven days a week. Admission fee.

Thomas Elfe House, 54 Queen Street; (843) 722–9161. This is the oldest home in Charleston open to visitors. Built in 1760, it was the home of the city's most famous cabinetmaker.

Fort Sumter Tours and SpiritLine Cruises; (843) 722–1691. Three cruises including a stop-off tour at Fort Sumter, where the Civil War began.

Fort Sumter National Monument, 1214 Middle Street, Sullivans Island; (843) 883–3123. Open from 9 A.M. to 5 P.M. every day except Christmas. The monument is part of historic Fort Moultrie; Edgar Allen Poe was stationed here and used Sullivans Island as the setting for *The Gold Bug*.

Ghost Walk; (843) 577–5931. A truly creepy evening tour.

Historic Charleston Foundation Museum Shop and Bookstore; (843) 724–8484. For information on tours of local historic houses, as well as a great assortment of local books.

Low Country and Resort Islands Tourism Commission; (800) 528–6870; www.southcarolinalowcountry.com.

Low Country Ghost Walk; (843) 853–4467. Based on the wonderful book *Charleston Ghosts*, by Margaret Rhett Martin.

Magnolia Plantation and Gardens, on Highway 61, ten miles from downtown Charleston; (843) 571–1266; www.magnoliaplantation.com.

Noble Dragon Bookshop, 106 Church Street, just below Broad Street; (843) 577–9334. Exquisite selection of used and out-of-print books in a setting that's something like a cozy library.

Old Exchange and Provost Dungeon, 122 E. Bay Street; (843) 727–2165. Admission fee. Wonderful exhibit takes you through three hundred years of "pirates, patriots, presidents and preservation."

Old Powder Magazine, 79 Cumberland Street; (843) 805–6730. Circa 1713, this is the city's oldest public building.

The Original Charleston Walks; (843) 543–4467; www.charleston walks.com. Wonderful tours include the Charleston Walk, Murders and Mysteries, the Lowcountry Ghost Walk, Churches and Graveyards of

Charleston, the Civil War, Historic Homes Walk, In Slavery and Freedom, and Pubs of the Old City.

Preservation Society of Charleston, 147 King Street; (843) 722–4630.
For information on tours of local historic homes and other sites. The
society shop boasts a wonderful collection of Charleston mementos—
sweet-grass baskets, regional fiction and history, posters; I even got my
much-coveted (by my boyfriend's sons, at least) Confederate saber
letter opener here.

Nathaniel Russell House, 51 Meeting Street; (843) 724–8481. Charleston's most-visited house museum, circa 1808.

Southern Literary Tradition, 84 Church Street; (843) 722–8430. Modern
first editions, regional history, and a marvelous selection of Southern
fiction. Books are catalogued by state, so memorize where your favorites
were born before you go searching.

Tour Charleston; (803) 723–1670 or (800) 854–1670; www.tour charleston.
com. Excellent tour focusing on Charleston and Low Country history.
Tours depart daily from Waterfront Park; reservations required.

Beaufort and Area

Beaufort Museum, 713 Craven Street, Beaufort; (843) 525–7077. Admission fee. Open from 10 A.M. to 5 P.M. daily, except Wednesdays and
Sundays. This 1798 brick and tabby building once housed an arsenal.
Tabby, a popular local construction material, is a cement first made in
South Carolina by Colonial Spaniards, who burned oyster shells to
extract lime, then mixed that with sand and shells and poured it into
wooden molds.

Beaufort Shrimp Festival, Beaufort; (843) 524–3163. Held in October
every year, this is the place to go if you want to taste all the varieties
of shrimp catalogued in *Forrest Gump*.

The Book Shop Bay Street Trading Company, 808 Bay Street, Beaufort;
(843) 524–2000.

Waterfront Park, off Bay Street in Beaufort. This pretty park was one of
the filming sites for *The Prince of Tides*. Events held here include the
annual Beaufort Water Festival in mid-July, with local arts and crafts
and a farmer's market.

Colleton Museum, 239 N. Jefferies Boulevard at Benson Street, Walter-
boro; (843) 549–2303. Open from 9 A.M. to 5 P.M. Tuesdays through

Fridays, 10 A.M. to 2 P.M. Saturdays, and 2 P.M. to 4 P.M. Sundays. Admission is free. The museum, housed in an 1855 jail, contains artifacts and information on the county's cultural heritage.

Daufuskie Island, near Hilton Head Island. This rural treasure was the setting for Pat Conroy's *The Water Is Wide*, which was made into the movie *Conrack*, starring Jon Voight. Excursions to Daufuskie are run out of Hilton Head by Adventure Cruises, (843) 785–4558, Vagabond Cruises, (843) 842–4155, and Calibogue Cruises, (843) 785–8242.

Edisto Beach State Park, eighty miles northeast of Beaufort; (843) 869–2156. Rural island with magnificent moss-draped oaks, open grasslands, and stands of palmetto palms. Many inhabitants are descendants of former slaves. Three miles of beach offer phenomenal shelling and camping.

Edisto Chamber of Commerce, Edisto Beach; (843) 869–3867.

Edisto Island Golden Age Tour; (843) 869–3867. Self-guided tour offered each October, focusing on the island's historic plantations and churches.

Edisto Island Museum, 2343 Highway 174; (843) 869–1954. Open 1 P.M. to 4 P.M. Tuesdays, Thursdays, and Saturdays. Admission fee. The museum contains exhibits on sea island plantation life, the Civil War, and Florida's Native Americans.

Fall Festival of Homes and History, Beaufort, annual weekend in mid-October, Historic Beaufort Foundation; (843) 524–6334. This annual festival focuses on the history and architecture of Beaufort and the Low Country.

George Parsons Elliott House, 1001 Bay Street, Beaufort. This Greek Revival house overlooking the Beaufort River was built in 1844 for planter and politician George Elliott. The house, which sports double verandahs and a raised foundation, served as a Union hospital during the Civil War and typifies the "Beaufort Style" described by Pat Conroy in *Beach Music*, although Conroy calls the town "Colleton."

Greater Beaufort Chamber of Commerce, 1106 Carteret Street, Beaufort; (843) 524–3163; www.beaufortsc.org.

Hilton Head Island Chamber of Commerce, Hilton Head; (843) 785–3673; www.hiltonheadisland.org.

Hunting Island State Park; (843) 838–2011. Eighteen miles southeast of Beaufort, this wonderful island has an 1,120-foot-long fishing pier that's among the lengthiest on the East Coast. Once an Indian hunting ground, the park boasts beautiful beaches, forest trails, and marshes. A 140-foot-tall, 1850s-era lighthouse makes it all visible from above for those willing to climb, and visitors can stay at campgrounds or in rental cabins.

John Mark Verdier House Museum, 801 Bay Street, Beaufort; (843) 524–6335. Open daily except Sundays from 10 A.M. to 4:30 P.M. Admission fee. This 1790s Federal-style home was built by a prosperous merchant and was taken over by Union officers as their headquarters during the Civil War. In 1825, the Marquis de Lafayette was a guest at the Verdier House, on his triumphant tour through the South.

ACCOMMODATIONS AND RESTAURANTS

Charleston

Ashley Inn Bed-and-Breakfast, Bee Street at Ashley Street; (843) 723–1848; www.cchat.com/Ashley. Festive pink-and-green architecture, circa 1832.

Barksdale House Inn, 27 George Street; (843) 577–4800. One of the city's oldest inns, circa 1778. Decor here includes borders and fabrics from the eighteenth and nineteenth centuries.

Battery Carriage House Inn, 20 S. Battery; (843) 727–3100 or (800) 775–5575. Built in 1843 during Charleston's golden age.

Mike Calder's Pub, 288 King Street; (843) 577–0123.

Cannonboro Inn Bed-and-Breakfast, 184 Ashley Avenue; (843) 723–8572. Charming 1853 historic home.

Carolina's Restaurant, 10 Exchange Street; (843) 724–3800. Historic downtown restaurant with luscious Low Country specialties.

Charleston Grill, 130 Market Street; (843) 577–4522.

Charleston Place Hotel, 130 Market Street; (843) 722–4900 or (800) 611–5545. Graceful and elegant. The lobby alone is worth a visit—Venetian-glass chandeliers, marble floors, antiques from Sotheby's.

East Bay Bed-and-Breakfast, 301 E. Bay Street; (843) 722–4186. Dating from 1807, this Federal-style house was the birthplace of Civil War heroine Phoebe Pember.

Elliott House Inn, 78 Queen Street; (843) 723–1855.

Embassy Suites Historic Charleston, 337 Meeting Street, on Marion Square; (843) 723–6900 or (800) 362–2779. This extraordinary hotel incorporates the original courtyard of the Citadel, transforming the former marching ground into a skylit atrium with stone flooring, palm trees, and a fountain. Some guest rooms of the 1822 building contain original gun ports, a not-so-subtle reminder of its beginnings as a fortification.

Gilligan's Steamer and Raw Bar, 160 Main Road, Johns Island; (843) 766–2244. Sit right back and you'll hear a tale . . . or several, and it might be more than a three-hour tour.

Historic Charleston Bed-and-Breakfast; (843) 722–6606 or (800) 743–3583. Reservations service.

Lodge Alley Inn, 195 E. Bay Street; (843) 722–1611.

Magnolias, 185 E. Bay Street; (843) 577–7771. Popular restaurant full of lovely etched glass, wrought iron, and candlesticks, set in an 1823 warehouse.

Mills House Hotel, 115 Meeting Street; (843) 577–2400 or (800) 874–9600. Reconstruction of an old hostelry in the historic district, run with charm and attention to period detail by Holiday Inns.

Planters Inn, 112 N. Market Street; (843) 722–2345 or (800) 845–7082; www.plantersinn.com. Circa 1844 old-world style inn with a beautiful outdoor eating area. Fabulous bird's-eye view of City Market from the new wing.

Poogan's Porch, 72 Queen Street; (843) 577–2337. Fresh seafood and Low-Country cuisine in a charming circa-1888 home. The restaurant is named after a pooch named Poogan, whose owners left him behind when they moved away from the house in the mid-1970s. After the house was turned into a restaurant soon after, Poogan became the official greeter from his regular front-porch perch. The much-loved little guy died in 1979, but the current owners call the restaurant his monument.

Pusser's Landing, Charleston City Marina, 17 Lockwood Drive; (843) 853–1000. Wonderful restaurant in the historic Rice Mill Building.

S.N.O.B. (Slightly North of Broad), 192 E. Bay Street; (843) 723–3424. Lordy, lordy, Miss Scarlett! A restaurant whose name actually pokes fun at the attitude sometimes found among Old South society. Does the Chamber of Commerce know about this?!? Set in a snazzy rehabilitated warehouse.

Sticky Fingers, 235 Meeting Street; (843) 853–7427 or (800) 671–5966. Their specialty is ribs done six different ways. The restaurant's name is completely appropriate.

Sword Gate Inn, 111 Tradd Street; (843) 723–8518. Circa-1800 mansion in a vibrant private courtyard setting.

The 27 State Street Bed-and-Breakfast was used for scenes in the miniseries *Scarlett and Queenie*.

Twenty-Seven State Street Bed-and-Breakfast, 27 State Street; (843) 722–4243. This dreamy bed-and-breakfast, circa 1800, is in the French Quarter of the original walled city of Charleston, two blocks from the harbor. Each carriage-house suite includes a bedroom-living room, private bath, and kitchenette. The inn stood in, so to speak, for a brothel in the TV-movie adaptation of *Scarlett*, in which Timothy Dalton, as Rhett, stepped out onto the shady outdoors breakfast nook upstairs. The miniseries *Queen*, based on the book by Alex Haley, also had scenes shot at 27 State Street.

Vickery's Bar and Grill, 15 Beaufain Street; (843) 577–5300. A half-block off King Street, with a bar that rocks till the wee hours.

Wentworth Mansion, 149 Wentworth Street; (843) 853–1886 or (888) 466–1886. Twenty-one-room manse with gorgeous decor and froufrou.

Beaufort and Area

Battery Creek Marina and Inn, 19 Marina Village Lane, Beaufort; (843) 521–1441.

Bay Creek Villa Rentals, 3701 Docksite Road, Edisto Beach; (843) 869–1848 or (800) 533–7145.

Bay Towne Grill, 310 West Street, Beaufort; (843) 522–3880. Favorite lunch spot for locals.

Beaufort Inn, 809 Port Republic Street, Beaufort; (843) 521–9000; www.beaufortinn.com.

Blackstone's Deli and Cafe, 915 Bay Street, Beaufort; (843) 524–4330. Full breakfasts with Southern specialties such as shrimp 'n' grits.

Broad River Seafood, 2601 Boundary Street, Beaufort; (843) 524–2001. Casual dining with a spectacular view of the marsh.

Cassina Point Plantation, 1642 Clark Road, Edisto Island; (843) 869–2535. You'll almost believe that you're Scarlett and Rhett in this antebellum fantasy of a bed-and-breakfast surrounded by fields once planted with Sea Island cotton. Graffiti left by Federal troops during their Civil War occupation can still be seen on the basement walls, and dolphins frequently frolic in the nearby creek. The Miss Ella and Miss Addie rooms are the best, overlooking the beautiful marsh at the rear of the home.

Craven Street Inn, 1103 Craven Street, Beaufort; (843) 522–1668.

Cuthbert House Inn, 1203 Bay Street, Beaufort; (843) 521–1315 or (800) 327–9275; www.cuthbert-bb-beaufort.com. Federal-style house built on the Carolina marshes in 1790 by the Cuthbert family of rice and cotton planters. Sherman slept here—in November 1861, the home was captured by Union forces, who hospitably welcomed their general on his march through the Confederacy. This was one building he refrained from burning. A marble mantle in the home retains the signatures of Union soldiers who sketched their names and home states on it.

Duke's BBQ of Beaufort, 3531 Trask Parkway, Beaufort; (843) 524–1128. Terrific family dining, with scrumptious barbecued and fried chicken.

Eleventh Street Dockside Restaurant, 1699 Eleventh Street, Port Royal; (843) 524–7433. Overlooking the shrimp-boat docks of Battery Creek.

Harry's Restaurant-John Cross Tavern, 812 Bay Street, Beaufort; (843) 524–3993. Harry's, downstairs, serves lunch and breakfast; John Cross Tavern upstairs serves dinner.

Old Point Inn, 212 New Street; (843) 524–3177.

Old Post Office Restaurant, 1442 Highway 174, five miles from Edisto Beach, Edisto Island; (843) 869–2339. Originally Bailey's General

South Carolina 213

Store and a U.S. Post Office, this restaurant on Store Creek specializes in serving *anything* with grits.

Ollie's Seafood Grille and Bar, 71 Sea Island Parkway, Beaufort; (843) 525–6333. Indoor and outdoor dining on the waterfront.

Plums, 904$^1/_2$ Bay Street, Beaufort; (843) 525–1946. Excellent casual dining in Waterfront Park.

Rhett House Inn and Fine Dining, 1009 Craven Street, Beaufort; (843) 524–9030. Named not for Margaret Mitchell's quintessential alpha Southern male, but for a prominent nineteenth-century South Carolina family.

Steamer Oyster and Steakhouse, 168 Sea Island Parkway, Beaufort; (843) 522–0210.

Whitehall Plantation Restaurant, 27 Whitehall Drive, Ladys Island, Beaufort; (843) 521–1700. A century-old Low-Country setting, with sensational views of the bay.

Greenville and the Up-Country

Short story author and novelist Dorothy Allison was born in Greenville in 1949 and grew up in a large extended family of entirely humble means. Her family's less-than-noble status informs every page of her writing, as does her unconventional sexuality—lesbianism, combined with dirt-poor economics, makes for an uneasy life in the Deep South. Allison's characters would have been the people that Faulkner's or Welty's characters called white trash and wrinkled their noses at if meeting them at the library or market.

Allison's characters are completely, sorrowfully aware of their place in Southern hierarchy. She writes in *Bastard Out of Carolina*, a finalist for the National Book Award in 1992:

> Aunt Alma had given me a big paperback edition of *Gone With the Wind*, with tinted pictures from the movie, and told me I'd love it. I had at first, but one evening I looked up from Vivien Leigh's pink cheeks to see Mama coming in from work with her hair darkened from sweat and her uniform stained. A sharp flash went through me. Emma Slattery, I thought. That's who I'd be, that's who we were.

Not Scarlett with baking-powder cheeks. I was part of the trash down in the mud-stained cabins, fighting with the darkies and stealing ungratefully from our betters, stupid, coarse, born to shame and death. I shook with fear and indignation.

Allison's writing is unflinching, spare, and unnerving to read, throwing a brutally bright light into the darkest corners of Southern rural life. In *Trash*, a collection of short stories, she writes:

Almost always, we were raped, my cousins and I. That was some kind of joke, too. *What's a South Carolina virgin? 'At's a ten-year-old can run fast.*
     It wasn't funny for me in my mama's bed with my stepfather, not for my cousin, Billie, in the attic with my uncle, nor for Lucille in the woods with another cousin, for Danny with four strangers in a parking lot, or for Pammie who made the papers. Cora read it out loud: "Repeatedly by persons unknown." They stayed unknown since Pammie never spoke again. Perforations, lacerations, contusions, and bruises. I heard all the words, big words, little words, words too terrible to understand.

The storytelling tradition, propelling Southern children to tell tales with an almost genetic urgency, prevented Allison's keeping quiet, no matter how horrible the subject. As she writes in *Bastard Out of Carolina*:

All the Boatwrights told stories, it was one of the things we were known for, and what one cousin swore was gospel, another swore just as fiercely was an unqualified lie. Raylene was always telling people that we had a little of the tarbrush on us, but the way she grinned when she said it could have meant she was lying to make somebody mad, or maybe she just talked that way because she was crazy angry to start with.

Allison's works are set mostly in and around Greenville, including her best-known novel, *Bastard Out of Carolina*, which was made into an acclaimed movie for Showtime. The film was originally slated for another cable network, which bowed out because of the controversial, highly autobiographical subject matter: sexual abuse of a twelve-year-old girl by her stepfather.

Allison's memories aren't entirely grim, however. In *Bastard*, she recalls the unmistakable languor of Southern heat through the eyes of her protagonist Ruth Anne:

> That was the summer it was so hot the katydids failed to sing and everyone spent their evenings out on the back porch with large glasses of ice tea and damp hand towels to cool the back of the neck. Alma wouldn't even start cooking until after the sun had gone down. Twilight came on early, though, a long-drawn-out dimming of the heat and glare that made everything soft and magical, brought out the first fireflies, and added a cool enchantment to the metallic echoes of the slide guitar playing on Alma's kitchen radio.
>
> Granny would plant herself in the porch rocker, leaving Alma's girls to pick through snap beans, hope for a rainstorm, and tease her into telling stories.
>
> I always positioned myself behind Granny, up against the wall next to the screen door, where I could listen to Kitty Wells and George Jones, the whine of that guitar and what talk there was in the kitchen, as well as the sound of Aunt Alma's twin boys thumping their feet against the porch steps and the girls' giggles as their fingers slipped through the cool, dusty beans.

And she gives the area's natural beauty its full due, also in *Bastard*:

> Greenville, South Carolina, in 1955 was the most beautiful place in the world. Black walnut trees dropped their green-black fuzzy bulbs on Aunt Ruth's matted lawn, past where their knotty roots rose up out of the ground like the elbows and knees of dirty children suntanned and dark and covered with scars. Weeping willows marched across the yard, following every wandering stream and ditch, their long whiplike fronds making tents that sheltered sweet-smelling beds of clover.
>
> Over at the house Aunt Raylene rented near the river, all the trees had been cut back and the scuppernong vines torn out. The clover grew in long sweeps of tiny white and yellow flowers that hid slender red-and-black striped caterpillars and fat gray-black slugs—the one that Uncle Earle swore would draw fish to a hook even in a thunderstorm.

LITERARY LURES AND SOUTHERN SIGHTS

Greater Greenville Convention and Tourism Bureau, Downtown Visitors Center, 206 S. Main Street; (800) 717–0023.
Greenville Online; www.greenvilleonline.com.

ACCOMMODATIONS AND RESTAURANTS

Chief's Wings and Firewater, 75 Orchard Park Drive, Greenville; (864) 288–4177. The name pretty much says it all. Not subtle, but tasty.

Cottage Cuisine, 615 S. Main Street, Greenville; (864) 370–9070. The ultimate in "comfort food" cuisine.

Creekside Plantation Bed-and-Breakfast, 3118 S. Highway 14, Greenville; (864) 297–3293.

Henry's Smokehouse, 240 Wade Hampton Boulevard, Greenville; (864) 232–7774. Old-fashioned barbecue served in amounts that you'll never, ever conquer.

Jefferson House Bed and Breakfast and Restaurant, 2835 Old Williamston Road, Anderson; (864) 224–0678. Century-old bed-and-breakfast built by plantation owner Quincy Hammonds.

Vince Perone's Restaurant, 1 E. Antrim Drive, Greenville; (864) 233–1621.

Pettigru Place Bed-and-Breakfast, 302 Pettigru Street, Greenville; (864) 242–4529. 1920s Georgian-Federalist–style home, listed on the National Register of Historic Places.

Red Horse Inn, 310 N. Campbell Road, Landrum; (864) 895–4968. Charming Victorian cottages on 190 acres in the midst of fox-hunting land.

Schell Haus Bed-and-Breakfast, 117 Hiawatha Trail, State Highway 11; (864) 878–0078. Victorian-style getaway in the Blue Ridge foothills, with a spectacular view of Table Rock.

Seven Oaks Restaurant, 104 Broadus Avenue, Greenville; (864) 232–1895. Sophisticated fare in a nineteenth-century mansion.

Stax's Peppermill, 30 Orchard Park Drive, Greenville; (864) 288–9320.

Strossner's Bakery, 1626 E. North Street, Greenville; (864) 233–3996. Just follow your nose to the chocolate, dough, and frosting.

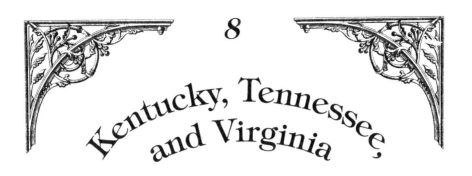

8

Kentucky, Tennessee, and Virginia

Spotting a sign for the battlefield, I became suddenly giddy. . . .
When I'd first read about and painted the battle as a boy, Shiloh—
"place of peace" in the Bible—sounded haunting and beautiful,
nothing like the bluntly named Bull Run or the Germanic towns of
Gettysburg and Fredericksburg. Only Antietam rolled off the
tongue in as lovely a way. But Antietam lay within the same fifty-
mile orbit of my boyhood home as the Virginia and Pennsylvania
battlefields.

Shiloh lay a world away, in a wilderness of lazy rivers, log
cabins and tersely named creeks: Dill, Owl, Snake, Lick. . . .
Now, the real battlefield lay before me in the predawn gloom. I
turned in at the park gate, switching off my headlights lest a ranger
apprehend me for entering outside of official hours. Inching along
in the dark, I parked near the spot on my tourist map labeled
Fraley Field. It was here in J. C. Fraley's cottonfield, at dawn on
April 6th, that Northern sentries first encountered the oncoming
rebel army.

—Tony Horwitz, *Confederates in the Attic*

he upper South comes across as being rougher, grittier, and more uncomfortably visceral than the cotton-field South of the Carolinas or Louisiana. Kentucky and Tennessee are places that, geography notwithstanding, seem almost *more* Southern, certainly more western, closer to that immense, wild "out there" of the Midwest and West. Up in the Kentucky and Tennessee mountains and valleys, where the bloodiest battles of the Civil War were waged—brother against cousin against in-law, across bluegrass fields and atop frosty ridges—the air seems always to carry the subtle scent of sweat, blood, devotion, revenge. Magnolias and bougainvillea can't disguise the psychic energy clinging to this land, molecular remnants left over from centuries of raw passion.

Likewise, the literature that comes from this region typically goes beyond the power to merely seduce, adding to its arsenal words that can stun, slam, and shame. A gentle linguistic blossom may find its way into the work of Bobbie Ann Mason or Peter Taylor, but you'll have to get past a lot of thorns to savor the sweetness.

KENTUCKY

The Bluegrass state grows authors as brazenly as other Southern realms; but its authors seem to have a distinct proclivity to move away and write about other places. Sue Grafton, Barbara Kingsolver, Michael Dorris—all Kentucky-born, all known for their intricate renderings of *other* places: Grafton for California, in her mystery series starring Kinsey Millhone; Native America in all its intricacies in Dorris's *Cloud Chamber* and *Broken Cord;* Africa and the American Southwest in Kingsolver's novels.

Despite their disparate themes and settings, what pervades all of these authors' writings is a palpable, distinctly Southern sense of place: the certainty that place determines personality and, to a much more profound degree, morality. *Where* we live, and that place's distinct yet always shifting layers of custom, culture, and the unexpected kindness or devastating meanness of one's neighbors makes us who we are, and Southern writers transfer that knowledge, that innate Southern-ness, to any setting they inhabit. The *New York Times Book Review*, in its piece on Kingsolver's *The Bean Trees*, called the book "as clean as air. It is the southern novel taken west, its colors as translucent and polished as one of those slices of rose agate from a desert shop."

LITERARY LURES AND SOUTHERN SIGHTS

Kentucky Department of Travel Development; (502) 564–4930 or (800) 225–8747; www.state.ky.us or www.kentuckytourism.com.
Kentucky's Historic Heartland; www.kyvacation.com.

ACCOMMODATIONS

Bed-and-Breakfast Association of Kentucky; (888) 281–8188; www.bbon line.com/ky/bbak. Lists nearly two hundred bed-and-breakfast homes and inns in all parts of the state.
Bluegrass Bed-and-Breakfast Reservation Service; (859) 873–3208. Represents about twenty lodgings, some exclusive to this service.

Western Kentucky

Bobbie Ann Mason, the contemporary writer who is probably most associated with rural Kentucky, spent decades living in the North before returning to her Southern origins. Her books, though, have always been deeply rooted in the farm country of western Kentucky, that fertile little triangle of earth jutting precociously out into land that, logically and geographically, should have been part of Tennessee or Illinois or Missouri.

It seems entirely appropriate that Mason would come from such a place; her characters show a similar tendency to push into uncharted or forbidden territory, sticking their noses—and their very souls—out on proverbial limb after limb. Mason's family came from that same feisty stock, and writing about them, she says, was harder than making things up. In 1999, she told *Bookpage* magazine that in writing her memoir, *Clear Springs*, it was "awfully hard working with facts—or even what you remember as facts. I had so much trouble writing this book because I had to be faithful to what I knew to be fact, and yet I was trying to write something that in so many ways was like fiction."

Mason was born in Mayfield in 1940, to a dairy-farming family. The fifty-three-acre farm was just off Kentucky Highway 45, in Graves County, a mile from Mayfield and a few miles from tiny Clear Springs, where her ancestors had settled in the early 1800s. She graduated from the University of Kentucky and then moved to New York, where she began her writing career with television scripts and movie magazines.

Her third book, *Shiloh and Other Stories*, published in 1982, won both the Ernest Hemingway Foundation Award and the PEN-Faulkner Award for Fiction. *Feather Crowns* (1993) is about a nineteenth-century version of a media circus that ensues when a Kentucky farm wife gives birth to quintuplets. The book won the Southern Book Critics Circle Award.

Her characters are working people, caught in the frenzied miasma of modern "development," with Taco Bells and Wal-Marts sprouting on corners once occupied by poultry farms and horse ranches. In *Shiloh*, for instance, her character Norma Jean "works at the Rexall drugstore, and she has acquired an amazing amount of information about cosmetics. When she explains to Leroy the three stages of complexion care, involving creams, toners, and moisturizers, he thinks happily of other petroleum products—axle grease, diesel fuel. This is a connection between him and Norma Jean."

Mason's most popular book, *In Country*, like so much of Southern literature, deals with "the War." In this case, however, she flashes forward a hundred years from *that* war, the one that's consumed Southern thinking since 1860, to the one that once again turned brother against brother, American against American: Vietnam. *In Country* tells the story of a teenage girl who tries to learn about her father, who was killed in Vietnam, through the eyes of an uncle who also served in the war.

Unlike many Southern writers, Mason denies any fixation with, or indeed knowledge *of*, the Civil War. She has told interviewers, "I think the culture I write about is very distinctly Southern," but also that "I don't think the people I write about are obsessed with the past. I don't think they know anything about the Civil War, and I don't think they care. They're kind of naive and optimistic for the most part; they think better times are coming."

The movie version of *In Country*, starring Bruce Willis and Emily Lloyd, was filmed at a private home in Mayfield, at the Graves County Courthouse, Maplewood Cemetery, Paducah Community College, and Ballard County Wildlife Management Area. The wildlife area, a popular local hunting and fishing spot, doubled for the murky swamps of Vietnam. The restaurant in the movie, Chuck's (the one with the chicken on top; you can't miss it), was a set built for the film but was based on Emma's in Mayfield, which does sport its own rooftop clucker.

Mason turned her pen to the most personal subject, her own family, with *Clear Springs: A Memoir*, published in 1999. As the *Lexington*

Herald-Leader put it in an April 1999 story about Mason, soon after the book's release, "She tells of picking blackberries, surviving childhood accidents and illnesses (she almost died of pneumonia), her obsession with jigsaw puzzles and the Hilltoppers (the quartet from Bowling Green), her fears of the dark and 'the booger man,' the flour-sack dresses she wore to school, her feelings of inferiority as a country girl and the books that inspired her and connected her to a larger world. She remembers her mother's endless work at home, canning, sewing, milking, churning, drying apples and tending the garden, and her sometimes jobs working in a clothing factory and managing a roadside restaurant.

"But this life was not for Bobbie Ann Mason," the article continues. "She wanted to get out and see the world and maybe write about it: 'I didn't want to be hulling beans in a hot kitchen when I was fifty years old.'" The book opens and closes at her mother's fish pond, which turns the tale into a mini-epic with echoes of *Moby-Dick* and *The Old Man and the Sea.*

About fifty miles from Mayfield, south and to the east, is Guthrie, a small hamlet on the Tennessee border that was the birthplace of Robert Penn Warren, whose books include *All the King's Men*, a quintessential look at Southern politics by way of Louisiana. Guthrie has turned Warren's birthplace into a nice little museum, with displays of his writings and personal belongings. You can also buy his works in the on-site gift shop.

Todd County, in which Guthrie sits, boasts its own wacky little contribution to the Civil War, albeit a century later. As explained by Tony Horwitz in *Confederates in the Attic:*

> Todd County wasn't rebel country, at least not historically. According to the volumes of local history I perused, most Todd Countians supported the Union in the Civil War. Like much of the upper South, the county split along geographic lines. Whites from the county's fertile plantations bordering Tennessee tended to side with the South. But the more numerous yeoman farmers in Todd County's hilly north (where slaves were few) supported the Union. Kentucky also stayed in the Union, though the first Confederate Congress optimistically allotted a star for Kentucky on the Confederacy's flag in hopes the state might secede.
>
> Despite this history, almost all whites I spoke to echoed Frances Chapman, proclaiming their county rebel territory and

believing it had always been so. As proof, they pointed to a 351-foot concrete spike soaring at the county's western edge. The obelisk marked the birthsite of Confederate president Jefferson Davis, who was born there in 1808. . . . Davis's parents were peripatetic folk; they moved to Louisiana when "little Jeff" was two. It seemed doubtful the Confederate leader had any memories of his old Kentucky home.

No matter. Each year on Davis's birthday, Todd Countians crowded around the spike for a bizarre rite: the crowning of a local teenager as "Miss Confederacy." Contestants were judged on their poise, hair, hooped skirt, and answers to questions such as, "What will you do while holding the title to promote and defend Southern heritage?"

Robert Penn Warren watched the monument's construction as a child. As recounted by Horwitz, he later "recalled the bemusement he felt as this 'immobile thrust of concrete' soared above his native soil."

Warren later wrote, "Remembrance of the Confederacy had never been of burning importance in Guthrie, where to a certain number of contemporary citizens the Civil War seemed to have been fought for the right to lynch without legal interference." But Todd County was determined to claim its scars on the Civil War battlefield, and preferred the sympathy that went to the losers. Indeed, as Warren wrote, "History, like nature, knows no jumps. Except the jump backward."

LITERARY LURES AND SOUTHERN SIGHTS

Clarksville Tourist Information, 180 Holiday Drive, Clarksville, Tennessee; (931) 551–3572. The closest major tourist information center to Guthrie, Kentucky, where Robert Penn Warren was born.

Good News Shoppe, 203 E. South; (270) 247–5217. Local bookstore.

Historic Drennon Springs Storytelling and Crafts Festival, 9 miles north of New Castle on Kentucky 202. This annual daylong event features local storytellers and craftspeople, and takes place in mid-October. For information, call the Mayfield-Graves County Chamber of Commerce.

Mayfield-Graves County Chamber of Commerce, 201 E. College Street; (270) 247–6101; www.2ldd.net/commerce/mayfield.

Robert Penn Warren Birthplace Museum, Third at Cherry Streets; (270) 483–2683. Open 11:30 A.M. to 3:30 P.M. Tuesdays through Saturdays,

2 P.M. to 4 P.M. Mondays. Admission free; donations appreciated. This historic house includes displays of Warren's writings and belongings, and has a gift shop where visitors can buy his books.

ACCOMMODATIONS AND RESTAURANTS

Budget Inn, 513 E. Broadway; (270) 247–6179.
Dairy Queen of Mayfield and Graves County, 914 Paducah Road; (270) 247–4000. Quit snickering; in any small Southern town, the local Dairy Queen is *the* place to get quickly up to speed on local customs, style, and gossip.
Days Inn, Highway 121 North; (270) 247–3700.
Emma's Restaurant, 514 N. Seventh; (270) 247–9208. Home of the giant rooftop chicken, Emma's had a Hollywood-built stand-in in the film version of *In Country*.
Linda's Market, 1306 Cuba Road; (270) 247–2761.
Majestic Family Restaurant, 700 S. Sixth; (270) 247–2541.

Bluegrass Country: Louisville, Frankfort, and Lexington

Like William Faulkner and Shelby Foote with their fictitious Mississippi worlds, Kentuckian Wendell Berry has created a wholly believable micro-universe in Port William, Kentucky, the setting for his novels. Berry has lived and farmed all his life in rural Henry County, north of Frankfort in the bluegrass country. The entire county, which was founded in 1789 and named for Revolutionary War hero Patrick Henry, boasts only 14,000 people in its 291-square-mile radius, which may explain some of Berry's renowned aversion to all things "city." New Castle, Henry County's largest town and county seat, is about thirty miles east of Louisville.

In addition to novels, Berry writes poetry, but he is perhaps best known as an insightful essayist whose pastoral vision serves as a piercing indictment of modern, materialistically driven society. Reading Berry's essays is a little like being lectured for wrongdoing by a beloved uncle; one doubly feels the shame of self-centered ambition, both for the careless acts committed and the loss of esteem.

In *A World Lost*, one of the Port William novels, Berry tells the World War II–era story of an uncle much like that: Andrew Catlett, a womanizer and fun-lover, whose death in a trivial ruckus is retold by his grown nephew and namesake, Andy. As reviewed on *Amazon.com,* Berry in this book is "uninterested in stylistic leaps or postmodern bravura: he is interested in a profound, well-told tale of honor and memory and community." Berry's Uncle Andrew was a man who many would consider an innocent, someone who relished "company, talk, some kind of to-do, something to laugh at." The character serves as a deft metaphor for pre-war America—robust and blessed with a self-deprecating sense of humor, yet ultimately troubled and uneasy with his responsibilities.

Berry's criticism of contemporary life has grown consistently more harsh. *Kirkus Reviews,* in reviewing *Sex, Economy, Freedom, and Community* (1994) noted:

> His pessimism seems to grow with each volume, as he sees the nation in a tailspin toward moral and economic chaos. His targets proliferate: The military and its Gulf War (he calls for a National Peace Academy); profiteering industrialists who ravage economies around the world; addiction to drugs, war, TV, and junk products; public schooling, which instills mediocrity in place of moral values; media exploitation of sexuality, which robs it of sacred meaning; "tolerant and multicultural people" who defend special interest groups but defame "people who haven't been to college, manual workers, country people, peasants, religious people, unmodern people, old people"—in other words, Berry's friends, neighbors, and comrades.
>
> If the diagnosis is bitter, so is the cure: "economic secession." For Berry, small communities based on the household are our only hope. He calls upon these localities to seize control of their economic and social lives, supporting home-grown agriculture, manufacturing, and education, and establishing moral codes that reflect eternal truths. Power-to-the-people, 90s style. A powerful emetic, worth a swallow.

Berry's reverence for the country people, among which he most definitely counts himself, came through strongly in an interview for Enviro Arts' Web page in 1999:

Rome destroyed itself by undervaluing the country people, too. I guess we should leave open the possibility that we'll be too stupid to change. Other civilizations have been. But at least it's more obvious now that this superstition is a superstition, because now there's no place else to go. The "other" places are gone. If we use up the possibility of life here, there's no other place to go, and so the old notion is bankrupt, though it still underlies most destructive practice.

Of those who feel disconnected from place—the children of the second half of the twentieth century, for whom moving every eighteen months or two years is as natural as breathing—Berry has this advice:

Stop somewhere! Because you can't recover what's lost. There's no going back to get it. You just have to start again, and I think what people have to experience—have to let themselves experience—is the knowledge and understanding and even happiness that come with long association with people and places and kinds of work.

Novelist Mary Ann Taylor-Hall set her delightful debut novel, *Come and Go, Molly Snow,* amid the bluegrass country, telling the story of fiddler Carrie Marie Mullins, who's living in Lexington after a "wildest-of-the-wild" period in which she gets pregnant by a stranger from Georgia.

When her baby girl dies in an accident and clinical depression starts to eat away at Carrie, her longtime boyfriend Cap Dunlap—still in love with her despite the Georgia transgression—takes her to his grandmother's farm to recover. The book serves as a lyrical testament to the healing power of Kentucky, both through its land and its people.

LITERARY LURES AND SOUTHERN SIGHTS

Louisville

A Reader's Corner, 115 Wiltshire Avenue; (502) 897–5578.
All Booked Up, 1555 Bardstown Road; (502) 459–6348.
Book Lady, 9908 Taylorsville; (502) 266–8831.

Booklink, 1504 W. Kentucky Street; (502) 584–2665.

Broadway Books, 632 W. Broadway; (502) 583–3724.

Hawley-Cooke Booksellers, 4600 Shelbyville Road, Suite 130, St. Matthews; (502) 893–0133.

Kentucky Derby Festival, 1001 S. Third Street; (502) 584–6383. If you're in town in the spring, you can't miss it.

Louisville and Jefferson County Convention and Visitors Bureau, 400 S. First Street; (502) 584–2121 or (800) 626–5646; www.louisville_visitors.com.

Frankfort and Area

Executive Mansion, 704 E. Capitol Avenue, just east of the Capitol; (502) 564–8004. Tours of public rooms from 9 A.M. to 11 A.M. Tuesdays and Thursdays. Free admission. Reportedly modeled after Marie Antoinette's summer villa, this Kentucky limestone mansion has been the governor's residence since 1914.

Frankfort Cemetery, 215 E. Main Street; (502) 227–2403. Open from 7 A.M. to 8:30 P.M. during the summer, 8 A.M. to 5:30 P.M. during winter months. This shady, tranquil cemetery contains the graves of Daniel and Rebecca Boone, who were originally buried in Missouri, where they lived the final years of their lives. In 1845, their remains were moved to Kentucky, and a monument was placed on the grave site in 1862. The grave site looks down on the Kentucky River and the State Capitol.

Frankfort-Franklin Tourist Information, 100 Capitol Avenue; (502) 875–8687; www.frankfortky.org.

Henry County Farmers Market, on the Court House lawn; 9 A.M. till the produce is gone every Saturday. You might run into Wendell Berry at this weekly local tradition. He's a dandy writer, no doubt about that, but word is he's a pretty good farmer, too.

Kentucky State Capitol, 702 Capitol Avenue; (502) 564–3449. Tours from 8 A.M. to 4:30 P.M. weekdays, 8:30 A.M. to 4:30 P.M. Saturdays and 1 P.M. to 4:30 P.M. Sundays. Admission is free. This French Renaissance–style building invites comparisons to the U.S. Capitol. It was constructed from 1905 to 1910 at the then-unthinkable price of $1.75 million. The grounds include the unusual Floral Clock, a thirty-four-foot-diameter timepiece with thousands of flowers covering its face.

Kentucky Military History Museum, East Main Street at Capitol Avenue; (502) 564–3265. Open from 9 A.M. to 4 P.M. Mondays through Saturdays, and from noon to 4 P.M. Sundays. Free admission. Operated by the Kentucky Historical Society, this museum is in the Old State Arsenal building. Its exhibits emphasize the Civil War and the Kentucky National Guard.

Kentucky Vietnam Veterans Memorial, Coffee Tree Road, on the grounds of the State Library and Archives. Open daily from dawn till dusk. A beautiful memorial to Kentucky natives who died in the war, the site features a sundial designed so that the points of its shadow touch the name of each veteran, etched on the ground in granite.

Lieutenant Governor's Mansion, 420 High Street; (502) 564-3449. Tours from 1:30 P.M. to 3:30 P.M. Tuesdays and Thursdays. Free admission. The Kentucky governor's mansion until 1914, this Federal-style home was completed in 1798 and is the oldest official executive residence still in use in the United States.

Lexington

Ashland (Henry Clay Estate), 120 Sycamore Road; (859) 266-8581. Open 10 A.M. to 4:30 P.M. Tuesdays through Saturdays, 1 P.M. to 4:30 P.M. Sundays. Admission fee. Henry Clay, the Kentucky lawyer known as the Great Compromiser, lived at Ashland from 1811 until his death in 1852. Clay's career included service as a U.S. senator and three runs for the presidency. The estate includes several original outbuildings and a crop of ginkgo trees, which Clay brought to Kentucky.

Black Swan Books, 505 E. Maxwell Street; (859) 252-7255.

Bodley-Bullock House, 200 Market Street; (859) 259-1266. Open by appointment for tours, 9 A.M. to 1 P.M. weekdays. Admission fee. This 1814 Federal-style house, built for a Lexington mayor, contains one of the few cantilevered staircases left in Kentucky. The home was used as a Union army headquarters during the Civil War, and one popular legend says that Yankee troops painted one of the hardwood floors red, white, and blue in a victory celebration.

Book Gallery, 3250 Nicholasville Road; (859) 272-1094.

Bookmark, 410 W. Vine Street; (859) 254-7863.

Caraway Book Company, 3516 Castlegate Wynd; (859) 266-9412.

Glover's Bookery, 862 S. Broadway; (859) 253-0614.

Hopemont (Hunt-Morgan House), 201 N. Mill Street; (859) 233-3290. Open 10 A.M. to 4 P.M. Tuesdays through Saturdays, 2 P.M. to 5 P.M. Sundays, with guided tours March 1 through December 22. Admission fee. Built in 1814 by John Wesley Hunt, the first millionaire west of the Alleghenies. The family also included Thomas Hunt Morgan, who won the 1933 Nobel Prize for Medicine.

Kennedy Book Store, 405 S. Limestone; (859) 252–0331.

Lexington Cemetery, 833 W. Main Street; (859) 255–5522. Open from 8 A.M. to 5 P.M. daily. Free admission. The office has free brochures pointing out the graves of famous Lexingtonians. Chartered in 1848, this beautiful graveyard is better known, at least on a national level, for its secondary purpose as an arboretum. More than two hundred varieties of trees grow in the cemetery, including the country's second-largest known linden tree. The cemetery is also home to more than 180 species of birds.

Lexington Convention and Visitors Bureau, 301 E. Vine Street; (859) 233–7299 or (800) 845–3959; www.visitlex.com.

Mary Todd Lincoln House, 578 W. Main Street; (859) 233–9999. Originally built in 1803 as a tavern, this childhood home of Abraham Lincoln's future wife was renovated into a family dwelling in the 1830s. The home, the first site restored to honor a First Lady, contains dozens of antiques and a collection of Mrs. Lincoln's personal belongings.

Loudoun House, 209 Castlewood Drive; (859) 254–7024. Open noon to 4 P.M. Tuesdays through Fridays, 1 P.M. to 4 P.M. weekends. Admission free. One of only five remaining castellated Gothic villas designed by architect A. J. Davis in the United States. Built in 1852, it currently houses the Lexington Art League.

Morgan Adams Books, 1439 Leestown Road; (859) 252–3612.

Waveland State Historic Site, 225 Waveland Museum Road, Lexington; (859) 272–3611. Open from 10 A.M. to 4 P.M. Tuesdays through Saturdays, 2 P.M. to 5 P.M. Sundays. Admission fee. Greek Revival mansion built in 1847 by Joseph Bryan, a relative of Daniel Boone.

ACCOMMODATIONS AND RESTAURANTS

Louisville

Ashton's Victorian Secret Bed-and-Breakfast, 1132 S. First Street; (502) 581–1914 (answered evenings and weekends). A hundred-year-old Victorian mansion in Old Louisville with fourteen rooms and eleven fireplaces. One of the few bed-and-breakfasts where children are welcome, and first-floor accommodations are available for those who have trouble climbing stairs.

Baxter Station Bar and Grill, 1201 Payne Street; (502) 584–1635. Fun little nightspot with a railroad motif.

Bluegrass Brewing Company, 3929 Shelbyville Road; (502) 899–7070. Recommended for anyone who loves beer. The *Insider's Guide* Web site; www.insiders.com, calls Bluegrass Brewing's product "well-crafted, largely true to the city's German heritage and pleasing to both the average person and the most rigorous beer snob."

Bristol Bar and Grille, 1321 Bardstown Road; (502) 456–1702; 300 N. Hurstbourne Parkway; (502) 426–0627. Great people-watching occurs here, especially at the Bardstown location. This is where writer Hunter S. Thompson and Johnny Depp dined to celebrate the twenty-fifth anniversary of Thompson's *Fear and Loathing in Las Vegas*.

Captain's Quarters, 5700 Captain's Quarters Road; (502) 228–1651. Riverside locale where you can dine on burgers or crab legs. The building has sections that date back before the Civil War.

Central Park Bed-and-Breakfast, 1353 S. Fourth Street; (502) 636–0295. Eighteen-room, three-story Victorian home built in 1884 and listed on the National Register of Historic Places. The Rose Blossom was built by Vernon D. Price, a vinegar manufacturer and president of the *Saturday Evening Post*. The house is across from Central Park in Old Louisville.

Check's Cafe, 1101 E. Burnett Avenue; (502) 637–9515. Family-oriented tavern featuring Germantown-style casual fare.

Club Grotto, 2116 Bardstown Road; (502) 459–5275. Urban feel that's unusual for Louisville, and a menu that includes both the innovative and the traditional.

Cunningham's Restaurant, 900 S. Fifth Street; (502) 587–0526. Local legend insists that Cunningham's was once a bordello, and it does sport several suspicious little rooms upstairs and those naughty saloon-style swinging doors. Whatever—it's been a restaurant since 1870, so your reputation should be safe within its doors.

Inn at the Park, 1332 S. Fourth Street; (502) 637–6930. Built in 1886 as the home of Russell Houston, founder of the L & N Railroad. Richardsonian Romanesque architectural touches include a sweeping grand staircase, hardwood floors, and high ceilings.

Jack Fry's, 1007 Bardstown Road; (502) 452–9244. Some of the best food in town, in a spot that just about guarantees good company.

Kunz's, 115 S. Fourth Avenue; (502) 585–5555. Owned and operated by the same family since 1892. Features steaks, seafood, and Dutch favorites such as *jaeger schnitzel* and *zweibel roastbraten*.

Lilly's, 1147 Bardstown Road; (502) 451–0447. Freewheeling culinary art—elements of Thai, Vietnamese, French, and Italian make surprise appearances—at the hands of renowned local chef Kathy Cary.

Melrose Inn, 13306 W. Highway 42; (502) 228–4893. Charming hotel located just across the county line, in dry Oldham County. Derby Pie was invented in the Melrose kitchen, and it's still on the menu.

The Old Louisville Inn, 1359 S. Third Street; (502) 635–1574. Built in 1901 for John Armstrong, president of the Louisville Home Telephone Co. The 10,000-square-foot mansion was restored in the early 1970s. The ten guest rooms are decorated with antiques, and five include marble baths.

Rudyard Kipling Restaurant, 422 W. Oak Street; (502) 636–1311. Restaurant featuring a funky blend of Kentucky, British Isles, Italian, French, vegetarian, and various other cuisines.

Frankfort and Area

Anna Banana's, 220 Hanna Place; (502) 226–3217.

Capitol Coffee and Tea, 149 Franklin Square Shopping Center; (502) 875–1970.

Chat 'n Nibble, 28 S. Penn Avenue, Eminence; (502) 845–9109. In Wendell Berry's Henry County, north of Frankfort.

Lyons 1900s Bed-and-Breakfast, 4575 N. Main Street, Eminence; (502) 845–1364.

Mom's Restaurant, 18 W. Cross Street, New Castle; (502) 845–7598. A Henry County favorite.

Miss Ramey's, 76C Michael Davenport Road; (502) 875–1236.

Our Best Restaurant, 5728 Smithfield Road, Smithfield; (502) 845–7682. The name says it all: the best dining Henry County has to offer.

Scotty's Pink Pig BBQ, 581 E. Main Street; (502) 223–7343.

Lexington

A. P. Suggins Bar-and-Grill, 345 Romany Road; (859) 268–0709. A neighborhood restaurant with terrific regional cuisine.

Beaumont Inn, 638 Beaumont Drive off of U.S. Highway 27, Harrodsburg; (859) 734–3381. Built in 1845, this Greek Revival mansion was
once the Greenville Female Institute. Specialties include yellow-legged
fried chicken, cured country ham, and corn pudding.

Boone Tavern Hotel, 100 Main Street, Berea; (859) 985–3700. Plentiful
traditional Kentucky cooking. Reservations required, and men must
wear jackets (if you forget yours, they'll loan you one).

The Brand House, 461 N. Limestone Street; (859) 226–9464 or (800)
366–4942. Historic, luxurious Federal-style bed-and-breakfast, in downtown Lexington.

Cafe Jennifer at the Woodlands, 111 Woodland Avenue; (859)
255–0709. A tucked-away restaurant with charming decor, it's one of
the few places in town that offers a full array of regional specialties.

Campbell House Inn, 1375 Harrodsburg; (859) 255–4281. Traditional
Southern fare in a graceful white-columned setting.

Canaan Land Farm Bed and Breakfast, 4355 Lexington Road, Harrodsburg; (859) 734–3984. All the comforts of paradise: feather beds, a
swimming pool and hot tub, beautiful hiking woods, and the pastoral
bleats of two flocks of sheep to keep you company. Guests stay in either
the 1795 brick farmhouse or in a big reconstructed log house. Close to
the Shaker Village. And don't miss Max, the llama who'll give you a
kiss if you let him.

Cherry Knoll Farm Bed and Breakfast, 3975 Lemons Mill Pike; (859)
253–9800 or (800) 804–0617. Set on twenty-eight acres of immaculate
bluegrass farmland, this Greek Revival manse was built in 1855 and is
on the National Register of Historic Places. Two spacious guest rooms,
with an upstairs verandah that overlooks a pastureful of grazing horses.

deSha's Grille and Bar, 101 N. Broadway; (859) 259–3771. 1870s-era
mansion at the southeast end of Victorian Square, Main and Broadway.

Homewood Farm, 5301 Bethel Road; (859) 255–2814. Peaceful, three-
hundred-acre cattle-and-horse farm that's been in the same family since
1846. The new country house built by Bob and Anne Young was
designed especially for bed-and-breakfast guests.

Merrick Inn, 3380 Tates Creek Road; (859) 269–5417. Regional cuisines
with continental style, all served in a Colonial inn amid brass chandeliers, working fireplaces, and candlelight.

Ramsey's Diner, 469 E. High Street; (859) 259–2708. Old-fashioned
home cooking.

Rosebud Bar and Grill, 121 N. Mill Street; (859) 254–1907. Quaint, tiny downtown bar.

Shaker Village Dining Room, 3500 Lexington Road, Harrodsburg; (859) 734–5411. The Shakers aren't around anymore—they practiced celibacy, which pretty much ensured their eventual demise—but their dining traditions survive nicely at the Shaker Village of Pleasant Hill. You'll find three big meals a day here, all served by women in traditional Shaker attire.

Silver Springs Bed and Breakfast, 3710 Leestown Pike; (859) 255–1784. Homey, Federal-style house that's big and sunny, with spotless hardwood floors and lots of antiques, set on a twenty-one-acre horse farm, five minutes from downtown.

Springs Inn, 2200 Harrodsburg Road; (859) 277–5751. Locally owned motel and dining room renowned for its Southern hospitality.

Swann's Nest at Cygnet Farm, 3463 Rosalie Lane; (859) 226–0095. It's only about twenty years old, but this Southern-style beauty has the feel of an antebellum dwelling. Close to the Keeneland Race Track, down a tree-lined drive that shields it from the traffic of the road.

True Inn, 467 W. Second Street; (859) 252–6166 or (800) 374–6151. Richardsonian Romanesque mansion, built in 1843 and chock-full of gorgeous architectural details.

TENNESSEE

Among contemporary authors, Trenton native Peter Taylor has probably best captured the rhythms and soul of Tennessee, at least the Tennessee of a generation or two ago. Some critics have said that his short stories and novels portray characters that, like the Old South, no longer exist—growling, posturing "Big Daddy" men; delicately suffering belles; resentful children. I'd say the only difference is that air-conditioning has helped everyone smell a little better, and you can make your mint juleps from a mix. Other than that, "the more things change, the more they stay the same" has never been as true as in the South, and Taylor sketched that dichotomy with every masterful word.

Completely dissimilar in style, but equally Tennessean, Lisa Alther sets her novels in the Knoxville area of eastern Tennessee, using keen humor to gently dissect its intricate, bizarre social structure. Her 1976 book, *Kinflicks*, opens: "My family has always been into death. My father, the major, used to insist on having an ice pick next to his placemat at meals so that he could perform an emergency tracheotomy *when* one of us strangled on a piece of meat." The protagonist's mother, meanwhile, would rather "repolish her obituary and worry over whether or not the Knoxville *Sentinel* would accept it for publication. . . . What could bring more posthumous humiliation than to have your obituary rejected by a paper like the Knoxville *Sentinel?*"

SOUTHERN SIGHTS

Tennessee Department of Tourism; (615) 741–2158 or (800) 836–6200; www.state.tn.us/tourdev.

ACCOMMODATIONS

Tennessee Bed-and-Breakfast Innkeepers Association; (800) 820–8144; www.bbonline.com/tbbia.

Memphis

Memphis was for years the home of a man who's sold more books than . . . well, just about anyone. After graduating from the University of Mississippi in Oxford, John Grisham practiced law for years in Memphis, and his familiarity with the city, not to mention the state's legal system, has made it a natural setting for many of his novels. Most scenes from the movie versions of *The Firm* and many from *The Client* were filmed on location in Memphis.

The historic Cotton Exchange Building, at 65 Union Avenue, was where Gary Busey and Holly Hunter had their run-down little detective agency in the movie, and the plaque in the building honors John Grisham. A few blocks away, at Front and Madison, is the Union Planters Building, which was used for exterior shots of Tom Cruise's evil law firm: Bendini, Lambert, and Locke. Other Memphis locales used in the film include the rooftop of the Peabody Hotel, the Blues Cafe, the Front Street Deli, the Mud Island Monorail, and the Mississippi River Museum. Jake's

Place, on North Main, served as the Boston bar where Tom Cruise waits tables while attending Harvard Law School, and the William Faulkner Lounge at Memphis State University stood in for a Harvard classroom.

The Client was filmed at John F. Kennedy Park on Raleigh-LaGrange Road, as well as at the Sterick Building, 9 N. Third Street (Susan Sarandon's law office), Memphis Regional Medical Center, 877 Jefferson Avenue (exterior hospital scenes), Memphis County Courthouse, 140 Adams Avenue, and the Criminal Justice Center, 201 Poplar Avenue, where the young protagonist, played by Brad Renfro, spends an unpleasant night.

About forty-five miles north of Memphis, the little hamlet of Henning is the birthplace of Alex Haley, author of *Roots* and *Queenie*. The ten-room turn-of-the-century bungalow was built in 1919 by Will E. Palmer, Haley's maternal grandfather, and was originally called Palmer House. Haley lived here, with his grandparents, from 1921 to 1929 and during some of the subsequent summers. Visitors can catch a breeze on the front porch, where young Alex first heard the tales of Kunta Kinte and his other African ancestors. Haley, who died in 1992, bought the home after the success of *Roots* and had it restored. He is buried on its front lawn.

LITERARY LURES AND SOUTHERN SIGHTS

Beale Street Historic District, 203 Beale Street; (901) 526–0110. Tours, exhibits, and relics from Beale Street's heyday.

Blues City Tours, 325 Union Avenue; (901) 522–9229.

Burke's Book Store, 1719 Poplar Avenue; (901) 278–7484. Zillions of selections, incredibly knowledgeable staff, and they've been around since 1875. Burke's was very good to John Grisham when he was getting started, and Grisham has repaid the favor by making Burke's one of the few bookstores where he still does signings.

Carriage Tours of Memphis, 393 N. Main Street; (901) 527–7542 or (800) 955–9248.

Center for Southern Folklore, 209 Beale Street; (901) 525–3655. Open daily; call for hours. Documents the people and traditions of the South via films and exhibits, with an emphasis on Memphis music, books, arts and crafts. Offers tours of Beale Street and the Delta region.

Chucalissa Archaeological Museum, 1987 Indian Village Drive; (901) 785–3160. Open from 9 A.M. to 5 P.M. Tuesdays through Saturdays. Admission fee. Reconstruction of prehistoric Native American village dating to the fifteenth century.

Davies Manor Plantation, 9336 Davies Plantation Road; (901) 386–0715. Open from noon to 4 P.M. Tuesdays through Fridays, April 1 through December 20. Admission fee. Shelby County's oldest home, built in 1807.

Elmwood Cemetery, 824 S. Dudley Street; (901) 774–3212. Walking maps available in the Victorian cottage at the gate. Founded in 1852, this cemetery contains more than 70,000 graves, as well as outstanding Victorian statues and monuments. Featured in *The Firm* as the site where . . . er, uncooperative . . . lawyers from Bendini, Lambert, and Locke were buried. Tom Cruise's character escaped that fate, but only barely.

Graceland, 3734 Elvis Presley Boulevard; (901) 332–3322 or (800) 238–2000. Open seven days a week; call for times. Admission fee. Literary landmark? Yes, thank you. Thank you very much. Two of the best biographies of this half of the century, Peter Guralnick's *Last Train to Memphis: The Rise of Elvis Presley* and *Careless Love: The Unmaking of Elvis Presley*, were written about the king of rock 'n' roll, not to mention hundreds of other tomes. Although now that I think about it, I'm not sure any books are actually *displayed* at Graceland. Oh, well. Elvis had other things on his mind.

Alex Haley House and Museum, 200 S. Church Street, Henning; (901) 738–2240. Open from 8 A.M. to 4:30 P.M. Mondays through Saturdays, and from 1 P.M. to 4 P.M. Sundays. Haley was born here, in his grandparents' house, and also is buried on the site.

Heritage Tours, 280 Hernando Street; (901) 527–3427. Specializing in cultural and historical tours.

Hunt-Phelan Home, 533 Beale Street; (901) 344–3166 or (800) 350–9009. Antebellum home that's been in the same family for more than 160 years. It boasts a first-rate Confederate pedigree—this is where General Grant planned the Battle of Vicksburg.

John F. Kennedy Park, 4575 Raleigh-LaGrange Road. That nasty murder at the beginning of *The Client* takes place in this park.

Lauderdale County Chamber of Commerce, 103 Jackson Avenue, Ripley; (901) 635–9541; www.lctn.com/chamber. For tourist information about the Henning area, birthplace of Alex Haley.

Thousands of tourists visit Graceland each year to see the grave of the King, whose name is misspelled on the bronze marker. His middle name was "Aron," not "Aaron."

The Map Room's Authentic Tours, 2 S. Main Street; (901) 579–9924. Custom strolls choreographed to Memphis rock 'n' roll, and driving tours in a perfectly reconditioned 1955 Cadillac. Great fun, great guides, very informative.

Memphis Pink Palace Museum and Planetarium, 3050 Central Avenue; (901) 320–6320. One of the largest museums in the Southeast, the Pink Palace is dedicated to the cultural and natural history of Memphis and vicinity. The museum, built of pink Georgia marble, was constructed as a private residence in the 1920s by grocery entrepreneur

Clarence Saunders, who founded Piggly-Wiggly. Among other exhibits, the museum features a replica of the first Piggly-Wiggly store and a shrunken head. The connection is unclear, but hey, it's interesting.

Memphis Visitor Information Center, 340 Beale Street; (901) 543–5333; www.memphistravel.com.

Mud Island, 125 N. Front Street; (901) 576–7241 or (800) 507–6507; www.mudisland.com. Open daily, call for hours. Admission fee. The island exhibits include the Mississippi River Museum and a 5-block-long scale rendering of the Mississipi River, all the way from its mouth to the Gulf of Mexico. This was the site of one of the big chase scenes in *The Firm*. If you want to try re-creating it, you'll have to bring your own Dave Grusin soundtrack. Mud Island is also home to the *Memphis Belle*, the first aircraft to successfully complete twenty-five missions during World War II.

National Civil Rights Museum, 450 Mulberry Street; (901) 521–9699; www.mecca.org/~crights/ncrm.html. Open every day but Tuesday; call for hours. Admission fee. Housed at the historic Lorraine Hotel, where Martin Luther King Jr. was gunned down in 1968. Exhibits and interactive displays trace the Civil Rights movement from Rosa Parks to Dr. King.

A. Schwaub Dry Goods, 163 Beale Street; (901) 523–9782. All of life's little necessities can be found in this wacky, crowded, dusty store, dating from 1876. We're talking dogs with wobbly heads for your rear dashboard, candy dispensers in the shape of teensy guitars, and frighteningly realistic piggy banks.

Slavehaven-Burkle Estate Museum, 826 N. Second Street; (901) 527–3427. Admission fee, reservations required. Fascinating museum that tells the story of the Underground Railroad in an actual way station. Visitors follow the escape route through tunnels, trapdoors and displays of ads, auctions, and slave artifacts.

ACCOMMODATIONS AND RESTAURANTS

Adam's Mark Hotel, 939 Ridge Lake Boulevard; (901) 683–2326.

The Arcade Restaurant, 540 S. Main Street; (901) 625–5757.

Blues Alley-Beale Street BBQ, 205-209 Beale Street; (901) 527–5840. Piano bar with everything from Memphis blues to country music, along with great Southern food.

Blues City Cafe, 138 Beale Street; (901) 526–3637. Steaks, ribs, jumbo shrimp, all done very Southern-style—i.e., spicy. In *The Firm*, this is where Cruise is first approached by an FBI agent, played by Ed Harris.

The Bridgewater House, 7015 Raleigh-LaGrange Road; (901) 384–0080; www.bbonline.com/tn/bridgewater. Greek Revival structure that once housed an 1890s schoolhouse, now a bed-and-breakfast with two spacious rooms, each with private bath, leaded-glass windows, fifteen-foot ceilings, and antique furnishings.

The Cupboard Too, 149 Madison Avenue; (901) 527–9111. Home cooking, with emphasis on tons of fresh veggies.

French Quarter Suites Hotel, 2144 Madison Avenue; (901) 728–4000 or (800) 843–0353. Reminiscent of an older, New Orleans–style inn.

Front Street Deli, 77 S. Front Street; (901) 522–8943. In *The Firm*, this is where Tom Cruise and Holly Hunter meet to plot their escape from the clutches of wicked, evil lawyers (or is that redundant?).

Little Tea Shop, 71 Monroe Avenue; (901) 525–6000. Plate lunches, soup and salad, and extra-gooey, extra-yummy cobbler.

Lowenstein-Long House Bed and Breakfast, 217 N. Waldran Boulevard; (901) 278–3000.

The Peabody, 149 Union Avenue; (901) 529–4000 or (800) PEABODY. The grande dame of Tennessee hotels is also the place every day, at 11 A.M. and 5 P.M., the famous Peabody Ducks march down their very own red carpet to the daunting strains of *King Cotton March* (not to mention the daunting flashbulbs) and hop into the lobby's fancy tiled water fountain. The mallards live in the Duck Palace on the hotel roof, but come down every day for a six-hour splash in the fountain. The gift shop sports everything you could possibly want in the way of duck decorations, from golf-club covers to gold lockets. Celebrities who've stayed at the Peabody include presidents Andrew Johnson and William McKinley, Confederate General Robert E. Lee, William Faulkner, and Charles Lindbergh.

The Pier Restaurant, 100 Wagner Place; (901) 526–7381.

Rendezvous Restaurant, 52 S. Second Street Rear; (901) 523–2746. Specialties are barbecued pork and charbroiled ribs.

Sleep Inn at Court Square, 40 N. Front Street; (901) 522–9700 or (800) 627–5337. Within walking distance of Mud Island and Beale Street.

Talbot Heirs Guesthouse, 99 S. Second Street; (901) 527–9772; www.talbothouse.com.

Chattanooga

Chattanooga, the largest city in southeast Tennessee, lies nestled south of Chickamauga Lake, almost at the Georgia border. The University of Tennessee at Chattanooga's Arts and Education Council hosts the annual Chattanooga Conference on Southern Literature, which for ten years has been delving into themes such as "A Sense of Place" (1999).

The conference, which takes place in April, includes readings of works by new authors and playwrights, full performances of Southern plays, and discussions on topics such as "Lace to Leather: The Portrayal of Women in Southern Literature" and "Fact or Fiction: Defining the Boundaries in Historical Writing."

Past speakers have included Bobbie Ann Mason, Kaye Gibbons, Barry Hannah, Wendell Berry, Lee Smith, Doris Betts, Clyde Edgerton, Elizabeth Spencer, Charles Frazier, Shelby Foote; attend this conference, and chances are good you'll be hobnobbing with Pulitzer Prize–winners and poet laureates. The conference's success over the last decade led the Fellowship of Southern Writers to make its headquarters in Chattanooga.

LITERARY LURES AND SOUTHERN SIGHTS

All Books-Mountain Herbs, 410 Broad Street; (423) 266–0501. Largest selection of antiquarian and used books in the area, including regional history, Civil War, Native American, and Southern literature.

Chattanooga Conference on Southern Literature; (423) 267–1218 or (800) 267–4232; www.artsedcouncil.org.

Chattanooga Convention and Visitors Bureau; (423) 756–8687 or (800) 322–3344; www.chattanoogafun.com.

Chattanooga Regional History Museum, 400 Chestnut Street; (423) 265–3247. Admission fee.

ACCOMMODATIONS AND RESTAURANTS

Adams Hilborne Restaurant and Mansion, 801 Vine Street; (423) 265–5000 or (800) IINN–JOY. European-style hotel with ten rooms, all with private baths and fireplaces.

Back Inn Cafe, 412 E. Second Street; (423) 265–5033. Continental bistro in a turn-of-the-century mansion with spectacular river views.

Big River Grille and Brewing Works, 222 Broad Street; (423) 267–2739.

Chattanooga Choo Choo, 1400 Market Street; (423) 266–5000. Have your meal aboard an authentic railway dining car, back at the "Station House," or drop by the Cafe Espresso for a cappuccino, espresso, or gourmet dessert.

The Loft, 328 Cherokee Boulevard; (423) 266–3601. Casual atmosphere, menu featuring prime rib, steaks, and fresh seafood.

Lookout Lake Bed and Breakfast, 3408 Elder Mountain Road; (423) 821–8088.

Renaissance Commons, 402 E. Second Street; (423) 265–5033. Elegant breakfasts in the beautiful River Room, with brunch offered on Sundays.

Nashville

Ironically, Peter Taylor made his home in Nashville for many years, although his most acclaimed book was called *A Summons to Memphis*. Taylor remains one of the few Tennessee authors to gain a national reputation, primarily through collections of stories such as *In the Miro District* and *The Oracle at Stoneleigh Court*. He studied at Vanderbilt University and Kenyon College, then spent much of his life teaching creative writing at universities, most recently the University of Virginia in Charlottesville, where he lived until his death in 1994.

A Summons to Memphis, winner of the 1987 Pulitzer Prize, tells the story of a prominent Nashville family's devastating social decline and their subsequent move to Memphis (an entire *city* on the other side of the tracks, in the view of many Nashvillians). Protagonist Phillip Carver believes he has escaped the family shame by moving to huge, anonymous, blissfully un-Southern Manhattan. But Carver finds he must confront lingering psychic scars when summoned home by his middle-aged, still-unmarried sisters on behalf of their father, a widower about to make an unsuitable union with a much younger woman.

Robert Penn Warren, who hailed from just north of the Tennessee border, in Guthrie, Kentucky, had this praise for Taylor's *A Woman of Means*: "No description of mere mortals or events of *A Woman of Means* can indicate the particular kind of excitement it possesses—the excitement of being constantly on the verge of deep perceptions and deep interpretations."

Nashville and the Tennessee Humanities Council sponsor one of the best literary festivals, the annual Southern Festival of Books, held each

October at War Memorial Plaza downtown. The 1998 festival included readings by Kurt Vonnegut, Charles Frazier, Ellen Gilchrist, and Reynolds Price, as well as the revelation of the mysterious K. C. McKinnon's true identity: Nashville author Cathie Pelletier. McKinnon-Pelletier caused shocked titterings in the literary world when she received a $1 million deal to write a second novel before the first one under that pseudonym, *Dancing at the Harvest Moon* (1997), had even come out.

Past speakers have included Tim Gautreaux, Nanci Kincaid, Ellen Gilchrist, Heather Graham, Rick Bragg, Sharyn McCrumb, and Kaye Gibbons, with topics as diverse as "The Civil War in the Upland South," "Redneck and Okie and the Sense of Human Worth: Southern Memoirs," "Families in Flux: Debut Novelists," and "Design of the South: Architecture and Urban Planning."

LITERARY LURES AND SOUTHERN SIGHTS

Belle Meade Plantation, 5025 Harding Road; (615) 356–0501 or (800) 270–3991. Admission fee. The "Queen of Tennessee Plantations," with good reason. A nineteenth-century thoroughbred stud farm, with antebellum mansion, carriage house, and eight outbuildings.

Davis-Kidd Booksellers, 4007 Hillsboro Road; (615) 385–2645. You'll find a good cafe on the second floor and frequent readings by Southern authors. The store is south of downtown, in the Green Hills area.

Elders Books, 2115 Elliston Place; (615) 327–1867. Specializing in Southern titles, dusty and musty and packed to the rafters. A collector's fantasy come true.

The Hermitage, 4580 Rachel's Lane; (615) 889–2941. Admission fee. Hundreds of the fabulous oaks on Andrew Jackson's plantation were damaged by tornadoes in 1998, but the estate retains its dignity and allure. Tours of the National Landmark include the mansion, period garden, original log cabins, and Jackson's tomb.

Nashville Convention and Visitors Bureau, 211 Commerce Street; (615) 741–2158 or (800) 657–6910; www.nashvillecvb.com.

Southern Festival of Books, Tennessee Humanities Council; (615) 320–7001, ext. 15; www.tn-humanities.org.

Tennessee State Museum, Fifth and Deaderick; (615) 741–2692 or (800) 407–4324. Open 10 A.M. to 5 P.M. Tuesdays through Saturdays, 1 P.M. to 5 P.M. Sundays. Admission free.

Travellers Rest Plantation, 636 Farrell Parkway; (615) 832–2962. Admission fee. Circa 1799, this is the oldest Nashville home open to the public. Covers one thousand years of Tennessee history, from its origins as a prehistoric Native American village and burial site to its role as a Civil War headquarters.

ACCOMMODATIONS AND RESTAURANTS

Apple Brook Bed, Breakfast, and Barn, 9127 Highway 100; (615) 646–5082. Turn-of-the-century farmhouse built in 1896; on five lush acres close to the Natchez Trace.

Carole's Yellow Cottage, 801 Fatherland Street; (615) 226–2952. Victorian cottage on the National Register of Historic Places, built in 1902 and near downtown. It has a resident cat for fur fanciers.

Hillsboro House Bed-and-Breakfast, 1933 Twentieth Avenue South; (615) 292–5501 or (800) 228–7851. Cozy Victorian with feather beds and homemade breakfasts, near Vanderbilt and Belmont Universities and Music Row.

Linden Manor Bed-and-Breakfast, 1501 Linden Avenue; (615) 298–2701. Romantic Victorian cottage in the historic Belmont-Hillsboro area.

Opryland Hotel, 2800 Opryland Drive; (615) 889–1000. Stunning, over-the-top, an adventure in itself.

Terrawinn, 304 Highland Heights Drive, Goodlettsville; (615) 859–0041. Very congenial bed-and-breakfast with just one bedroom suite.

VIRGINIA

One would naturally suspect that it doesn't get much more "true Southern" than Virginia, capital of the Confederacy. Yet overall, the commonwealth, as noted by Nancy Lemann in *The Fiery Pantheon*, has much more the feel of the Northeast about it:

> The place seemed Northern. There was no hint of the tropics, of the Stewarts' customary Gulf Coast environs. It was more American than Southern, this genteel old Virginia; it could have been the Adirondacks. There was no hint of the blazing tropic sun. A view to the mountains and the white-painted wood of some

columned mansions in green groves, seen from the rambling verandahs and turrets and spires of the Virginia Hotel, showed the hills and valleys that were once the haunts of the Confederates. But the place was neutral now.

Virginia has played home and host to many Southern literary luminaries, from William Faulkner to Peter Taylor to the man revered as one of America's most brilliant scholars, Thomas Jefferson. In the 1990s, the state's role as home to the Federal Bureau of Investigation's training center at Quantico has made Virginia the unofficial headquarters for contemporary mysteries and thrillers, from Thomas Harris's *The Silence of the Lambs* and *Hannibal* to Patricia Cornwell's Richmond-based series starring Kay Scarpetta, the state's fictitious chief medical examiner. And we can probably expect a John Grisham novel or two to be set here in the future; the world's best-known writer of legal thrillers recently moved to Charlottesville in central Virginia.

Cornwell described the FBI facility—apparently not one of Virginia's more bucolic spots—in her 1991 novel *Body of Evidence*. "The FBI National Academy in Quantico, Virginia, is a brick and glass oasis in the midst of an artificial war," Cornwell writes in the voice of her heroine, Dr. Kay Scarpetta. "I would never forget my first stay there years ago. I went to bed and got up to the sound of semi-automatics going off, and when I took a wrong turn on the fitness course one afternoon, I was almost flattened by a tank."

One of the most beloved authors of the late twentieth century, Lee Smith, was born in Grundy, a coal-mining hamlet just miles from the Kentucky border in western Virginia, and spent her late teenage years in Richmond. While a student at Hollins College in Roanoke, she and fellow student Annie Dillard became go-go dancers for an all-girl rock band, the Virginia Woolfs. Her first novel, *The Last Day the Dog Bushes Bloomed*, a coming-of-age story, was published in 1968. In the mid-1970s, Smith and her family moved to Chapel Hill, North Carolina, and she now teaches at North Carolina State University, in Raleigh.

On her Web site, www.leesmith.com, she talks about growing up surrounded by natural storytellers:

I didn't know any writers, but I grew up in the midst of people just talking and talking and talking and telling these stories. My

> Uncle Vern, who was in the legislature, was a famous storyteller, as were others, including my dad. It was very local. I mean, my mother could make a story out of anything; she'd go to the grocery store and come home with a story.

Smith describes herself, with true Southern flair, as a "deeply weird" child who wrote her first story at the age of nine or ten, a tale about Adlai Stevenson and Jane Russell heading out West together to become Mormons. Those same themes, of religion and flight, still pervade her writing today. *Saving Grace* (1995), about the perpetually terrified eleventh child of a traveling evangelist who holds snakes and guzzles strychnine to confirm his faith, was praised by one reviewer as raising "questions of sin and salvation in a way that invokes the spirit of Flannery O'Connor."

Smith, like other writers of the region, makes deft use of the Southerner's peculiar dalliance with story, the nudging back and forth and over and around and under before ever really getting to the point. "The way southerners tell a story is really specific to the South," she told the editors of *Growing Up Southern*. "It's a whole narrative strategy, it's an approach. Every kind of information is imparted in the form of a story. As for directions in the South? It's not just, *turn left*. It's *I remember the time my cousin went up there and got bit by a mad dog*."

LITERARY LURES AND SOUTHERN SIGHTS

Bed and Breakfast Association of Virginia; (540) 672–6700 or (888) 660–BBAV; www.bbonline.com/va/bbav.
Virginia Division of Tourism; (800) 321–3244; www.virginia.org.

Charlottesville

Charlottesville, home of that eighteenth-century hyphenate Thomas Jefferson—architect-writer-president-scholar—seems to magnetically pull in writers in their later lives, many of them as professors at the classically lovely University of Virginia. Jefferson founded the University of Virginia in 1819 with a faculty of ten and sixty-eight students. The former president planned UVA as the first secular college in America, confident in his belief that education led to enlightenment. As with everything else, Jefferson was revolutionary in his approach and not afraid of shaking up the status quo.

"Science is progressive," he wrote. "What was useful two centuries ago is now become useless, e.g., one-half the professorships at William and Mary."

William Faulkner was a writer-in-residence at UVA during the last years of his life. He had purchased a home in Charlottesville, but died at a hospital not far from his beloved Rowan Oak, in Mississippi. Oddly enough, John Grisham—who, like Faulkner, hails from Oxford, Mississippi—recently moved his primary residence from Oxford to Charlottesville and can occasionally be seen strolling the aisles at local bookstores.

Another visitor of note to UVA was Edgar Allan Poe, who enrolled as a student on St. Valentine's Day, in 1826. The room Poe occupied on West Range has been carefully preserved, with an appearance similar to the way it looked when Poe was here. The furniture all looks slightly shabby, such as what one might expect an aspiring writer to be able to afford, including a replacement table for the one Poe threw into the fireplace one icy night. Poe's first book of poetry, *Tamerlane and Other Poems*, was written in this room on breaks from studying and gambling, his other passions. He stayed at UVA only a brief time, however, and returned to Richmond when his money ran out in December 1826.

LITERARY LURES AND SOUTHERN SIGHTS

Albemarle County Historical Society, the McEntire Building, 200 Second Street; (804) 296-1492. Exhibits, photo collection, research library, walking tours.

Ash Lawn-Highland, James Monroe Parkway; (804) 293-9539. President James Monroe's estate, near Jefferson's Monticello.

Charlottesville-Albemarle County Visitors Center, Virginia Route 20, south of Interstate 64; (804) 293-6789.

Monticello, Route 53, about 2 miles southeast of Charlottesville; (804) 984-9822 or (888) 293-1776; www.monticello.org. Open 8 A.M. to 5 P.M. March through October, 9 A.M. to 4:30 P.M. the remainder of the year. Admission fee. Mountaintop estate designed by President Thomas Jefferson, who called it his essay in architecture. Tour includes the main house, gardens, Jefferson's grave, and a well-stocked gift shop.

University of Virginia, University Avenue; (804) 924–7969; www.uva.edu/wlam.html. Free tours daily. Ask for directions at the UVA information desk in the Rotunda, on McCormick Road, to Edgar Allan Poe's room, appropriately enough No. 13, on the West Range.

Virginia Festival of the Book, each March; (804) 924–3296; www.vabook.org. This annual celebration of literature and literacy is sponsored by the Virginia Foundation for the Humanities. The festival typically features more than 150 writers in nearly two hundred programs, with more than 15,000 people attending. Participants have included Alice McDermott, John Grisham, Gay Talese, Rita Dove, Sharyn McCrumb, Lois Lowry, and Nikki Giovanni. Programs range from author readings and book signings to how to run a bookstore to freelancers' rights. All programs are open to the public, and most are free.

ACCOMMODATIONS AND RESTAURANTS

Awful Arthur's Seafood Company, 333 W. Main Street; (804) 296–0969. Located in the heart of downtown in a historic brick building.

Bizou, 119 W. Main Street; (804) 977–1818. Classic home cooking.

The Boar's Head Inn, Route 250 West; (804) 296–2181 or (800) 476–1988; www.boarsheadinn.com. 1830s gristmill on fifty-three rolling acres.

The Brick Oven, 1966 Rio Hill Shopping Center, Highway 29 North; (804) 978–7898. Superb Old World–style cooking, including the best pizza in town.

Carrsbrook Bed and Breakfast, 313 Gloucester Road; (804) 973–8177. Circa-1794 manor house where Mr. Jefferson once entertained.

The 1817 Historic Bed and Breakfast, 1211 W. Main Street; (804) 979–7353. Perfect location, one block from the University of Virginia, minutes from Monticello and Michie Tavern. Built in the Federal style, the Eighteen Seventeen is completely furnished in antiques, all of which are for sale. The inn was built by James Dinsmore, Thomas Jefferson's master craftsman, who also did work at Monticello and the university.

Guesthouses; (804) 979–7264; www.va-guesthouses.com. Reservation service for more than sixty private homes, guest suites, and estate cottages in the Blue Ridge Mountains.

Historic Michie Tavern, 683 Thomas Jefferson Parkway; (804) 977–1234. Eighteenth-century mill and tavern, still serving Colonial fare.

Inn at the Crossroads, 5010 Plank Road; (804) 979–6452. Historic 1820s inn on four acres, close to Charlottesville.

The Inn at Monticello, Highway 20 South, 1188 Scottsville Road; (804) 979–3593; www.innatmonticello.com. Charming ambience with antique canopy beds and fireplaces.

Keswick Hall, 701 Club Drive, Keswick; (804) 979–3440 or (800) ASHLEY1; www.keswick.com. The place to stay if you're in that "landed gentry" mood, Keswick Hall sits amid a six-hundred-acre estate. The forty-eight-room country house hotel, owned by Sir Bernard Ashley, features fabrics and wallpapers by his late wife—that would be *Laura* Ashley—in each room. Expensive, definitely an indulgence, but you'll feel ultra-pampered.

Rococo's, 2001 Commonwealth Drive; (804) 971–7371. Homemade delights with specialties of pasta, gourmet pizza, and wood-grilled seafood.

Silver Thatch Inn, 3001 Hollymead Drive; (804) 978–4686. One of the oldest buildings in central Virginia, the original portion of the Silver Thatch was built in 1780 by Hessian soldiers who were captured during the Revolutionary War during the Battle of Saratoga, New York, then marched south to Charlottesville. The central part of the inn was built in 1812 and served for a time as a boys' school.

Richmond

Richmond was the childhood home of Boston-born Edgar Allan Poe, whose work pretty much defines the term "Southern Gothic."

The city's tribute to its adopted literary son, the Poe Museum, is built around the city's oldest standing structure, the Old Stone House, dating from about 1737. The museum grounds also include the Enchanted Gardens, with an array of his favorite plants and flowers, and a shrine built from the bricks of the building where he put together his magazine, the *Southern Literary Messenger*. None of the actual homes Poe occupied in Richmond has survived the twentieth century, but the museum contains the meager possessions the writer left behind: a trunk, a walking stick, a pair of boot hooks, and a mirror and trinket box that belonged to his wife.

Literary pilgrims can take home all manner of Poe souvenirs: posters, photos, busts, raven puppets, mouse pads, even a pillbox (in defiance of the unspoken rule that it's not nice to mention drug addiction on the premises; tour guides will tell you all that drug stuff about Poe was an invention of his first biographer). If your visit to the Raven Room leaves you a bit chilled, you can buy a sweatshirt proclaiming your preoccupation, "dreaming dreams no mortal ever dreamed before."

LITERARY LURES AND SOUTHERN SIGHTS

Annabel Lee Riverboat, 3011 Polk Street; (804) 644–5700 or (800) 752–7093. Historic four-hundred-passenger paddlewheeler named for the heroine of Edgar Allan Poe's classic poem.

Historic Richmond Tours, 707 E. Franklin Street; (804) 780–0107.

Metro Richmond Convention and Visitors Bureau, 550 E. Marshall Street; (804) 358–5511 or (888) RICHMOND.

Edgar Allan Poe Museum, 1914 E. Main Street; (804) 648–5523; www.poemuseum.org. Guided tours daily; call for times. Admission fee. This museum features the world's largest collection of Poe memorabilia, located inside Richmond's oldest house. Don't miss the eerie Raven Room, hung with illustrations inspired by his most famous work.

Lee vs. Grant: The 1864 Campaign, Metro Richmond CVB; (804) 782–2777. Visitors can trace Grant's 1864 campaign trail on this fifty-two-stop tour through central Virginia.

The Library of Virginia, 800 E. Broad Street; (804) 692–3500. Exhibits and rare books tracing the commonwealth through four hundred years of history.

The Museum and White House of the Confederacy, 1201 E. Clay Street; (804) 649–1861. Admission fee. Victorian jewel nousing the nation's most extensive collection of Confederate artifacts.

Richmond Metro Visitors Center, 1710 Robin Hood Road, exit 78 off Interstate 95; (804) 358–5511.

Tuckahoe Plantation, 12601 River Road; (804) 784–5736. Tours by appointment. Thomas Jefferson's boyhood home, including the one-room schoolhouse where that fine mind was first honed.

Valentine Museum and 1812 Wickham House, 1015 E. Clay Street; (804) 649–0711. Admission fee. Museum of Richmond's life and history, with rotating exhibits. Exceptional collection of costumes and photographs.

Virginia Historical Society: The Museum of Virginia History, 428 N.
Boulevard; (804) 358–4901. Admission fee.

Virginia State Capitol, Ninth at Grace Streets; (804) 698–1788. Graceful and spare, designed by master architect (and president) Thomas
Jefferson after a Roman temple in the south of France.

ACCOMMODATIONS AND RESTAURANTS

Amici Ristorante, 3343 W. Cary Street; (804) 353–4700. Cozy atmosphere with game specialties such as stuffed quail, buffalo Gorgonzola,
and ostrich.

The Berkeley Hotel, 1200 E. Cary Street; (804) 780–1300. Small fifty-five-
room hotel with a distinctive flair combining old world and New South.

Emmanuel Hutzler House, 2036 Monument Avenue; (804) 353–6900.
Circa-1914 home, gloriously restored with beautiful architectural detail.

The Jefferson Hotel, 101 W. Franklin at Adams Streets, downtown; (804)
788–8000. Five-diamond historic hotel with two on-site restaurants.
The thirty-six-step grand staircase of this Gilded Age resurrection was
reputedly used as the model for the staircase in the scene in *Gone With
the Wind* where a drunken Rhett carries Scarlett up before . . . well,
you know the rest.

La Petite France, 2912 Maywill Street; (804) 353–8729. Specialties
include lobster whiskey, chateaubriand, and Dover sole amandine.

Linden Row Inn, 100 E. Franklin Street; (804) 783–7000 or (800)
348–7424. Built in 1847, beautifully preserved and listed on the
National Register of Historic Places.

Virginia Cliffe Inn, 2900 Mountain Road; (804) 266–7344 or (800)
827–1874.

Chincoteague Island

If you or your children have read Marguerite Henry's classic children's
book of the 1940s, *Misty of Chincoteague,* this is where you can get a
glimpse of those wild ponies. Chincoteague Island is in Virginia's Tidewater region, about one hundred miles northeast of Norfolk. Every
summer, on the last Thursday in July, the ponies from Assateague Island
are driven (by firemen, oddly enough) across the channel to Chincoteague, where they are sold at auction. Those that remain unsold swim
back home.

Legend has it that the ponies first arrived on Assateague in the six-teenth century, when a group of horses swam ashore from a Spanish galleon shipwrecked offshore.

William Styron, a Tidewater native, wrote about the region's melan-choly beauty in his 1951 book *Lie Down in Darkness*:

> Riding down to Port Warwick from Richmond, the train begins to pick up speed on the outskirts of the city, past the tobacco fac-tories with their ever-present haze of acrid, sweetish dust and past the rows of uniformly brown clapboard houses which stretch down the hilly streets for miles . . . Suddenly the train is burrow-ing through the pinewoods, and the conductor, who looks middle-aged and respectable like someone's favorite uncle, lurches through the car asking for tickets . . . and when you ask him how far it is to Port Warwick and he says, "Ab*oot* eighty miles," you know for sure that you're in the Tidewater.
>
> You look out once more at the late summer landscape and the low, sorrowful beauty of tideland streams winding through marshes full of small, darting, frightened noises and glistening and dead silent at noon, except for a whistle, far off, and a distant rumble on the rails.

LITERARY LURES AND SOUTHERN SIGHTS

Assateague Island National Seashore, Tom's Cove Visitor Center; (757) 336–6577.

Assateague Island Tour, 6262 Marlin Street; (757) 336–6155.

Chincoteague Island Chamber of Commerce, 6733 Maddox Boulevard; (757) 336–6161.

Pony Swim and Auction, every July, from the northeast end of Assateague Island across the channel to Chincoteague Island; (757) 336–6161.

ACCOMMODATIONS AND RESTAURANTS

Anchor Inn Motel, 3775 Main Street; (757) 336–6313.

Channel Bass Inn, 6228 Church Street; (757) 336–6148. Rambling, unpretentious guest rooms and a lovely tea room.

Driftwood Motor Lodge, Beach Road; (757) 336–6557. Large rooms over-looking the wildlife refuge and the candy-striped red-and-white Assateague Lighthouse.

1848 Island Manor House Bed and Breakfast, 4160 Main Street; (757) 336–5436.

Landmark Crab House, 6162 Main Street; (757) 336–5552.

The Mariner Motel, 6273 Maddox Boulevard; (757) 336–6565 or (800) 221–7490, ext. 001.

Miss Molly's Inn, 4141 Main Street; (757) 336–6686.

Sea Shell Motel, 3720 Willow Street; (757) 336–6589. Family motel close to the beach and wildlife refuge.

Sting-Ray's, 26507 Lankford Highway; (757) 331–2505. Behind the Cape Center's gas station-souvenir shop, this homey restaurant features fresh seafood and barbecue.

Suggested Reading and Internet Resources

to Stir the Southern Soul

What follows is a highly personal, subjective list of Southern literature, nonfiction and travel guides, magazines and literary journals, as well as Internet sites for people whose noses are perpetually buried in books—people like us. It is meant solely as a starting point for inspiration, not the wellspring. That's up to y'all, constant readers.

As you've learned by now, these Southern scribes have a tendency to pack up and move a lot, albeit usually to another Southern state. In an admittedly frustrating attempt to tie them down in one spot, at least for purposes of this appendix, I've mostly put books *about* authors under the state where they were born or spent the majority of their lives; books *by* Southern authors are categorized mostly according to where the books are set.

ALABAMA

Alabama Literary Review, Troy State University, Troy, Alabama.
Beidler, Philip D., ed., *Many Voices, Many Rooms; The Art of Fiction in the Heart of Dixie: An Anthology of Alabama Writers.*
Capote, Truman, *Other Voices, Other Rooms; Breakfast at Tiffany's.*
Childress, Mark, *Tender; Gone for Good; Crazy in Alabama.*
Lee, Harper, *To Kill a Mockingbird.*
Morris, Willie, *The Ghosts of Medgar Evers.*
Plimpton, George, *Truman Capote: In Which Various Friends, Enemies, Acquaintances, and Detractors Recall His Turbulent Career.*
Southern Humanities Review, Auburn University, Auburn, Alabama.

FLORIDA

Apalachee Quarterly, Tallahassee, Florida.

Barry, Dave, *Dave Barry's Greatest Hits; Dave Barry Turns 40; Dave Barry Slept Here: A Short History of the United States; Dave Barry's Only Travel Guide You'll Ever Need.*

Buchanan, Edna, *Miami, It's Murder; Suitable for Framing; Act of Betrayal; Contents Under Pressure; Margin of Error; Nobody Lives Forever; The Corpse Had a Familiar Face.*

Campbell, Frank D., *John D. MacDonald and the Colorful World of Travis McGee.*

Capitman, Barbara Baer, *Deco Delights: Preserving the Beauty and Joy of Miami Beach Architecture.*

The Florida Review, University of Central Florida, Orlando, Florida.

Fodor's Miami and the Keys.

Fowler, Connie May, *Before Women Had Wings; Sugar Cage; River of Hidden Dreams.*

Frommer's Miami and the Keys.

Frommer's Miami by Night.

Hemingway, Ernest, *Death in the Afternoon; The Green Hills of Africa; To Have and Have Not.*

Hiassen, Carl, *Naked Came the Manatee* (ed.); *Double Whammy; Lucky You; Native Tongue; Strip Tease; Stormy Weather; Team Rodent: How Disney Devours the World.*

Hurston, Zora Neale, *Their Eyes Were Watching God; Spunk: The Selected Stories of Zora Neale Hurston; Dust Tracks on the Road.*

Kaufelt, David, *The Fat Boys Murders* series.

Kaufelt, Lynn Misuko, *Key West Writers and Their Houses.*

Keith, June, *Postcards From Paradise; More Postcards From Paradise.*

Lurie, Alison, *The Last Resort.*

MacDonald, John D., *Condominium; Cinnamon Skin; Darker Than Amber; Bright Orange for the Shroud; Free Fall in Crimson; The Girl in the Plain Brown Wrapper;* and the rest of the Travis McGee series.

Matthiessen, Peter, *Killing Mister Watson; Lost Man's River; Bone by Bone; The Snow Leopard.*

McCarthy, Kevin M., ed., *The Book Lover's Guide to Florida.*

Rawlings, Marjorie Kinnan, *Cross Creek; The Yearling.*

Shearer, Victoria and Vanessa Richards, *The Insiders' Guide to the Florida Keys and Key West.*

Tampa Review, University of Tampa Press, Tampa, Florida.

Willeford, Charles, *Miami Blues.*

Williams, Joy, *The Florida Keys: A History and Guide.*

GEORGIA

Allison, Dorothy, *Cavedweller.*
Berendt, John, *Midnight in the Garden of Good and Evil.*
Burns, Olive Ann, *Cold Sassy Tree; Leaving Cold Sassy.*
The Chattahoochee Review, DeKalb College, Dunwoody, Georgia.
DeBolt, Margaret Wayt, *Savannah Spectres and Other Strange Tales.*
Edwards, Anne, *Road to Tara: The Life of Margaret Mitchell.*
Five Points, Georgia State University, Georgia.
Fodor's Pocket Savannah and Charleston.
Frommer's The Carolinas and Georgia.
Gaines, Ernest, *The Autobiography of Miss Jane Pittman; A Lesson Before Dying.*
The Georgia Review, University of Georgia, Athens, Georgia.
Gournay, Isabelle, *AIA Guide to the Architecture of Atlanta.*
Groom, Winston, *Forrest Gump.*
Lady Chablis and Theodore Bouloukos, *Hiding My Candy: The Autobiography of the Grand Empress of Savannah.*
McCullers, Carson, *The Member of the Wedding; The Heart Is a Lonely Hunter.*
McKenzie, Barbara, *Flannery O'Connor's Georgia.*
Mitchell, Margaret, *Gone With the Wind; Lost Laysen.*
O'Briant, Don, *Looking for Tara.*
O'Connor, Flannery, *The Habit of Being; A Good Man Is Hard to Find; Wise Blood; The Violent Bear It Away; Collected Works.*
Price, Eugenia, *Savannah; To See Your Face Again; Before the Darkness Falls; Stranger in Savannah.*
Ripley, Alexandra, *Scarlett: The Sequel to Margaret Mitchell's Gone With the Wind; Fields of Gold.*
Siddons, Anne Rivers, *Fox's Earth; Homeplace; Peachtree Road; King's Oak.*
Smith, Deborah, *A Place Called Home; When Venus Fell.*
White, Bailey, *Mama Makes Up Her Mind; Quite a Year for Plums.*
Wittish, Rich and Betty Darby, *The Insiders' Guide to Savannah.*
Wolfe, Tom, *A Man in Full.*

KENTUCKY

Beattie, L. Elisabeth, ed., *Conversations With Kentucky Writers.*
Berry, Wendell, *Sex, Economy, Freedom and Community; Another Turn of the Crank; Home Economics; A Continuous Harmony; Fidelity; A World Lost.*
Day, Teresa, ed., *Kentucky: Off the Beaten Path.*
Giles, Janice Holt, *Tara's Healing; 40 Acres and No Mule; The Believers; The Enduring Hills; Hannah Fowler; The Kentuckians.*
Knowles, Susan Williams, *Kentucky Tennessee Travel-Smart.*

Mason, Bobbie Ann, *Shiloh and Other Stories; In Country; Feathered Crowns; Clear Springs: A Memoir; Midnight Magic: Selected Stories.*
Nold, Chip, *The Insiders' Guide to Louisville, Kentucky, and Southern Indiana.*
Schenkkan, Robert, *The Kentucky Cycle.*
Taylor-Hall, Mary Ann, *Come and Go, Molly Snow.*
Walter, Jeff, and Susan Miller (contributor), *The Insiders' Guide to Lexington and the Kentucky Bluegrass.*
Ward, William Smith, *A Literary History of Kentucky.*

LOUISIANA

Bosworth, Sheila, *Slow Poison; Almost Innocent.*
Bultman, Bethany, *Compass American Guides: New Orleans.*
Burke, James Lee, *Black Cherry Blues; Neon Rainbow; Heaven's Prisoners; Burning Angel;* and everything else in the Dave Robicheaux detective series.
Chase, John Churchill, *Frenchmen Desire Good Children.*
Chopin, Kate, *The Awakening; Bayou Folk.*
Dickinson, Joy, *Haunted City: An Unauthorized Guide to the Magical, Magnificent New Orleans of Anne Rice.*
Double Dealer Redux, New Orleans, Louisiana.
Faulkner, William, *Mosquitoes.*
Fodor's New Orleans.
Florence, Robert and Mason, *New Orleans Cemeteries: Life in Cities of the Dead.*
Gaines, Ernest J., *A Lesson Before Dying; The Autobiography of Miss Jane Pittman.*
Gilchrist, Ellen, *In the Land of Dreamy Dreams; Rhoda, The Age of Miracles; Net of Jewels.*
Girardi, Robert, *Madeleine's Ghost.*
Grau, Shirley Ann, *The House on Coliseum Street; The Keepers of the House.*
Kennedy, Richard S., ed., *Literary New Orleans; Literary New Orleans in the Modern World.*
Keyes, Francis Parkinson, *Dinner at Antoine's; Steamboat Gothic.*
Laughlin, Clarence John, *Ghosts Along the Mississippi.*
Leblanc, Guy, *Irreverent Guides: New Orleans.*
Lemann, Nancy, *The Fiery Pantheon; Lives of the Saints.*
Leverich, Lyle, *Tom: The Unknown Tennessee Williams.*
Martin, Valerie, *A Recent Martyr.*
Louisiana Literature, Southeastern Louisiana University, Hammond, Louisiana.
New Delta Review, Louisiana State University, Baton Rouge, Louisiana.
New Orleans Architecture, eight-volume series by Pelican Publishing, Gretna, Louisiana.
Percy, Walker, *The Moviegoer; The Last Gentleman; Lancelot.*
Rice, Anne, *The Vampire Chronicles; Tales of the Mayfair Witches; The Feast of All Saints.*

Ripley, Alexandra, *New Orleans Legacy*.

Samsway, Patrick, *Walker Percy: A Life*.

Sexton, Richard and Randolf Delehanty, *New Orleans: Elegance and Decadence*.

Smith, Julie, *New Orleans Mourning; The Axeman's Jazz; Jazz Funeral; New Orleans Beat; House of Blues; The Kindness of Strangers; Crescent City Kill*.

Sternberg, Mary Ann, *Along the River Road*.

Strahan, Jerry E., *Managing Ignatius: The Lunacy of Lucky Dog and Life in the Quarter*.

Toledano, Roulhac, *The National Trust Guide to New Orleans*.

Tolson, Jay, *Pilgrim in the Ruins: A Life of Walker Percy*.

Toole, John Kennedy, *A Confederacy of Dunces*.

Wells, Rebecca, *Divine Secrets of the Ya-Ya Sisterhood; Little Altars Everywhere*.

Williams, Tennessee, *A Streetcar Named Desire; Cat on a Hot Tin Roof; Camino Real; The Glass Menagerie*.

Wyatt-Brown, Bertram, *The House of Percy: Honor, Melancholy, and Imagination in a Southern Family*.

Mississippi

Barry, John M., *Rising Tide: The Great Flood of 1927 and How It Changed America*.

Blotner, Joseph, *Faulkner, A Biography*.

Brown, Larry, *Father and Son; Big Bad Love*.

Douglas, Ellen, *A Family's Affairs; A Lifetime Learning; The Rock Cried Out*.

Faulkner, William, *The Sound and the Fury; As I Lay Dying; Sanctuary; Light in August; The Hamlet*.

Foote, Shelby, *Jordan County: A Landscape in Narrative*.

Grisham, John, *A Time to Kill; The Firm; The Client; The Pelican Brief*.

Hise, Dan, *Faulkner's Rowan Oak*.

McHaney, Pearl, *Eudora Welty: Writers' Reflections Upon First Reading Welty*.

Mississippi Review, University of Southern Mississippi, Hattiesburg, Mississippi.

Morris, Willie, *The Last of the Southern Girls; Yazoo; North Toward Home; Good Old Boy; Terrains of the Heart and Other Essays on Home; The Ghosts of Medgar Evers: A Tale of Race, Murder, Mississippi, and Hollywood*.

Tolson, Jay, *The Correspondence of Shelby Foote and Walker Percy*.

Waggett, Gerard J., *The John Grisham Companion: A Fan's Guide to His Novels, Films, Life, and Career*.

Welty, Eudora, *One Writer's Beginnings; The Collected Stories of Eudora Welty; A Curtain of Green; The Optimist's Daughter; The Robber Bridegroom; Delta Wedding*.

Wright, Richard, *Native Son; Black Boy*.

North Carolina

Betts, Doris, *The Astronomer and Other Stories; Beasts of the Southern Wild and Other Stories; Souls Raised From the Dead; The Sharp Teeth of Love*.

Carolina Quarterly, University of North Carolina, Chapel Hill, North Carolina.

Chappell, Fred, *Farewell, I'm Bound to Leave You; It Is Time, Lord.*

Compass American Guides: *North Carolina.*

Crucible, Barton College, Wilson, North Carolina.

DoubleTake Magazine, Center for Documentary Studies, Durham, North Carolina.

Frazier, Charles, *Cold Mountain.*

Frommer's *The Carolinas and Georgia.*

Gabaldon, Diana, *The Drums of Autumn.*

Gibbons, Kaye, *A Virtuous Woman; Ellen Foster; Charms for the Easy Life; Sights Unseen; On the Occasion of My Last Afternoon.*

Godwin, Gail, *Evensong; A Southern Family; Father Melancholy's Daughter.*

The Greensboro Review, University of North Carolina, Greensboro, North Carolina.

Gurganus, Allan, *Oldest Living Confederate Widow Tells All; White People; Plays Well With Others.*

Karon, Jan, *At Home in Mitford; A Light in the Window; These High, Green Hills; Out to Canaan; A New Song.*

Kuralt, Charles, *North Carolina Is My Home; Charles Kuralt's America.*

McCrumb, Sharyn, *Foggy Mountain Breakdown; The Rosewood Casket; She Walks These Hills; The Ballad of Frankie Silver; The Hangman's Beautiful Daughter; Lovely in Her Bones.*

Mitchell, Ted, *Thomas Wolfe: A Writer's Life.*

More From Mitford Newsletter, Penguin Books, New York, New York.

North Carolina Literary Review, *East Carolina University, Greenville, North Carolina.*

Price, Charles, *Freedom's Altar; Hiwassee: A Novel of the Civil War.*

Price, Reynolds, *Roxanna Slade; Kate Vaiden.*

Sandburg, Carl, *Abraham Lincoln: The War Years; Complete Poems.*

Sparks, Nicholas, *The Notebook; Message in a Bottle.*

Spencer, Elizabeth, *The Stories of Elizabeth Spencer; The Light in the Piazza; The Salt Line; Jack of Diamonds and Other Stories.*

Tyler, Anne, *If Morning Ever Comes; The Tin Can Tree; A Slipping-Down Life.*

The Smithsonian Guides to Historic America, *The Carolinas and the Appalachian States.*

Walser, Richard, *Literary North Carolina: A Historical Study.*

Wolfe, Thomas, *Look Homeward, Angel; You Can't Go Home Again.*

SOUTH CAROLINA

Allison, Dorothy, *Bastard Out of Carolina; Cavedwellers; Trash; Skin; Two or Three Things I Know for Sure.*

Ballantine, Todd, *Tideland Treasure.*

Conroy, Pat, *The Water Is Wide*; *The Great Santini*; *The Prince of Tides*; *The Lords of Discipline*; *Beach Music*.

Compass American Guides: *South Carolina*.

Fodor's Pocket Savannah and Charleston.

Martin, Margaret Rhett, *Charleston Ghosts*.

Poe, Edgar Allan, *Edgar Allan Poe Reader* (includes *The Gold Bug* and *Annabel Lee*, both set in South Carolina).

Powell, Padgett, *Edisto*; *Edisto Revisited*; *A Woman Named Drown*; *Aliens of Affection*.

Ripley, Alexandra, *Charleston*; *On Leaving Charleston*; *Scarlett: The Sequel to Margaret Mitchell's Gone With the Wind*.

Sanders, Dori, *Clover*; *Her Own Place*.

Siddons, Anne Rivers, *Lowcountry*.

The Smithsonian Guides to Historic America, *The Carolinas and the Appalachian States*.

The South Carolina Review, Clemson University, Clemson, South Carolina.

Worthington, Curtis, *Literary Charleston: A Lowcountry Reader*.

Yemasee, University of South Carolina, Columbia, South Carolina.

TENNESSEE

Alther, Lisa, *Kinflicks*; *Original Sins*; *Other Women*.

Haley, Alex, *Roots*; *Queenie*; *The Autobiography of Malcolm X*.

Murphree, Mary Noailles, *In the Tennessee Mountains*.

O'Brien, Tim, *Tennessee Off the Beaten Path*.

Olmstead, Marty, *Hidden Tennessee*.

Paschall, Douglass, and Alice Swanson, eds., *Homewords: A Book of Tennessee Writers*.

Taylor, Peter, *A Summons to Memphis*; *A Long Fourth*; *The Widows of Thornton*.

Tickle, Phyllis, *Home Work: A Book of Tennessee Writers*.

Van West, Carroll, ed., *The Tennessee Encyclopedia of History and Culture*.

VIRGINIA

Baker, Russell, *Growing Up*.

Brown, Rita Mae, *Bingo*; *Six of One*; *Southern Discomfort*; *Riding Shotgun*; *High Hearts*.

Compass American Guides: *Virginia*.

Cornwell, Patricia, *Postmortem*; *All That Remains*; *Cruel and Unusual*; *The Body Farm*; *From Potter's Field*; *Cause of Death*; *Hornet's Nest*; *Unnatural Exposure*.

Dillard, Annie, *Pilgrim at Tinker Creek*.

Fodor's Virginia and Maryland.

Glasgow, Ellen, *Barren Ground*; *Vein of Iron*; *This Our Life*; *The Sheltered Life*.

Goodman, Susan, *Ellen Glasgow: A Biography*.

Harris, Thomas, *The Silence of the Lambs; Hannibal.*
Rubin, Louis D., *No Place on Earth: Ellen Glasgow, James Branch Cabell, and Richmond-in-Virginia.*
Smith, Lee, *Oral History; Me and My Baby View the Eclipse; The Devil's Dream; Saving Grace; Family Linen; News of the Spirit.*
The Smithsonian Guides to Historic America, *Virginia and the Capital Region.*
Styron, William, *The Confessions of Nat Turner; Tidewater Morning; Lie Down in Darkness.*
Triglani, Adriana, *Big Stone Gap.*
The Virginia Quarterly Review, Charlottesville, Virginia.
William and Mary Review, College of William and Mary, Williamsburg, Virginia.

GENERAL

Auchmuicy, Jim, and Lea Donosky, eds., *True South: Travels Through a Land of White Columns, Black-Eyed Peas, and Redneck Bars.*
America's Best Bed and Breakfasts, Fodor's.
American Literary Review, University of North Texas, Denton, Texas.
The American Voice, Kentucky Foundation for Women, Louisville, Kentucky.
Andrews, Peter, *Inns of the Mid-Atlantic and the South.*
Applebome, Peter, *Dixie Rising: How the South Is Shaping American Values, Politics, and Culture.*
Berman, Eleanor, *Away for the Weekend—Southeast: Great Getaways for Every Season in Alabama, Georgia, North Carolina, South Carolina, Tennessee.*
Book magazine.
Brightleaf: A Southern Review of Books, Raleigh, North Carolina.
Brown, Fred and Jeanne McDonald, *Growing Up Southern: How the South Shapes Its Writers.*
Cantor, George, *Pop Culture Landmarks: A Traveler's Guide.*
Chesnut, Mary Boykin, *A Diary From Dixie.*
Emblidge, David, and Barbara Zheutlin, *The Writer's Resource.*
Fodor's The South.
Foote, Shelby, *The Civil War: A Narrative; Shiloh: A Novel.*
Garrison, Webb, *Southern Tales: A Treasury of Stories From Virginia, North Carolina, South Carolina, Georgia, Florida, Alabama, Kentucky, Tennessee, and Mississippi.*
Gieseking, Hal, *Historic Inns of the South.*
Gordon, William A., *Shot on This Site.*
Granta, New York, New York.
Hall, B. C., and C. T. Wood, *The South.*
Hauck, Dennis William, *Haunted Places: The National Directory. A Guidebook to Ghostly Abodes, Sacred Sites, UFO Landings, and Other Supernatural Locations.*
Hendrickson, Robert, *The Literary Life and Other Curiosities.*

Hills, Rust, ed., *Lust, Violence, Sin, Magic: 60 Years of Esquire Fiction.*

Horwitz, Tony, *Confederates in the Attic.*

Humphreys, J. R., *Timeless Towns and Haunted Places.*

Jones, Suzanne W., ed., *Growing Up in the South: An Anthology of Modern Southern Literature.*

Lawliss, Chuck, *Robert E. Lee Slept Here: Civil War Inns and Destinations.*

Literature of the American South: A Norton Anthology.

Lonely Planet *Deep South.*

Louisiana State University Press, *Voices of the South* series (reprints of long-out-of-print Southern classics, a marvelous series).

Oxford American, Oxford, Mississippi.

Pitzer, Sara, *Dixie: A Traveler's Guide.*

Price, Eugenia, and Mary Bray Wheeler, *Eugenia Price's South: A Guide to the People and Places of Her Beloved Region.*

Ravenel, Shannon, ed., *New Stories From the South* (anthology series, 1986–1999).

Rubin, Louis D., *The History of Southern Literature.*

Sherr, Lynn, and Jurate Kazickas, *Susan B. Anthony Slept Here: A Guide to American Women's Landmarks.*

The Smithsonian Guides to Historic America, *The Deep South.*

Southern Humanities Review, Auburn University, Auburn, Alabama.

The Southern Review, Louisiana State University, Baton Rouge, Louisiana.

Story, Cincinnati, Ohio.

Twain, Mark, *Life on the Mississippi.*

Watkins, James H., ed., *Southern Selves: From Mark Twain and Eudora Welty to Maya Angelou and Kaye Gibbons* (autobiographical writings).

Wilson, Charles, and William Ferris, *Encyclopedia of Southern Culture.*

INTERNET SITES

Amazon Books, www.amazon.com.

Barnes and Noble, www.barnesandnoble.com.

Bookpage, www.bookpage.com.

Brightleaf, www.brightleaf-review.com.

Frommer's Publications, www.frommers.com.

Insiders Guides, www.insiders.com.

Literary Traveler, www.literarytraveler.com.

Lonely Planet Publications, www.lonelyplanet.com.

Salon, www.salonmagazine.com.

University of North Carolina: The American South site, www.sunsite.unc.edu/south.

Society for the Study of Southern Literature, www.dept.usm.edu/~soq/sssl.html.

Y'all.com: The Webzine of the South, www.y'all.com.

Index of Authors
and Characters

Fictional characters are given in italics.